This Is My Beloved

This Is My Beloved

Embracing the Bridal Love of Jesus

LISA SMITH

WIPF & STOCK · Eugene, Oregon

THIS IS MY BELOVED
Embracing the Bridal Love of Jesus

Copyright © 2024 Lisa Smith. All rights reserved. Except for brief quotations in critical publications or reviews, no part of this book may be reproduced in any manner without prior written permission from the publisher. Write: Permissions, Wipf and Stock Publishers, 199 W. 8th Ave., Suite 3, Eugene, OR 97401.

Wipf & Stock
An Imprint of Wipf and Stock Publishers
199 W. 8th Ave., Suite 3
Eugene, OR 97401

www.wipfandstock.com

PAPERBACK ISBN: 979-8-3852-3060-0
HARDCOVER ISBN: 979-8-3852-3061-7
EBOOK ISBN: 979-8-3852-3062-4

12/13/24

Unless otherwise indicated, all Scripture quotations are from The ESV® Bible (The Holy Bible, English Standard Version®), © 2001 by Crossway, a publishing ministry of Good News Publishers. Used by permission. All rights reserved.

Scripture quotations marked MSG are taken from *The Message*, copyright © 1993, 2002, 2018 by Eugene H. Peterson. Used by permission of NavPress. All rights reserved. Represented by Tyndale House Publishers.

Scripture quotations marked (NASB®) are taken from the New American Standard Bible®, Copyright © 1960, 1971, 1977, 1995, 2020 by The Lockman Foundation. Used by permission. All rights reserved. lockman.org.

Scripture quotations marked (NIV) are taken from the Holy Bible, New International Version®, NIV®. Copyright © 1973, 1978, 1984, 2011 by Biblica, Inc.™ Used by permission of Zondervan. All rights reserved worldwide. www.zondervan.com. The "NIV" and "New International Version" are trademarks registered in the United States Patent and Trademark Office by Biblica, Inc.™

Scripture quotations marked (NKJV) are taken from the New King James Version®. Copyright © 1982 by Thomas Nelson. Used by permission. All rights reserved.

Scripture quotations marked (NLT) are taken from the *Holy Bible*, New Living Translation, copyright ©1996, 2004, 2015 by Tyndale House Foundation. Used by permission of Tyndale House Publishers, Carol Stream, Illinois 60188. All rights reserved.

Scripture quotations marked TPT are from The Passion Translation®. Copyright © 2017, 2018, 2020 by Passion & Fire Ministries, Inc. Used by permission. All rights reserved. ThePassionTranslation.com.

Book epigraph reproduced from *Butterfly Nebula* by Laura Reece Hogan by permission of the University of Nebraska Press. Copyright 2023 by Laura Reece Hogan.

For Jesus
This is my beloved and this is my friend (Song of Songs 5:16b)

The Soul should always stand ajar
That if the Heaven inquire
He will not be obliged to wait
Or shy of troubling Her.

Emily Dickinson, 1055

When he waits at the window,
when he waits at his just-open window,
I pray murmurations of starlings; that one
might swoop through the slender silence
he has left ajar
for me.

Laura Reece Hogan, "Exchange," *Butterfly Nebula*

Contents

Acknowledgments ix
A Note on the Texts xi
Introduction 1

RESPONDING TO OUR BRIDEGROOM

1. Awakening to Him: Samson Occom   15
   Song of Songs 1:1–11
2. Choosing Him: Edward Taylor   31
   Song of Songs 1:12—2:17
3. Pursuing Him: Jonathan Edwards   54
   Song of Songs 3:1–5
4. Encountering Him: Sarah Edwards   77
   Song of Songs 3:6—5:1a

MINISTERING WITH OUR BRIDEGROOM

Introduction   103
Song of Songs 5:1b

5. Interceding for Others: Dorothy Ripley   107
   Song of Songs 5:2—6:3
6. Encouraging Others: Sarah Osborn and Susanna Anthony   131
   Song of Songs 6:4—7:13
7. Loving our Bridegroom: Sarah Jones   156
   Song of Songs 8:1–7

8	Bearing His Authority: Julia A. J. Foote Song of Songs 8:8–14	186
Conclusion: John Winthrop		208
Bibliography		215

Acknowledgments

I GREATLY APPRECIATE THE opportunity to thank those who improved and supported this project.

My sincere appreciation to my readers: Kristen Cummins, whose personal and theological knowledge of our Bridegroom exceeds and inspires my own, and Katie Frye, whose scholarly eye and tender heart enhanced and clarified my writing and thought. You each blessed me greatly with your own insights on the material, and the book is much better for your input.

Pepperdine University librarians Elizabeth Parang and Sally Bryant—thank you for your invaluable assistance with the bibliographic components of this book.

Thanks to the Beinecke Rare Book and Manuscript Library, Yale University, for the use of the manuscripts of Edward Taylor's poetry in the Edward Taylor Collection, General Collection, and appreciation to Daniel Patterson, Emeritus Professor of English, Central Michigan University, and The Kent State University Press for the use of Patterson's transcriptions of Taylor's poems. Thanks also to the Special Collections Research Center, William & Mary Libraries, for the use of the Sarah Anderson Jones Diary, and to Chad Sandford, MA, for the use of his transcription. Thanks to the Massachusetts Historical Society for the use of the electronic edition of the Winthrop Family papers, and to the University of Nebraska Press and Laura Reece Hogan for the use of Hogan's poem "Exchange" in the book's epigraph.

Michael Ditmore, my sounding board for all things early American, thank you for sharing your encyclopedic knowledge and consistent encouragement.

Lindsey Sullivan, Ned Bustard, and Laura Reece Hogan—your excitement for the project inspired me.

Profound gratitude and love to my family and friends for their support, prayers, and love.

My deepest love and appreciation to Jesus, who loves me eternally and taught me the lessons I share in this book.

A Note on the Texts

THE WRITINGS REPRINTED IN this book are from the seventeenth, eighteenth, and nineteenth centuries and have been accessed through various sources. *Early American Imprints, Series I: Evans*, published by Readex, a division of NewsBank, offers writings published in America during the seventeenth and eighteenth centuries and is available at most university libraries and some public libraries. Some writings quoted or excerpted here have been obtained through historical societies and special collections departments at university libraries, noted in the acknowledgments. Other works have been accessed via Google Books, Internet Archive, and the HathiTrust Digital Library. Complete bibliographic information for all texts can be found in the bibliography.

To make these writings accessible to readers, I have silently modernized spelling and punctuation, expanded some contractions, updated archaic words, adjusted paragraphing, and added subtitles where needed. Square brackets denote insertions for clarity, and footnotes offer additional information on people, places, and events that appear in the documents.

Introduction

What a heavenly home God has set for the sun,
shining in the superdome of the sky!
See how he leaves his celestial chamber each morning,
radiant as a bridegroom[1] ready for his wedding,
like a day-breaking champion eager to run his course.
He rises on one horizon, completing his circuit on the other,
warming lives and lands with his heat.[2]

IS ANYONE EVER AS eager and excited as a bridegroom? The morning of his wedding, he awakens to the realization that the long-awaited day has finally come—the day he joins himself forever to the one he loves. This is the moment he will finally possess his beloved completely and be possessed completely by her. From this time forward, they will share an intimacy unique among human relationships as they embark upon their journey of life, embracing joys, sorrows, surprises, and challenges together. No wonder King David in Ps 19 compares the sun to an exuberant bridegroom who bursts out of his chamber on his wedding day, dazzling and passionate, impatient to embark upon his race across the skies. Only a groom displays that level of anticipation and zeal!

Humans around the globe experience the warmth and radiance of the earth's sun every day, but Christians are also blessed to know and

---

1. Although we typically use the shortened form of this word today to refer to a man on his wedding day—"groom"—the word *bridegroom* dates from very early in the English language, possibly even to Old English. *Oxford English Dictionary*, s.v. "bridegroom (n.)."

2. Ps 19:5–6 (TPT). All chapter epigraphs are from TPT.

enjoy the sun of righteousness, Jesus Christ.³ And like the sun, Jesus eagerly embarked upon his journey to redeem mankind "for the joy that was set before him," persisting through the pain and shame of the cross to accomplish salvation for humanity and create a people who will know and love him.⁴ Those of us who have chosen to follow Jesus as our Lord and Savior have been forgiven for our sins, have received the Holy Spirit to dwell inside us, and have entered into a relationship with God himself. We are on a journey of ever-deepening intimacy with Jesus, the sun of righteousness.

But did you know that like the sun in Ps 19, the Bible also depicts Jesus as a bridegroom? In fact, Jesus is presented in the Bible as the bridegroom of the church. What does it mean that Jesus is our bridegroom? And what does it mean that the church is his bride?

In the simplest sense, it means that Jesus relates to those who follow him as a bridegroom relates to a bride—pursuing her, loving her, caring for her, and always desiring increasing intimacy with her. And a bride responds to that pursuit by receiving the love of the bridegroom and offering her love in return. Perhaps most importantly, they both eagerly anticipate their eventual union, which for Jesus and his bride will occur when the earth ends and God's eternal kingdom begins: "Hallelujah! For the Lord our God the Almighty reigns. Let us rejoice and exult and give him the glory, for the marriage of the Lamb has come, and his Bride has made herself ready. . . . Blessed are those who are invited to the marriage supper of the Lamb."⁵ According to Revelation, the final book of the Bible, the earthly love shared by Jesus the Lamb of God and his bride the church will culminate in a celestial wedding at the end of time, inaugurating the everlasting kingdom of God. So, just as Jesus is our Savior, teacher, king, shepherd, and master, among other roles, he is also our eternal bridegroom.

How does thinking of Jesus as your bridegroom make you feel? Excited? Uncomfortable? Confused? Fearful? If you're like me, you might experience a combination of emotions when considering Jesus in this way. Perhaps it is a new concept for you. I myself spent decades as a Christian rarely considering Jesus' role as bridegroom of the church or how to relate to him as such; his other roles were much more comfortable

---

3. Mal 4:2.
4. Heb 12:2.
5. Rev 19:6b–7, 9a.

for me. And I don't think I'm alone in that response. It's easy to picture Jesus as our Savior, since symbols of his sacrifice adorn every church, and sermons often end with altar calls. Jesus as teacher is very accessible as well, since his lessons are continually propounded and urged upon us from pulpits and flickering screens. And there is certainly no dearth of contemporary worship songs extolling Jesus as our powerful king.

But whenever I contemplated Jesus as my bridegroom, a peculiar mixture of emotions arose in me. On the one hand, I was a bit uncomfortable with the concept. As a wife, I had experience with human marriage, and I knew there were biblical passages presenting Jesus and the church in a marriage context, but to personally relate to Jesus in that way was totally unfamiliar. Was it important to view Jesus in that role? How should I even do it? Should I use different terms to address him or adopt different physical positions in prayer? Would he say different words to me, express different affections, require different acts of obedience? And, honestly, would it feel a little *weird* to relate to him in that way?

Looking back, I suspect what I feared the most when considering Jesus in this role was the deep intimacy that is characteristic of the marriage relationship. After all, a bridegroom represents such intense relational realities as unequivocal exclusivity, profound closeness, fierce passion, and unwavering commitment. Lord, judge, shepherd, redeemer—roles such as these did not require me to connect with Jesus in such a familiar way, although of course he always seeks intimacy with us in every context. But *bridegroom*? Surely that connoted an entirely different level of relationship.

Yet, at the same time, the idea of sharing with Jesus the profound intimacy of a marriage relationship also evoked in me a real longing. In a healthy marriage, who is closer than a spouse? Who is more understanding, more intimate, more loving, more tender, more loyal? What would it be like to share *that* kind of relationship with Jesus, the lover of my soul? Isn't it possible that it would be absolutely amazing?

For me, learning to embrace Jesus in his role as my bridegroom *was* amazing. Absolutely amazing. And challenging and terrifying and stressful and surprising. It took time and work, but, eventually, a truly seismic shift occurred in my relationship with Jesus when I learned to relate to him as his bride, and that shift mostly involved a deepened intimacy and the startling discovery of how very *real* a relationship with Jesus can be. A *real* friendship, a *real* sharing of thoughts and desires, a *real* feeling of being cared for and loved.

I discovered that Jesus related to me in unique ways as my bridegroom, unlike the ways he connected with me as my teacher, leader, and master. A bridegroom has different desires for his bride than a teacher has for a student. A bridegroom feels different emotions for his bride than a leader feels for a follower. A bridegroom cares differently for his bride than a master cares for a servant. Only as my bridegroom did Jesus touch some of the deepest, most intimate places of my heart.

Where are you on the journey to embrace Jesus as your bridegroom? Maybe the idea excites you, and you long to make it real in your life. Maybe you have never even considered the concept of Jesus as bridegroom, or maybe you aren't even sure it is biblically accurate. Connecting with Jesus as a bride can be a daunting, unfamiliar task, especially when personal relationship history or gender are considered. Or maybe you have already been pursuing Jesus as a bride and have experienced his intense passion and affection for you. This book is written for Christians in all of these places—for anyone who desires to grow in knowing and experiencing the power and intimacy of Jesus' bridal love.

EMBARKING ON THE JOURNEY

Throughout history, Christians have embraced their identity as Jesus' beloved bride both on a corporate level as a church, and, by extension, on an individual level.[6] Third-century theologian Origen (ca. 185–ca. 253) is often credited with advancing the allegorical reading of the Song of Songs as a picture of Jesus as bridegroom, an approach supported by other ancient writers such as Athanasius (ca. 293–373), Augustine of Hippo (354–430), and Jerome (ca. 347–420), and maintained by later medieval Christians such as Bernard of Clairvaux (1090–1153) and St. John of the Cross (1542–91).

Seventeenth-century English and American Puritans consistently envisioned and celebrated the individual Christian life as that of a bride of Jesus, preaching and publishing numerous sermons on Song of Songs and the parable of the ten virgins and emphasizing the attractiveness and beauty of Jesus the bridegroom as a force that draws the heart of the believer and produces devotion.[7] John Cotton (1585–1652), a leading

---

6. For detailed studies of historical interpretations of the Song of Songs as delineating Jesus as the bridegroom of the church and the individual Christian, see Robinson, *Companion*; Schellenberg, *Through the Ages*; Hogan, *I Live*, 101–2, especially note 34.

7. For more on the history among the Puritans of Jesus as the bridegroom in Song

minister and theologian of the early Puritan Massachusetts Bay Colony, published an exposition on Song of Songs as "a work very useful and seasonable to every Christian," particularly because the biblical book could be applied "to express the mutual affection and fellowship between Christ and every Christian soul."[8]

Early evangelicals in the eighteenth century also embraced the bridal narrative, commonly referring to their conversion to Christ with phrases reminiscent of engagement such as "the day of my espousals" or "the time of my first espousals."[9] Jesus' role as the bridegroom of the Christian was a key element of eighteenth-century revivals such as the First Great Awakening. In Philadelphia in 1739, transatlantic preaching sensation George Whitefield (1714–70) used the bridegroom metaphor as the centerpiece of one of his most famous and impactful sermons.[10] Methodists throughout the eighteenth century employed bridal language to speak of their relationship to Jesus. English Methodist leader Mary Fletcher (1739–1815) encourages young women in the society to avoid "spiritual adultery" and pursue holy devotion to their "heavenly Bridegroom" in her popular pamphlet *Jesus, Altogether Lovely*.[11]

In the nineteenth century, Jesus' role as bridegroom was also viewed as central to an understanding of the Christian life. English preaching sensation Charles Spurgeon (1834–92) asserts in his sermon on Song 5:16 that "all the patriarchs, all the prophets, all the apostles, all the confessors, yea, and the entire body of the church have left us no other testimony" than that our bridegroom Jesus is "altogether lovely."[12] Even today, Catholic religious orders and Protestant prayer and worship movements continue to promote and celebrate Jesus' identity as our eternal bridegroom. Thus, in keeping with this tradition, the suggestions proposed

---

of Songs, see Won, "Communion with Christ," 116–31; Hammond, "Bride in Redemptive Time," 78–101; Robinson, *Companion*, 327–57.

8. Cotton, *Brief Exposition*, title page, 9–10. For all historical writings quoted or excerpted in this book, I have silently modernized spelling and punctuation, expanded some contractions, updated archaic words, adjusted paragraphing, and added subtitles where needed for ease of reading. Square brackets denote insertions for clarity.

9. For examples, see Hopkins, *Memoirs of Osborn*, 315, and Hopkins, *Memoirs of Anthony*, 49.

10. Whitefield, *Wise and Foolish Virgins*. For more on early evangelicals and the bridegroom metaphor, see Roberts, "Calvinist Couplet," 412–31.

11. Fletcher, *Jesus Altogether Lovely*, 3.

12. Spurgeon, *Spurgeon's Sermons*, 5:323.

in this book are designed to help every Christian connect with Jesus as a bride.

The book is organized around the idea that embracing Jesus as our bridegroom is a two-part process that begins with Jesus drawing our hearts to himself with the passion of a bridegroom and ends with us ministering with Jesus and sharing that same passion for him and his kingdom. Thus, the first section of the book focuses on Jesus' pursuit of us as his bride and how we should *respond* to him—awakening to him, choosing him, pursuing him, and encountering him. The second section examines the *ministries* we then undertake with our bridegroom in the context of our mature, consummated love—interceding for others, encouraging others, loving our bridegroom, and bearing his authority.

For me, the journey of connecting with Jesus as my bridegroom involved input from many sources, but two were key and provide the bulk of the material presented in this book. The first source is the Bible, specifically the Old Testament book Song of Songs. Traditionally ascribed to King Solomon of the tenth century BC, third king of Israel and King David's son,[13] Song of Songs combines poetry, symbols, passion, and longing to create a story of fierce and unstoppable bridal love and pursuit. The book presents in eight chapters the words and affections of a bridegroom-king, traditionally seen as Solomon, as he pursues his bride; the responses of the bride, traditionally seen as a Shulamite commoner; and the commentary of the friends of the bride on the unfolding romance.[14]

Although numerous interpretations of the text have been offered throughout the ages—a poetic celebration of the historical marriage between King Solomon and one of his wives, a Christian guide to human sexuality and marriage, an allegory representing Jesus' love for and pursuit of his church—the last interpretation allowed me to read the book as a literary demonstration of the process of becoming the bride of Jesus, a bridegroom "greater than Solomon."[15] As I watched King Solomon woo his Shulamite bride-to-be in the first four chapters of Song of Songs and then minister with her in the next four, I encountered a powerfully

---

13. See Song 1:1.

14. The bride is called a Shulamite in Song 6:13, which is traditionally understood as denoting a person from the Israelite city of Shunem, a person from Jerusalem (Salem), or a feminine form of the name *Solomon*; see Josh 19:18 and 1 Kgs 1:3. Although in this book I refer to the lovers in Song of Songs as "Solomon" and "the bride," I am using these names to represent the roles of bridegroom and bride in Song of Songs and am not referencing the historical Solomon nor any of his historical wives.

15. See Matt 12:42 and Luke 11:31.

illustrative picture of how Jesus draws and matures his bride. Thus, the chapters of this book are organized around Song of Songs' evolving bridal narrative, and each chapter uses one section from Song of Songs to provide the topic and infrastructure for that chapter. I recommend that you read the corresponding Song of Songs section as you begin each chapter.

The second important source that inspired me to pursue Jesus as my bridegroom might surprise you, but it is the writings of Christians who lived in early America, in the years 1600–1800. While this may seem like a time period far removed from our own in terms of culture and ideology, much about early America actually connects closely to our own time.

For instance, America from its inception was diverse. As we know, Native peoples had lived in the Americas for centuries and had their own extremely varied languages, cultures, and ways of life. Indigenous tribes in the northeastern woodlands differed vastly from tribes in the Pacific Northwest, for example, and some estimate the number of Native American languages to have been more than one thousand. When Europeans began to develop settlements in the early 1600s, they added radically to the diversity in terms of race, culture, and values. Jamestown was founded in Virginia by English settlers interested in financial gain, while English Puritans started the Massachusetts Bay Colony for religious freedom. Maryland was settled by Catholics, the Carolinas were modeled on the Caribbean plantation system, and Georgia began as an English penal colony. Florida was settled by the Spanish, New York by the Dutch, and New Orleans and Detroit by the French. Early Americans were farmers, hunters, traders, ministers, merchants, laborers, artisans, free and indentured and enslaved, and all races, ethnicities, and backgrounds mingled in what truly was a melting pot of humanity.

Early America was also quite dynamic. Indigenous peoples shifted alliances with each other and with settlers and re-formed themselves into larger, more powerful tribal communities. Colonial towns changed ownership and governments, land disputes were endless, and European wars wreaked continual havoc on commerce and trade. Even the thirteen original English colonies each had its own government, currency, and borders. So, while much is different in our time, the diversity and vibrancy of early America allows it to still speak to our culture today.

But perhaps the most important reason I turned to early American Christians to inform my understanding of Jesus as our bridegroom is the fact that, for these believers, Jesus' role as bridegroom of the church was central to their understanding of the Christian life, more central than it is for Christians today. Presbyterians, Congregationalists, Methodists, Puritans, Quakers, and other groups all employed the bridal framework to represent the relationship of the believer to Jesus, and their stories offer their own experiences with Jesus in this context. As a professor of early American literature, I have been privileged to encounter these real-life accounts of Christians pursuing a bridal calling, and these experiences have deepened my understanding of my identity as a bride of Christ.

In fact, these stories, told in the writers' own words, are what prompted this book. I wanted to curate for modern readers a collection of the most interesting, instructive, and inspiring accounts of early Americans who embraced the bridal love of Jesus, so each chapter includes both the life story and one piece of writing of an American Christian who has something to teach us. The writers are as varied as was early America—male and female, rich and poor, minister and lay person, Puritan and Methodist and Quaker, Native American and African American and Anglo American. The texts themselves include personal journal entries, letters, a missionary diary, poems, a published sermon, and spiritual narratives and have been silently modernized where necessary to make them accessible for the reader. I suspect you will be pleasantly surprised by the passion and power of these voices from the past and by how much they can inspire us to pursue the love and affection of Jesus our bridegroom.

My hope is that these two sources, the bride's experience in Song of Songs and the transformative stories and writings of early Americans, will provide a unique approach that makes the journey toward embracing the bridal love of Jesus understandable, practical, accessible, and appealing for all readers. Before we commence our discussion, let's lay the foundation for where in the Bible we get our understanding of Jesus as the bridegroom of the church.

JESUS THE BRIDEGROOM OF THE CHURCH

Perhaps the best place to start when examining Jesus as bridegroom in the Bible is at the end instead of the beginning. As noted above, we learn from the final book of the Bible, Revelation, that the end-time kingdom of God will commence with the wedding of the Lamb of God, Jesus Christ, and his bride, the church. Written by John the apostle, Revelation has as its stated purpose "the revelation of Jesus Christ, which God gave him to show to his servants the things that must soon take place,"[16] and Jesus is compellingly revealed in Revelation to be a conquering king who will return to judge the world and establish his everlasting kingdom. At the end of the book, after all the (literally) earth-shattering warnings, judgments, angelic messages, and celestial battles, the heavenly marriage of the Lamb and his bride magnificently initiates the glorious kingdom of God: "Then I saw a new heaven and a new earth, for the first heaven and the first earth had passed away, and the sea was no more. And I saw the holy city, new Jerusalem, coming down out of heaven from God, prepared as a bride adorned for her husband."[17]

John is stunned by the beauty and glory of Jesus' bride, as he records, "Then came one of the seven angels who had the seven bowls full of the seven last plagues and spoke to me, saying, 'Come, I will show you the Bride, the wife of the Lamb.' And he carried me away in the Spirit to a great, high mountain, and showed me the holy city Jerusalem coming down out of heaven from God, having the glory of God, its radiance like a most rare jewel, like a jasper, clear as crystal."[18] John spends the next twenty-one verses describing this city of "pure gold, like clear glass"—its twelve gates, each made of a single pearl inscribed with the name of a tribe of Israel; its twelve foundations, engraved with the names of the twelve apostles and adorned with twelve types of jewels; its endless source of light coming from the Lamb; and its river of the water of life, flowing from God's throne into the center of the city and feeding the tree of life with its twelve fruits that offer healing to the world. Nothing impure exists in this city, and only those "whose names are written in the Lamb's book of life" dwell there. Perfect intimacy between the Lamb and his bride is finally realized as "they will see his face, and his name will be on their foreheads."[19] No wonder John ends his book by crying out for Jesus' return with the words "The Spirit and the Bride say, 'Come.'"[20]

But for students of the New Testament, the centrality of Jesus' end-time wedding is not really a surprise, as the bridal relationship of Jesus and his church appears in the writings of other prominent disciples of Jesus besides John the apostle. For example, John the Baptist uses a powerful bridal metaphor to locate his preaching and baptizing within the

16. Rev 1:1a.
17. Rev 21:1, 2.
18. Rev 21:9–11.
19. Rev 21:12—22:5.
20. Rev 22:17a.

context of Jesus' emerging public ministry: "You yourselves can testify that I said, 'I am not the Messiah but am sent ahead of him.' The bride belongs to the bridegroom. The friend who attends the bridegroom waits and listens for him, and is full of joy when he hears the bridegroom's voice. That joy is mine, and it is now complete. He must become greater; I must become less."[21]

Similarly, in his second letter to the Christian church in Corinth, the apostle Paul utilizes bridal language when referring to those who have become believers through his ministry: "Do bear with me! For I feel a divine jealousy for you, since I betrothed you to one husband, to present you as a pure virgin to Christ."[22] And, of course, Paul's well-known comparison of the earthly marriage relationship to Christ and his church in the book of Ephesians highlights explicitly the connection between Jesus as bridegroom and the church as his bride: "Therefore a man shall leave his father and mother and hold fast to his wife, and the two shall become one flesh. This mystery is profound, and I am saying that it refers to Christ and the church."[23] The use of explicit bridal imagery by both John the Baptist and Paul reveals the importance of Jesus' role as bridegroom of the church in their minds.

Of course, bridal imagery in the Bible begins even before the writings of the New Testament, as there are many passages in the Old Testament that identify God as the bridegroom of his bride Israel. Sadly, many of these Old Testament passages present Israel as a consistently unfaithful bride to her lovingly faithful husband Yahweh. For example, God complains about his people to the prophet Hosea, the last great prophet to the northern kingdom of Israel from 753–715 BC, with these words: "Rebuke your mother, rebuke her, for she is not my wife, and I am not her husband. . . . She said, 'I will go after my lovers.'"[24] One hundred years later, Jeremiah, prophet to the southern kingdom of Judah, shares a similar message with the people of Israel from the broken heart of God: "I remember the devotion of your youth, your love as a bride," but now "as a treacherous wife leaves her husband, so have you been treacherous to me, O house of Israel."[25] Several decades later, as Ezekiel prophesies to the Israelites in captivity in Babylon, he uses sixty-three verses

21. John 3:28–30 (NIV).
22. 2 Cor 11:1b-2.
23. Eph 5:31–32.
24. Hos 2:2a, 5b (NIV).
25. Jer 2:2, 3:20.

to deliver an anguished condemnation of Israel as a traitorous spouse, including this rebuke: "Adulterous wife, who receives strangers instead of her husband!"[26]

But despite Israel's consistent infidelity, God remains a faithful husband. In Hosea, God promises to reclaim his wife Israel: "But then I will win her back once again. I will lead her into the desert and speak tenderly to her there. . . . You will call me 'my husband' instead of 'my master'. . . . I will make you my wife forever, showing you righteousness and justice, unfailing love and compassion. I will be faithful to you and make you mine, and you will finally know me as the LORD."[27] In Jeremiah, God promises mercy to his wandering bride: "Return, faithless Israel, declares the LORD. I will not look on you in anger, for I am merciful."[28] Even Ezekiel closes his book with twelve chapters detailing Israel's restoration under the hand of God, including this promise from God: "I will make a covenant of peace with them. It shall be an everlasting covenant with them. And I will set them in their land and multiply them, and will set my sanctuary in their midst forevermore."[29] Thank God for his unyielding faithfulness and love![30]

There are many additional biblical passages that use bridal imagery which we will examine throughout this book, but one truth we can glean from this short introductory discussion is that Jesus himself designed his relationship with us to include his role as bridegroom, and embracing that role for ourselves not only fulfills Jesus' desire for his church but our deepest desires as well. That is why learning to see Jesus as our bridegroom matters. If I saw my husband only as a financial provider, a co-parent, a lifestyle partner, or a friend, how much depth and joy in our relationship would I be missing? Jesus wants to share with us the profound love, intimacy, passion, and pleasure found in marriage, and his ultimate goal as bridegroom of the church is to draw his bride to himself, loving and caring for her as an affectionate husband and maturing her into the perfect partner who will reign with him throughout eternity, to their mutual benefit and delight. This is what Paul assures us of in Eph 5:25b–27: "Christ loved the church and gave himself up for her, that he

26. Ezek 16:32.
27. Hos 2:14, 16b, 19–20 (NLT).
28. Jer 3:12a.
29. Ezek 37:26.
30. For a detailed discussion of Jesus as the bridegroom through the eyes of Jewish tradition and scripture, see Pitre, *Jesus the Bridegroom*.

might sanctify her, having cleansed her by the washing of water with the word, so that he might present the church to himself in splendor, without spot or wrinkle or any such thing, that she might be holy and without blemish."

So, let's begin our journey into the heart of Jesus the bridegroom and his relentless yet tender pursuit of our hearts. I pray you will be surprised, delighted, captivated, and inspired by Jesus' passionate bridal love for you.

Responding to Our Bridegroom

1

Awakening to Him: Samson Occom
Song of Songs 1:1–11

Let him smother me with kisses—his Spirit-kiss divine.
So kind are your caresses,
I drink them in like the sweetest wine!
Your presence releases a fragrance so pleasing—
over and over poured out.
For your lovely name is "Flowing Oil."
No wonder the brides-to-be adore you.
Draw me into your heart.
We will run away together into the king's cloud-filled chamber.[1]

OUR JOURNEY INTO THE bridegroom heart of Jesus begins with romance—the premarital romance of a future bride and bridegroom, as revealed in the first four chapters of Song of Songs. And, as is sometimes the case in life, one party is initially much more eager for a lifelong union than is the other! In this instance, although the bride-to-be is attracted to her aspiring groom, she is not truly awakened to all that he is and to all that their relationship will become. No matter. The groom-to-be is remarkably optimistic, unswervingly committed, desperately in love, and eternally patient. He will have his bride.

---

1. Song 1:2–4a.

As those who aspire to relate more deeply to Jesus as our bridegroom, we must begin our journey by recognizing that Jesus himself initiates and directs the process of making us his bride. Thankfully, it is not up to us to kick-start the romance, so we can breathe a huge sigh of relief. Jesus, creator and Savior of the universe, is the one who made our union with himself possible when he died on the cross to save us from our sins, Jesus is the one who gives every follower the Holy Spirit to ensure our continual growth in holiness and relationship with him, and Jesus is the one who will wed us to himself at the start of his eternal kingdom. Jesus does it all!

That is why the four chapters in the first section of this book focus on Jesus' pursuit of us as his bride and the *responses* he desires us to have to his overtures. We are not called to initiate and direct our bridal relationship with Jesus, but we are called to respond to his promptings. Thus, our discussion of becoming Jesus' bride begins by examining four responses we hope to have to Jesus—awakening to him, choosing him, pursuing him, and encountering him. These responses will move our hearts nearer to the heart of our beloved bridegroom.

AWAKENING TO JESUS

In this chapter, we focus on our first desirable response to Jesus as his bride—having our hearts awakened to his love for us. Our spirits must be roused to the fact that Jesus is our bridegroom and that he desires to relate to us in an intimate way. Just as we first awakened to Jesus as our Savior when we received salvation and later as our Lord when we learned to obey him, so we must deliberately turn our attention to opening our hearts to him as our loving bridegroom.

Becoming awakened suggests in one sense a straightforward, uncomplicated experience. When we awaken physically from sleep, we become aware of the life going on around us that we were missing while we were slumbering. In the same way, awakening to Jesus as our bridegroom is straightforward. We learn the basic truth that Jesus loves his church with a bridal love. It's that simple.

Yet, in another sense, there is a deeper experience of awakening, isn't there? We've all sleepwalked through enough early morning work meetings, late-night "meaningful" conversations, and lazy Sunday afternoons to know that sometimes we can be technically awake but not really engaged at a meaningful level. If we're not careful, we can end up in that exact place with Jesus—recognizing that he loves us as a bridegroom but not really connecting meaningfully with him in that role.

I know this pitfall is real because I fell into it at least two times myself on my journey to embrace Jesus' bridal love. The first time was in my late twenties when I first heard the truth that Jesus loved me as a bride. Although the reality of this message struck me with such force that I actually taught on the subject at a few women's conferences over the next several years, I did not really know how to process the revelation deeply or how to integrate it into my relationship with Jesus in practical ways. Thus, it remained mostly intellectual for me, and I eventually forgot about it.

A second encounter with Jesus' bridal love occurred a decade later when Paul's words in 2 Cor 5:11–21 and Col 1:21–29 helped me realize that my ministry to the church, even as a layperson, was done in partnership with Jesus as his bride. However, I limited this second experience of Jesus as my bridegroom solely to a ministry context, again not really allowing it to penetrate my heart profoundly or permanently.

But the passion of our bridegroom is nothing if not astonishingly tenacious! Another decade later, Jesus tried once again to reach my heart, and this time the dart struck deeply, effectively, and irrevocably. At that time, I had been sensing in my spirit that the lessons I had been working on in my spiritual life were ending and that new lessons would soon begin. What this new learning stage would be, however, I really could not determine. Then, one night while I was in prayer, Jesus spoke to my heart that it was time for me to get to know him as my bridegroom. Despite my uncertainty and fear about how to proceed toward that goal, I embarked on the journey with him. This time, thankfully, I became truly awakened to his bridal love, watching as my life changed forever, just like it had when I had embraced him many years before as my Savior.

What was the difference between my first significant but still limited encounters with Jesus' bridal love and the powerful, life-altering awakening I later experienced? Certainly, in one sense, important truths need time to move into the depths of our hearts, so initial, less impactful realizations can be necessary stepping stones to future deeper revelation. But, in another sense, a life-changing awakening has two characteristics that less influential insights do not. A real awakening to Jesus as our bridegroom is both *deep* and *wide*. Deep, because it reaches a place that brings true change; wide, because it affects our life as a whole and not just one part. The first two times I encountered Jesus as my bridegroom, the impact was limited and soon faded. But the final time, Jesus' bridal love sent shock waves across all areas of my life and has stayed with me. My devotional practices, my sense of identity, my spiritual and earthly goals, my relationships with others—all these and more were affected permanently by my new recognition and acceptance of Jesus as my bridegroom. This is a true awakening.

So how do we position our hearts so they can truly awaken to Jesus as our bridegroom in the deepest, widest, most profound sense? I believe the bride in Song of Songs and one of the greatest Native American preachers of all time can help us find our answers.

THE BRIDE'S HEART AWAKENS: SONG 1:1-11

The first eleven verses of Song of Songs show us the bride as she awakens her heart and begins responding to the overtures of her bridegroom, the king. Her opening words reveal to us that she both appreciates her bridegroom and desires to deepen her relationship with him, as she asserts in verses two and three: "For your love is better than wine; your anointing oils are fragrant; your name is oil poured out; therefore virgins love you." She also expresses her desire to move into a bridal relationship with the king when she requests to enter his bedchamber: "Let him kiss me with the kisses of his mouth. . . . Take me away with you—let us hurry! Let the king bring me into his chambers."[2]

Yet despite these beautiful sentiments, the bride has two challenges ahead of her, and these challenges can become obstacles to awakening her heart. Her first challenge is that she does not know how to find her bridegroom in this deeper way; she asks, "Tell me, you whom my soul loves, where you pasture your flock, where you make it lie down at noon."[3] Although she values and loves her king, she does not yet know how to access him in this new role as bridegroom.

Perhaps the bigger obstacles for the bride are her feelings of unworthiness and shame. Although she claims that she is "lovely," she also begs, "Do not gaze at me because I am dark, because the sun has looked upon me. My mother's sons were angry with me; they made me keeper of the

---

2. Song 1:2a, 4 (NIV).
3. Song 1:7a.

vineyards, but my own vineyard I have not kept!"[4] This is not a concern about race, ethnicity, or socioeconomic status but a feeling that she is not attractive to the king because she has been unable to tend to her "own vineyard," traditionally understood to symbolize her inward spirit.[5]

Thus, the bride encounters two obstacles to awakening her heart to her bridegroom—lack of knowledge about the bridegroom himself and lack of security in her identity as the one he desires. For us as well, connecting with Jesus as a bride can be difficult when we don't know much about him in that role or when we do not feel worthy of his spousal love and attention. Thankfully, the bride in Song of Songs not only reveals these obstacles but also shows us how to overcome these challenges.

First, as we read in verse seven, the bride has the humility to admit her weakness and need and to ask the bridegroom for help in finding him. And he answers her immediately! "If you do not know [where to find me], O most beautiful among women, follow in the tracks of the flock, and pasture your young goats beside the shepherds' tents" is his reply in the very next verse.[6] This is important for us to remember when we desire to awaken our heart to our beloved: Jesus is not a reluctant bridegroom, waiting for us to meet him halfway. When we admit to him that we need him and that we desire to awaken to him in a deeper, more intimate way, he will respond to us. He longs to be the one to meet all of our needs if we would only ask because he is not just loving but is love itself.[7] He will never leave us alone and forsaken on our journey to him; he will respond to our cries because he loves us.

In fact, I would argue that Jesus responds to us in a special way when we are willing to admit our need and ask for his help. We can learn and grow greatly in the Christian life through strength. We can develop self-discipline, we can learn to focus our thoughts, we can recall and stir up our faith in God's promises, and we can resist and reject temptation when it seeks to master us. But awakening our heart to our bridegroom cannot be accomplished through strength because our weakness is what moves his heart. When we admit to Jesus that we need him, he can move closer to us because our heart is open to him. Love, especially perfect love, does not force itself on the beloved but waits to be invited because then the connection is authentic. Jesus knows that when we admit our weakness

---

4. Song 1:5a, 6.
5. See, for example, Henry, *Commentary*, 3:1057–58.
6. Song 1:8.
7. 1 John 4:8.

and ask for help, this act positions our heart where he can awaken us. The process of becoming the bride of Jesus must be undertaken in weakness, not in strength, and asking for help is the first step in the process.

The second wise choice of the bride in Song of Songs is accepting the bridegroom's vision of herself and allowing his perspective to shift her view of herself away from shame and unworthiness and toward approval and love. While she sees herself as "darkened by the sun" and an unfit companion for the king,[8] her bridegroom offers a contrasting view when he declares in verses nine and ten, "I compare you, my love, to a mare among Pharaoh's chariots. Your cheeks are lovely with ornaments, your neck with strings of jewels." Solomon does not see his bride as inadequate but as utterly appealing, and the more the bride can accept his view of her, the more easily she will relate to Solomon as her bridegroom.

Although this may be hard for you to believe, Jesus sees you as beautiful. He does not see you as unworthy, unattractive, or deficient. He loves you, enjoys you, believes in you, and is supremely attracted to you. For *you*, he left heaven and came to earth to die brutally and shamefully on a cross.

If you would like to see how you appear in Jesus' eyes, read Ps 45. Composed by those who served in the temple of Israel, this psalm was written for an historic wedding between a king, possibly Solomon, and his bride, but the song is also a prophetic picture of bridegroom Jesus and his bride the church, as identified in Heb 1:8–9. The first half of the psalm addresses the king on his wedding day, offering him both beautiful words of praise and an exhortation to ride onward in triumphant conquest. The second half of the psalm does the same for the bride. She is exhorted to listen to her king and choose him, leaving behind her people and her family because "your royal husband delights in your beauty."[9] Look at how the psalm describes the bride: "The bride, a princess, looks glorious in her golden gown. In her beautiful robes, she is led to the king, accompanied by her bridesmaids. What a joyful and enthusiastic procession as they enter the king's palace!"[10] This is how Jesus sees you—lovely and desirable, his perfect partner. And while it might be challenging to accept the fact that the king of the universe longs for a profoundly intimate relationship with you, embracing this truth is actually a crucial step in awakening your heart to him.

8. Song 1:6a (NIV).
9. Ps 45:10–11 (NLT).
10. Ps 45:13–15 (NLT).

If you are struggling to align your view of yourself more closely with how Jesus sees you, I would offer a few suggestions. First, simply confess to him that you are struggling with accepting his view of you and ask for his help in shifting your perspective. Ultimately, he must work in our hearts to make this change, so it's best to bring him into the process at the beginning! Second, confess and verbally reject any incorrect view of yourself as inadequate, deficient, unlovable, too needy, and so on, even if you actually believe those descriptions are true of you. They are not. Consistently and persistently reject those descriptors; Jesus does not see you in those ways, and his view is the only view that counts. Third, begin to fill your mind and speech with truths from the Bible about how Jesus *does* see you. Verses from Song of Songs can be very helpful here as can the lyrics of many hymns and worship songs. Meditate on biblical passages like this one from Zeph 3:17: "The LORD your God is in your midst, a mighty one who will save; he will rejoice over you with gladness; he will quiet you by his love; he will exult over you with loud singing." The Holy Spirit will use biblical truth to move your heart into accepting that Jesus finds you stunningly beautiful and desirable. After all, what bridegroom marries a bride he is not attracted to?

SAMSON OCCOM'S CALL TO THE "WEDDING DAY"

The bride in Song of Songs is not the only voice that can teach us how to awaken our hearts to our bridegroom Jesus. Samson Occom (1723–92), one of the best-known Native American Christian preachers in the eighteenth century, is in some ways our perfect guide in this matter because he himself was both awakened to Jesus and became an awakener of others.

Born a member of the Mohegan tribe in Connecticut, Occom was believed to be descended from a famous Mohegan chief. His life was permanently changed at age sixteen by the eruption in his region of the First Great Awakening, an evangelical religious revival that swept through Great Britain and the American colonies beginning in 1739. Fiery evangelistic preachers visited Occom's area, and Occom attended many revival meetings, experiencing his own religious awakening at seventeen and converting to Christianity. At the age of twenty, Occom began a four-year course of study for the ministry with Congregational minister Eleazar Wheelock (1711–79), himself a passionate supporter of the Awakening who had traveled for a time as an itinerant preacher. Occom was ordained as a Presbyterian minister in 1759 and enjoyed a thirty-year career as a traveling minister.[11]

Occom's urgency and passion as a religious awakener is what prompted me to feature him in this chapter. Occom worked as a missionary to Indigenous tribes; his only surviving sermon from his early years as a missionary uses the metaphor of "awakening" to explain the necessity of the new birth highlighted in Eph 5:14 to his audience of Montauks in New York.[12] He spent two years traveling throughout England in partnership with English evangelist George Whitefield and others to raise money for Wheelock's Indian school, which would become Dartmouth College, preaching more than three hundred sermons throughout the country.[13] In the colonies, Occom preached thousands of sermons throughout New England and the mid-Atlantic to congregations of diverse races, denominations, and socioeconomic statuses, his extemporaneous preaching style enabling him to deliver a message with power and fervor. Fellow pastor and friend Samuel Buell (1716–1798) had this to say of Occom's preaching: "As a preacher of the gospel, he seems always to have before his eye the great end of the ministry, the glory of God, and the salvation of men."[14] Occom spent his later years helping establish and grow the Brotherton tribe, a newly organized tribe of Christian Native Americans from various communities that formed in 1773 and eventually settled in New York. When he died in 1792, hundreds attended the funeral of this powerful awakener.[15]

Beyond his achievements in ministry, Occom's life highlights many of the challenges and successes Indigenous peoples faced in the colonies. Native Americans and Anglo American colonists had varied and intricate connections in their daily lives—through land treaties, missionary endeavors, educational institutions, military skirmishes and all-out wars, commerce and trade, captivities and ransoms, and shared social encounters. Colonial towns and communities were a diverse mix of ethnicities, backgrounds, and interests.

As a convert to Christianity, Occom had strong connections with Anglo American Christians, studying and ministering with them. As

---

11. Brooks, *Collected Writings of Samson Occom*, 13–14.

12. Brooks, *Collected Writings of Samson Occom*, 161; see pages 166–70 for the complete sermon.

13. Brooks, *Collected Writings of Samson Occom*, 161.

14. Buell, *Excellence and Importance*, viii.

15. Brooks, *Collected Writings of Samson Occom*, 27.

his ministry progressed, however, Occom felt an increasing burden for his own people and grew concerned that Anglo American interests were too often opposed to those of Native Americans. Ultimately, he shifted his energies to Native American causes and challenged Anglo American ministers to fully support Indigenous rights and ministries.

The excerpt included in this chapter is an example of that refocus. *A Sermon, Preached at the Execution of Moses Paul, an Indian*, Occom's only published sermon, was delivered in September 1772 before a large, racially mixed crowd in New Haven, Connecticut, at the request of Moses Paul himself, who was to be executed for the crime of murder. The sermon was well-received and went through nineteen published editions over many decades.[16]

In the sermon, Occom shares his belief that salvation through Christ is necessary for happiness in both this life and the next, regardless of ethnicity or status: "This must be the unavoidable portion of all impenitent sinners, let them be who they will—great or small, honorable or ignoble, rich or poor, bond or free. Negroes, Indians, English, or of whatsoever nation, all that die in their sins must go to hell together, for the wages of sin is death."[17] Occom uses his opportunity to fearlessly and unapologetically preach the gospel message that all people, regardless of race, socioeconomic status, or reputation, need Jesus to save them from their sins.

THE BEAUTY AND PASSION OF JESUS

There are two aspects of Occom's sermon that I believe will help awaken our hearts to Jesus as our bridegroom. First, notice Occom's focus on the person of Jesus himself—his kindness, sufficiency, and mercy. Occom works hard in his oration to present to his listeners the person of Jesus in all his glory and attractiveness as our magnificent redeemer. In the same way, as those who are seeking to awaken our hearts to Jesus' bridal love, we also should center our thoughts, emotions, and attention on Jesus.

However, I would argue that while any focus on Jesus is beneficial, concentrating specifically on his *beauty* is the best choice for awakening to him as bridegroom. Throughout the ages, beauty has been thought to combine aspects of harmony, symmetry, integrity, perfection, splendor,

16. Brooks, *Collected Writings of Samson Occom*, 162.
17. Occom, *Sermon*, 17.

and radiance. There is a balance, consistency, excellence, and exquisiteness in beauty that pleases and touches us deeply as humans. Writers have long known this truth; nineteenth-century American author and literary critic Edgar Allan Poe (1809–49) remarks, "That pleasure which is at once the most intense, the most elevating, and the most pure is, I believe, found in the contemplation of the beautiful."[18] Similarly, English writer Joseph Addison (1672–1719) notes that "there is nothing that makes its way more directly to the soul than beauty."[19]

The attribute of beauty has often been applied to Jesus—and rightly so. Cathedrals throughout the world are filled with artwork presenting the absolute loveliness of our Savior. This is not physical beauty based on appearance or cultural representations of Jesus but a beauty that comes from the perfect consistency, integrity, virtue, and attractiveness of his *person*. In his commentary on Ps 45, church father Augustine of Hippo asserts the all-surpassing beauty of Jesus:

> To us, however, now that we are believers, let the Bridegroom, wheresoever he is, appear beautiful. . . . He then is "beautiful" in heaven, beautiful on earth, beautiful in the womb, beautiful in His parents' hands, beautiful in His miracles, beautiful under the scourge, beautiful when inviting to life . . . beautiful on the cross, beautiful in the sepulcher, beautiful in heaven.[20]

Verses two through nine of Ps 45 extol Jesus' beauty, with perhaps the best-known line being the first part of verse two: "You are fairer than the sons of men."[21]

The flawless beauty of Jesus awakens our hearts to him as our bridegroom in ways his mercy, gentleness, power, and even holiness do not. Jesus' beauty attracts and delights us, and attraction is necessary for successful courtship and marriage. We *want* to pursue the beautiful, and we are drawn to Jesus through his loveliness. When I was first learning to awaken my heart to Jesus as my bridegroom, I spent a lot of time meditating on biblical passages that reveal the beauty of Jesus such as Pss 2, 45; Song 5:10–16; Isa 52:13—53:12; Rev 1:12–16; Rev 5; and Rev 19:11–16. I listened to worship songs that admired the beauty of Jesus, and, in my personal praise times, I focused my adoration on his loveliness. Truly,

---

18. Poe, "Philosophy of Composition," 164.
19. Addison, *Spectator*, no. 412.
20. Augustine, Bishop of Hippo, *Expositions*, 2:230.
21. NKJV.

the ravishing beauty of our bridegroom awakens our hearts to him as nothing else can, and I believe you will enjoy reading Occom's eloquent descriptions of our lovely Savior.

Second, I appreciate how Occom reminds us of how absolutely relentlessly Jesus pursues his bride. When we are in the beginning stages of opening up to our bridegroom, we are encouraged when we remember that he is passionate about pursuing us and thus will *never* abandon the quest to awaken our hearts. Notice how Occom assures the convicted Moses Paul of Jesus' determination to find him: "Must Christ follow you into the prison by his servants and there entreat you to accept of eternal life, and will you refuse it? And must he follow you even to the gallows and there beseech you to accept of him, and will you refuse him? Shall he be crucified [close] by your gallows, as it were, and will you regard him not?"[22] Occom offers his listeners a poignant image of Jesus pursuing the one he loves through the jail cell and onto the actual scaffold. What an arresting picture of the unwavering passion of our bridegroom! Remembering Jesus' never-ending desire for us can help us remain encouraged when we first begin the journey of relating to him as a bride.

So, let's turn to the sermon excerpt from our awakener Samson Occom and let our hearts be stirred by his picture of Jesus, our beautiful bridegroom. As Occom assures Moses Paul, "Oh, what a joyful day would it be if you would now openly believe in and receive the Lord Jesus Christ . . . instead of a melancholy day, it would be a wedding day to your soul."[23]

SERMON: A SERMON, PREACHED AT THE EXECUTION OF MOSES PAUL, AN INDIAN[24]

Romans 6:23
For the wages of sin is death, but the gift of God is eternal life through Jesus Christ our Lord.

---

22. Occom, *Sermon*, 25.
23. Occom, *Sermon*, 25.
24. Selections are from Occom, *Sermon*, 5, 20–21, 23–26. Throughout this book, non-contiguous passages in original documents are presented together for ease of reading.

Jesus Our Beautiful Redeemer

We proceed in the next place to show that this life which we have described is the free gift of God through Jesus Christ our Lord.

Sinners have forfeited all mercy into the hand of divine justice and have merited hell and damnation to themselves, for the wages of sin is everlasting death, but heaven and happiness is a free gift. It comes by favor, and all merit is excluded, and especially if we consider that we are fallen, sinful creatures and there is nothing in us that can recommend us to the favor of God, and we can do nothing that is agreeable and acceptable to God, and the mercies we enjoy in this life are altogether from the pure mercy of God—we are unequal to them.

Good old Jacob cried out, under a sense of his unworthiness, "I am less than the least of all thy mercies,"[25] and we have nothing to give to God. If we [attempt] to give all the service that we are capable of, we should give him nothing but what was his own, and when we give up ourselves to God, both soul and body, we give him nothing, for we were his before. He had right to do with us as he pleased, either to throw us into hell or to save us. There is nothing that we can call our own but our sins, and who is he that dares to say, "I expect to have heaven for my sins"? For our text says that the wages of sin is death. If we are thus unequal and unworthy of the least mercy in this life, how much more are we unworthy of eternal life?

Yet God can find it in his heart to give it. And it is altogether unmerited; it is a free gift to undeserving and hell-deserving sinners of mankind. It is altogether of God's sovereign good pleasure to give it. It is of free grace and sovereign mercy and from the unbounded goodness of God; he was self-moved to it.

And it is said that this life is given in and through the Lord Jesus Christ. It could not be given in any other way, but in and through the death and sufferings of the Lord Jesus Christ. Christ himself is the gift, and he is the Christian's life: "For God so loved the world that he gave his only

---

25. Gen 32:10.

begotten Son, that whoever believes in him should not perish, but have everlasting life."[26] The word says further, "For by grace you are saved through faith, and that not of yourselves, it is the gift of God."[27] This is given through Jesus Christ our Lord. It is Christ that purchased it with his own blood, he prepared it with his divine and almighty power, and by the same power and by the influence of his Spirit he prepares us for it, and by his divine grace preserves us to it. In a word, he is all in all in our eternal salvation; all this is the free gift of God.

But let us now turn to a more pleasant theme. Though you [Moses Paul] have been a great sinner, a heaven-daring sinner, yet hark and hear the joyful sound from heaven, even from the King of kings and Lord of lords, that the gift of God is eternal life through Jesus Christ our Lord. It is a free gift and offered to the greatest sinners, and upon their true repentance towards God and faith in the Lord Jesus Christ, they shall be welcome to the life which we have spoken of. It is offered upon free terms. He that has no money may come; he that has no righteousness, no goodness, may come; the call is to poor undone sinners. The call is not to the righteous, but sinners, calling them to repentance. Hear the voice of the Son of the most high God, "Come to me, all you that labor and are heavy-laden, and I will give you rest."[28] This is a call, a gracious call to you, poor Moses, under your present burdens and distresses.

And Christ alone has a right to call sinners to himself. It would be presumption for a mighty angel to call a poor sinner in this manner, and were it possible for you to apply to all God's creatures, they would with one voice tell you that it was not in them to help you. Go to all the means of grace, they would prove miserable helps, without Christ himself. Yes, apply to all the ministers of the gospel in the world, they would all say that it was not in them, but would only prove as indexes to point out to you the Lord Jesus Christ, the only Savior of sinners of mankind. Yes, go to all the angels in heaven, they would do the same. Yes, go to God

---

26. John 3:16.
27. Eph 2:8.
28. Matt 11:28.

the Father himself—without Christ, he could not help you, to speak after the manner of humans, he would also point to the Lord Jesus Christ and say, "This is my beloved Son, in whom I am well pleased; hear him."[29] Thus you see, poor Moses, that there is none in heaven or on the earth that can help you, but Christ; he alone has power to save and to give life.

God the eternal Father appointed him, chose him, authorized, and fully commissioned him to save sinners. He came down from heaven into this lower world and became as one of us and stood in our [place]. He was the second Adam. And as God demanded perfect obedience of the first Adam, the second fulfilled it; and as the first sinned and incurred the wrath and anger of God, the second endured it; he suffered in our [place]. As he became sin for us, he was a man of sorrows and acquainted with grief; all our stripes were laid upon him.[30]

Yes, he was finally condemned because we were under condemnation, and at last was executed and put to death for our sins, was lifted up between the heaven and the earth, and was crucified on the accursed tree. His blessed hands and feet were fastened there; there he died a shameful and ignominious death; there he finished the great work of our redemption; there his heart's blood was shed for our cleansing; there he fully satisfied the divine justice of God for penitent, believing sinners, though they have been the chief of sinners.

Jesus Our Passionate Bridegroom

Oh, Moses! This is good news to you in this last day of your life: here is a crucified Savior at hand for your sins. His blessed hands are outstretched, all in a gore of blood for you. This is the only Savior, an almighty Savior, just such as you stand in infinite and perishing need of. Oh, poor Moses! Hear the dying prayer of a gracious Savior on the accursed tree, "Father forgive them for they know

29. Matt 17:5.
30. Isa 53:3, 5.

not what they do."[31] This was a prayer for his enemies and murderers, and it is for you, if you would only repent and believe in him.

Oh, why will you die eternally, poor Moses, since Christ has died for sinners? Why will you go to hell from beneath the bleeding Savior, as it were? This is the day of your execution, yet it is the accepted time, it is the day of salvation if you will now believe in the Lord Jesus Christ. Must Christ follow you into the prison by his servants and there entreat you to accept of eternal life, and will you refuse it? And must he follow you even to the gallows and there beseech you to accept of him, and will you refuse him? Shall he be crucified [close] by your gallows, as it were, and will you regard him not?

Oh, poor Moses, now believe on the Lord Jesus Christ with all your heart, and you shall be saved eternally. Come, just as you are, with all your sins and abominations, with all your filthiness, with all your blood-guiltiness, with all your condemnation, and lay hold of the hope set before you this day. This is the last day of salvation with your soul; you will be beyond the bounds of mercy in a few minutes more.

Oh, what a joyful day would it be if you would now openly believe in and receive the Lord Jesus Christ. It would be the beginning of heavenly days with your poor soul. Instead of a melancholy day, it would be a wedding day to your soul. It would cause the very angels in heaven to rejoice and the saints on earth to be glad. It would cause the angels to come down from the realms above and wait hovering [near] your gallows, ready to convey your soul to the heavenly mansions, there to take the possession of eternal glory and happiness and join the heavenly choirs in singing the songs of Moses and the Lamb, there to set down forever with Abraham, Isaac, and Jacob in the kingdom of God's glory. And your shame and guilt shall be forever banished from the place, and all sorrow and fear forever fly away, and tears be wiped from your face, and there shall you forever admire the astonishing and amazing and infinite mercy of God in Christ Jesus in pardoning such a monstrous sinner

---

31. Luke 23:34.

as you have been. There you will claim the highest note of praise, for the riches of free grace in Christ Jesus.

CHAPTER SUMMARY AND FURTHER READING[32]

I hope you were inspired by this chapter to seek a deep and wide awakening of your heart to the matchless love of your bridegroom Jesus. As Samson Occom reminds us, he is a beautiful Savior who relentlessly pursues us. And as the bride in Song of Songs models for us, asking for his help and embracing how passionately he loves us are two important first steps in awakening our hearts.

If you are interested in learning more about Samson Occom, I would recommend Joanna Brooks's *The Collected Writings of Samson Occom, Mohegan: Leadership and Literature in Eighteenth-Century Native America*. Brooks offers an interesting introduction to Occom's life and times as well as reprints of many of his sermons, letters, original hymns, and journal entries, including tribal documents that reveal Occom's important role among the Mohegans. For a discussion of Occom and American evangelicalism during the years of the First Great Awakening, see the chapter "Samson Occom and Evangelical Christian Indian Identity" in Julius H. Rubin's *Tears of Repentance: Christian Indian Identity and Community in Colonial Southern New England*. Angela Calcaterra's chapter "Fire and Chain: Samson Occom's Letters, Anglo-American Missions, and Haudenosaunee Eloquence" in *Literary Indians: Aesthetics and Encounters in American Literature to 1920* offers a look into Occom's life among both Anglo American and Indigenous Christians.

---

32. Full bibliographic information for the works suggested for further reading in each chapter can be found in the bibliography.

2

Choosing Him: Edward Taylor
Song of Songs 1:12—2:17

Listen! I hear my lover's voice.
I know it's him coming to me—
leaping with joy over mountains,
skipping in love over the hills that separate us,
to come to me.
Let me describe him:
he is graceful as a gazelle,
swift as a wild stag.
Now he comes closer,
even to the places where I hide.
He gazes into my soul,
peering through the portal
as he blossoms within my heart.
The one I love calls to me:
"Arise, my dearest. Hurry, my darling.
Come away with me!
I have come as you have asked
to draw you to my heart and lead you out.
For now is the time, my beautiful one."[1]

1. Song 2:8–10.

TIMING IS EVERYTHING, AS the saying goes, but often timing is not up to us, especially when it comes to choices. How true this is for everyone—the college student forced to declare a major by sophomore year, the employee faced with an early retirement package, the professional athlete who weighs risk of injury versus length of playing career, the daughter or son whose elderly parent is beginning to struggle with living alone. None of us has the power to create perfectly timed choices in our lives; we all must face decisions when they come to us, whether we feel prepared for them or not.

Having begun the journey of allowing our hearts to awaken to our bridegroom and his love for us, we are now faced with a choice—will we follow him in this new direction, or will we pull back? Deliberately choosing to embrace Jesus as our bridegroom and everything that decision entails is the second response he desires us make to his overtures of love. But what exactly is this choice and why is it important?

THE IMPORTANCE OF CHOICE

Perhaps you are surprised by my suggestion that we must deliberately *choose* Jesus as our bridegroom. After all, we've decided to open our hearts to be awakened by his love, so isn't that enough to start us on the journey?

Well, yes and no. Certainly, awakening is the first step in the journey, but at some point, we must decide to actually begin walking. Perhaps an example will clarify. Living in Southern California, I have the enviable opportunity to hike and enjoy nature most days of the year. I know this is true, I enjoy hiking, and I am open to hiking when given the opportunity. However, if I want to *actually* hike, I have to strap on my shoes, leave my house, and start down the trail. Likewise, after beginning the process of awakening our hearts to our bridegroom, we must *actually* embrace becoming his bride by moving forward with him. It's possible, even at this point, to stop the process and decide to remain where we are. Are we happy relating to Jesus simply as a servant? As a student? As a sheep? Or are we ready to begin consistently connecting with him also as a bride?

In my college classes, the vast majority of my students only relate to me as a teacher, and that is fine; it is my job to be their instructor. However, other students look for a different, deeper relationship with me and pursue it, asking me about my research or my family, inviting me to lunch, speaking with me about their spiritual lives, or sharing projects with me from their programs of study. With these students, I begin to develop real friendships, and thus it is with Jesus. If we want to press in to relate more closely to him as our bridegroom, we must say yes to his promptings and begin to pursue that course. He is always happy when we make the choice to relate to him in new ways and seek new experiences with him.

Our response of choosing Jesus as our bridegroom is in reality a very important step in our journey for two reasons. First, when we willingly choose Jesus, we are ensuring that our relationship with him will be one of authentic love because true love requires both parties to say yes. Real love doesn't happen when only one person is committed and the other is apathetic, opposed, or pursuing someone else. Choice is key to love. You can't force someone to love you. Jesus knows this truth, which is why he gave us free will in the first place. Surely, he could have created us in such a way that we would be programmed to "love" him, thereby eliminating the risk that we would reject him, but that wouldn't be genuine love, would it? Instead, he has gifted us with the freedom to choose to love him willingly, thereby ensuring that our relationship with him is authentic on both sides.

The second reason our choice to love Jesus as our bridegroom is significant is because it fulfills one of his deepest desires—the desire to be wanted. Believe it or not, Jesus longs for you to want him. Like any true lover, he wants you to desire him, pine for him, languish for him, and yearn for him desperately. I distinctly remember when this truth hit my heart as I was learning to relate to Jesus as a bride. I wrote in my journal, "I can't really believe one thing—that he so badly wants to be wanted."

I was honestly flabbergasted by that truth. Isn't Jesus perfectly self-sufficient? I had learned this lesson in Sunday School: Jesus doesn't need humans.

But maybe Jesus *wants* humans? Maybe we, made in the image of God, can look to our own deep need to be wanted and desired and surmise that this trait reflects Jesus' heart also? After all, isn't the entire Bible simply the story of God pursuing the people he loves, hoping they will turn and choose him? Jesus is holding back the coming of his eternal kingdom to give everyone on earth the chance to respond to his offer of love: "The Lord is not slow to fulfill his promise [of final judgment] as some count slowness, but is patient toward you, not wishing that any should perish, but that all should reach repentance."[2] Jeremiah assures the Jewish exiles in Babylon with God's promise that "you will seek me and find me, when you seek me with all your heart."[3] No one, not even Jesus, enjoys being in a relationship with someone who is not committed, so our deliberate decision to choose Jesus as our bridegroom reveals that we desire him and is thus significant for our journey of becoming his bride.

WHAT CHOICE LOOKS LIKE

But what, then, does choosing Jesus as our bridegroom look like? Is it simply a verbal affirmation? Does it involve practical actions, a shift in thinking, a change of affections, a long and demanding tutelage? I believe that choosing to follow Jesus as our bridegroom often involves three key pieces. The first is what I call holy dissatisfaction. Think about the last time you were dissatisfied with something in your life. Maybe you became bored in your job, felt stagnant in a relationship, longed for better physical health, or tired of your tried and true hobbies. What did that dissatisfaction feel like? Most likely, you felt restless, unhappy, uncomfortable, and ready for a change. You realized the status quo no longer satisfied you, and you longed for something else—a more challenging job, a new friendship, a healthier body, a more engaging hobby.

Dissatisfaction can occur in our spiritual lives as well. We can reach a point in our relationship with Jesus where we want something more, something else. We are no longer happy with the status quo; we want something deeper and more fulfilling from our connection with him. The good news is that this is not a bad thing—it is a wonderful thing! Spiritual dissatisfaction means that we have outgrown our current level of intimacy with the Lord and are ready to progress. In fact, God himself is the one who grants us the desire for more in our spiritual lives. If you are feeling a holy dissatisfaction in your relationship with Jesus, that is a sign that the Holy Spirit is stirring you toward a deeper connection with your bridegroom. Be grateful! Your holy discontent is what will propel you into choosing to pursue Jesus as a willing, expectant bride.

But launching forward with our bridegroom requires a second step, and that is a commitment to a personalized journey. Jesus loves you uniquely, for yourself, in a way he loves no one else in creation. Because

2. 2 Pet 3:9.
3. Jer 29:13.

of that, he will curate for you a specific path to help you grow into his bride. If you are hoping your journey will look like that of your mentor, your parents, your pastor, your best friend, your favorite social media influencer, or your spouse, you will be sadly disappointed. As a growing bride of Jesus, you must commit to pursuing the path he has for you, regardless of how different it looks from others' paths. I am not recommending becoming a lone ranger Christian who rejects fellowship or accountability within the body of Christ. Instead, I am suggesting that to become Jesus' bride, we must realize that our path to him is uniquely our own, and we must be willing to respond to him in ways that are personal.

Consider Jesus' first followers and how varied their lives were as members of the early church. John was tasked with caring for Jesus' mother, became a leader in the church in Jerusalem, and ended up exiled to the island of Patmos; Peter preached the sermon at Pentecost, ministered to the Jews, and is traditionally thought to have been crucified for his faith; Paul was sent to the gentiles and wrote much of the New Testament; Nympha hosted a church in her home in Colossae; and Priscilla and her husband Aquila worked as tentmakers and teachers in the church that met in their house.[4] Like these early lovers of Jesus, we can expect that our path will be individualized, and we can rejoice in the personal attention our bridegroom extends to us to confirm and keep us on the perfect route to him.

Lastly, in choosing our bridegroom, we want to grow in cultivating a consistent habit of saying yes to him. Recall from the last chapter that our journey as a bride is undertaken in weakness. Thus, since we are looking to Jesus to accomplish our growth and direct our course, we must make the conscious choice to agree with his decisions for us, obey his commands, trust his leadership, and align our will with his. This is all accomplished by simply saying yes to him as a choice of our will. Saying yes to Jesus does not require us to understand all that he is doing. Saying yes to Jesus does not mean we like all of his choices for us. Saying yes to Jesus does not assume we are without fear for the future. Saying yes to Jesus *does* mean that we give him our genuine, conscious affirmation that we trust him, love him, and will follow him, and we give it consistently, unconditionally, and humbly again and again and again.

If you say yes consistently to your personal trainer, your physical health will improve. If you say yes consistently to your teacher, you will

---

4. For Nympha, see Col 4:15b; for Priscilla and Aquila, see Acts 18:2–3; Rom 16:3–5a; 1 Cor 16:19.

learn. If you say yes consistently to your employer, you will progress in the company. And if you say yes consistently to your bridegroom, you will grow as his bride. Jesus doesn't need us to fully understand or completely predict all that he is working out in our lives. He just needs our yes. And with Jesus, every yes is important, no matter how big or small the choice seems to us. Every yes we give him moves his heart. So even though as humans we will fail countless times in this area, we can be encouraged that nurturing and protecting a heartfelt, unswerving commitment to saying yes to our bridegroom, through all our mistakes, will keep us on the path of growing closer to him.

So, what about the bride in Song of Songs? Having awakened her heart to her bridegroom-king, she is now presented with a choice as he calls her to follow him in a new direction. What will she do? Will she choose to embark upon this journey with him, or will she refuse him? And what can we learn from her choice?

THE BRIDE'S FATEFUL CHOICE: SONG 1:12—2:17

Our bride in Song of Songs has started strong in her journey to her bridegroom. She has asked where she can find him, she has turned to him for help, and she has allowed her heart to be awakened to him. How lovely to hear them confess their love for each other in verses fifteen and sixteen of the first chapter:

> *He*: Behold, you are beautiful, my love; behold, you are beautiful; your eyes are doves.
> *She*: Behold, you are beautiful, my beloved, truly delightful.

The bride acknowledges in verse five of the next chapter that she has been completely captivated by her bridegroom: "Sustain me with raisins; refresh me with apples, for I am sick with love."

"Sick with love," or "lovesick," as it appears in some translations,[5] is not a word we hear often today. The Oxford English Dictionary defines *lovesick* as "overwhelmed by . . . love; languishing for or with love."[6] Lovesickness connotes a love that incapacitates or overwhelms the lover by its sheer force. Some versions of the Bible translate this phrase as "weak

---

5. See, for example, NKJV and NASB.

6. *Oxford English Dictionary*, s.v. "lovesick (adj.)." Use of the word can be traced back to as early as the fifteenth century and can be found in the writings of William Shakespeare, John Dryden, Charles Dickens, and Charlotte Brontë, to name a few.

with love"[7] or "faint with love"[8] to express the devastating intensity of the experience.

As Jesus' bride, it is important that we understand the concept of lovesickness because lovesickness grows specifically in the realm of bridal love. When we begin connecting with Jesus as his bride, instead of as his servant or student, we begin to experience lovesickness. The power of lovesickness may take us by surprise, and understanding it can help us embrace it as a healthy, beneficial part of our relationship with our bridegroom.

First, we do not want to confuse lovesickness with hurtful encounters we may have had with love simply because *lovesick* contains the word *sick*. Damaging experiences with love subject us to the pain of betrayal, indifference, or mistreatment. This pain often lodges in our heart and causes negative consequences in our life such as questioning our identity or worth, feeling bitter or angry, or struggling with depression or anxiety. In these cases, our heart needs to be healed and made whole again, and the circumstances that caused the damage must be altered.

Conversely, lovesickness has its challenging aspects, but it is ultimately beneficial for us and does not cause us harm. On the one hand, when we are lovesick, our affections and desires are pulled so fiercely toward our beloved that we can feel like we are at the mercy of love. We miss the one we love, we think about them, we recall pleasant experiences together. These bittersweet thoughts and emotions can overwhelm us so forcefully that we may feel powerless to resist or diminish the drawings of love.

But, on the other hand, it is this intensity that makes lovesickness uniquely helpful for us. Lovesickness creates in us a healthy desperation for our beloved that pushes us past the normal obstacles to loving someone well—our own selfishness, laziness, insecurity, or pride. Our heart is motivated to pursue greater, deeper, purer love. Lovesickness grows love in a way that is especially effective and transformative, and our relationship with our bridegroom Jesus is strengthened and deepened as we become lovesick for him.[9] Thus, we are free to embrace lovesickness as a bride and all the intensity that it brings.

---

7. NLT.

8. NIV.

9. On the topic of lovesickness in his commentary on Song of Songs, Matthew Henry notes, "This is a sickness which is a sign of a healthy constitution of soul, and will certainly end well, a sickness that will be not of death, but life." Henry, *Commentary*,

The bride in Song of Songs has embarked on her own journey of lovesickness, erupting with joy as she sees her lover coming to her: "Behold, he comes, leaping over the mountains, bounding over the hills."[10] The bridegroom, certainly encouraged by the bride's words of passion and affirmation, arrives and asks the bride to follow him along this new path of intimacy:

> Arise, my love, my beautiful one,
>   and come away,
> for behold, the winter is past;
>   the rain is over and gone.
> The flowers appear on the earth,
>   the time of singing has come,
> and the voice of the turtledove
>   is heard in our land.
> The fig tree ripens its figs,
>   And the vines are in blossom;
>   they give forth fragrance.
> Arise, my love, my beautiful one,
>   and come away.[11]

The bridegroom is calling his beloved to a new season as spring has come and new life has blossomed in the earth. He asks her to follow him to the mountains of deeper intimacy, further into their bridal love.

But, sadly, at this early stage in her growth as a lovesick bride, she chooses not to follow her lover. Note her response in verse seventeen: "Until the day breathes and the shadows flee, turn, my beloved, be like a gazelle or a young stag on cleft mountains." The bride asks her bridegroom to return to the hills alone, without her. For some reason, she cannot choose him at this time.

We see from the bride's refusal to follow her bridegroom in Song of Songs that our own choice of Jesus as our bridegroom is not a foregone conclusion. Jesus himself knows this possibility and warned his listeners of this during his time on earth. Recall his parable of the wedding banquet, recorded in Matt 22:1–14 and Luke 14:15–24. According to Matthew, a king sends his servants to invite his intended guests to the wedding feast of his son, but those invited, with whom we assume the king has some kind of relationship, either ignore the invitation, choosing

---

3:1083.

10. Song 2:8b.

11. Song 2:10b–13.

instead to focus on their homes and businesses, or seize and kill the king's servants. The king is hurt and furious and sends his servants instead to invite anyone they can find from the roads and highways until his banquet hall is full. In the version in Luke, the parable ends with the king's chilling promise that "none of those men who were invited shall taste my banquet." The wedding feast has been closed to them.

Jesus didn't share this parable to terrify his listeners, but he did want to communicate the importance of choice in the lives of his followers. We don't know exactly why the bride refuses her bridegroom at this point. Is she afraid of what lies ahead? She mentions in verse seventeen a desire to wait until "the shadows flee." Is she worried the challenge will be too much for her? She notes the strength and grace of her bridegroom in verses eight and nine and might be afraid she will not be able to keep up with him on the mountains. Is she overwhelmed by the effort she believes joining him will require and thus simply requests in verse seventeen that he go on without her?

I suspect that the bride has misunderstood her lover's invitation. From her words, she appears to assume that he is asking her to steel her resolve, gather her strength, and work hard to join him on the mountains. But notice his actual request in Song 2:14: "O my dove, in the clefts of the rock, in the crannies of the cliff, let me see your face, let me hear your voice, for your voice is sweet, and your face is lovely." This is not a call to expend extra effort or make additional sacrifices. This is a call to deeper intimacy, an invitation to the bride to leave her place of hiddenness and move closer to the bridegroom, revealing her face and her voice, connecting with him in a more vulnerable, more personal way. He desires her to fall more profoundly in love, to embrace even more completely the lovesickness she is already beginning to experience. Would the bride have said yes if she had understood her bridegroom's true request?

We often make the same mistake when Jesus calls us to go deeper with him. We assume he is requesting that we work harder, embrace more sacrifice, and strengthen our determination. The increased labor we think is necessary to connect more closely with Jesus can seem daunting or even impossible and can weaken our motivation to move forward with him. And while struggle and sacrifice are certainly part of the Christian life, intensifying our effort is not really an effective way to grow in intimacy with our bridegroom and is not what he is asking of us. Like the bridegroom in Song of Songs, Jesus simply wants to see our face, hear our voice, and draw us into increasing lovesick desire for him.

While we will never know for certain the reasons behind the bride's fateful choice in Song 2, we can see that she is unable to follow her bridegroom at this time. However, not all brides of Jesus make this unfortunate decision. For a different perspective, let's turn to a seventeenth-century Massachusetts pastor to be encouraged to choose our bridegroom as a lovesick bride when he calls us to follow him to deeper places of intimacy.

EDWARD TAYLOR'S LOVESICK HEART

Edward Taylor (c. 1642–1729) learned the importance and consequences of making choices at an early age. Growing up in England during a time of severe turmoil as political and religious factions battled for control of the country and church, Taylor's family were Protestant Dissenters, which meant they were Christians who chose to worship outside of the official Church of England. At the time, making this choice carried with it grave repercussions—Dissenters faced barriers to a university education and careers in public service, fines and job loss, and even imprisonment. When Taylor himself refused to sign the Act of Uniformity to pledge his allegiance to the Church of England, he watched his opportunities vanish.

Eventually, in his mid-twenties, Taylor left England to join the Puritan Massachusetts Bay Colony, a colonial settlement welcoming to Dissenters. Three years later, he graduated from Harvard and became the minister of a frontier parish in Westfield, Massachusetts, marrying the love of his life and fathering eight children. Taylor's life in the colonies had heartache—five of his children died in infancy, and his wife died when Taylor was in his late forties. Even with shorter life expectancies and higher infant mortality rates in the colonial period, this is a significant amount of loss. Thankfully, Taylor eventually remarried and had an additional six children as he spent his life pastoring the remote Westfield church for more than fifty years.

Taylor used his free time to write, and he wrote prodigiously, producing a diary covering his early years in the colonies, 438 handwritten pages of his *Metrical History of Christianity*, 485 handwritten pages of his *Harmony of the Gospels*, sermons, church records, and 400 manuscript pages of a leather book of handwritten poems with seventy-eight additional pages of poetry crammed into the binding.[12] Except for one poem, his writings were unpublished during his lifetime, passed down in

---

12. Stanford, *Poems of Edward Taylor*, 519, 520, 502.

manuscript through his family. Eventually donated to Yale University in 1883, Taylor's works remained untouched in the library until 1937, when his writings finally were discovered and published. Almost immediately, Taylor's poetical genius was acknowledged by scholars, albeit more than two hundred years after he stopped writing!

Although Taylor loved writing, his real passion was his bridegroom Jesus. Consider Taylor's words in the sermon he preached to his church in Westfield on the day of its founding:

> Consider, soul, that you are called to enter here, if prepared. Christ speaks to you in his language to his spouse, Song of Songs 2:10–13, "Arise, my love, my fair one, and come away...." What do you say to this? Poor soul, can you withstand such soul-ravishing rhetoric? I think it should be like sweet wine that causes the lips of him that is asleep to speak and answer. Oh, then, attend on the call and reply to the same, saying, "I come, Lord."[13]

Taylor preached this sermon when he was in his late thirties.

More than thirty years later, as Taylor was entering his seventies, he embarked upon a twelve-year study of the Song of Songs, composing fifty-one poems based on his meditations. The last poem he wrote in his lifetime was on the statement by the bride in Song 2:5: "I am sick with love." Here is the final stanza of Taylor's poem:

> Had I but better thou shouldst better have.
>   I naught withold from thee through [stinginess]
> But better than my best I cannot save
>   From any one, but bring my best to thee.
>   If thou accepts my sick Love's gift I bring
>   Thy it accepting makes my sick Love sing.[14]

Truly, Taylor spent a lifetime choosing and delighting in his eternal bridegroom.

---

13. Davis and Davis, *Edward Taylor's "Church Records,"* 152–53. For a brief background on the foundation day sermon for the Westfield Church, see pp. xiii–xv.

14. Meditation 165, *Preparatory Meditations before my Approach to the Lord's Supper*, Second Series, hereafter cited as *Preparatory Meditations*. The manuscripts of Edward Taylor's poetry are held by Yale University, catalogued as the Edward Taylor Collection, General Collection, Beinecke Rare Book and Manuscript Library, Yale University, and used with permission. My quotations of Taylor's poetry are taken from Patterson, *Critical Edition*, with permission from The Kent State University Press and the author. I have made limited silent adjustments to the transcriptions for the reader. This excerpt is from Patterson, *Critical Edition*, 512.

I suspect that Taylor's lovesick heart for Jesus is what helped him continue to choose his bridegroom through the persecution he experienced as a Dissenter, the deaths of his children and wife, and his many challenging years of isolated ministry. We can see this in how Taylor processed the passing of two of his children. In a poem he wrote entitled "Upon Wedlock, and Death of Children," his only poem published during his lifetime, Taylor notes the overwhelming grief of his children's deaths and the temptation he faced to accuse God of wrongdoing. However, Taylor resists this temptation because the will of his bridegroom is his "Spell, Charm, Joy and Gem."[15] These are surprising words to use to describe God's will in a time of such extreme grief, but words that recall the admonition in Ps 37:4: "Delight yourself in the LORD, and he will give you the desires of your heart." According to Taylor, it is not his willpower or self-discipline that enable him to continue to choose to follow Jesus during this difficult time. Instead, it is his delight in his bridegroom and his lovesick heart, charmed under the spell of joyful, precious love, that strengthen him in his grief.

Despite being a male poet, Taylor is very comfortable using overt bridal language in his poetry, often referring to Jesus as his bridegroom, spouse, and even husband.[16] While we know from passages such as John 4:24 that God is spirit and thus nongendered, it still can be challenging for male readers to connect with Jesus as a bridegroom because Jesus was himself male when he walked the earth.[17] In his poetry, Taylor offers some ways to move past this challenge.

First, Taylor always views Jesus as his bridegroom within the bigger picture of God's agape love, which Taylor calls "The Best of Love," perhaps to distinguish it from romantic love or infatuation.[18] He emphasizes the honor he feels as the spouse of Jesus, and he highlights the affection he experiences from Jesus as his "bridegroom, bright, and Friend."[19] He is moved by the condescension Jesus displays in uniting with him, as if

---

15. Taylor's poem was published in Mather, *Right Thoughts*, n.p.

16. Although current-day conceptions envision gender as a spectrum, I am using the traditional binary understanding of gender as male and female in this book. In early America, gender was seen exclusively as binary.

17. Also see Isa 49:15, Isa 66:13, and Luke 13:34 for times when God compares himself to a female.

18. Meditation 115, *Preparatory Meditations*, Second Series. Patterson, *Critical Edition*, 421.

19. Meditation 115, *Preparatory Meditations*, Second Series. Patterson, *Critical Edition*, 420.

"Kings wed Worms," and also appreciates Jesus' pursuit of him: "I am so base and Froward [disobedient] to him, He / Appears as Wonder's Wonder, wedding me."[20] Lastly, Taylor values the significance and uniqueness of the marriage commitment Jesus makes to him; this pledge encourages Taylor to pledge himself to Jesus: "I then shall be thy Bride Espoused by thee / And thou my Bridegroom Dear Espoused shall be."[21] By focusing on agape love, Jesus' pursuit of him, and the inexpressible honor of sharing with his beloved the most sacred and eternal of commitments, Taylor is able to embrace the essence of what being a bride of Jesus means and celebrate Jesus as his bridegroom despite his own maleness.[22]

READING EDWARD TAYLOR

Reading Edward Taylor's poetry is a unique treat; I doubt you will have read much like it before. In some ways, his poems remind us of the Old Testament book of Psalms. Like many of the psalms, Taylor's poems often are addressed directly to God. Also, like many of the psalmists, Taylor is not afraid to be honest about his struggles. For example, he willingly reveals his frustration at not loving God as he would like with lines such as this one from Meditation 1: "But oh! my straitened[23] Breast! my Lifeless Spark! / My Fireless Flame! What Chilly Love, and Cold?" Taylor often cries to God to help his love grow: "Lord blow the Coal: Thy Love Enflame in me."[24] He expresses strong emotions throughout his writing

---

20. Meditation 23, *Preparatory Meditations*, First Series. Patterson, *Critical Edition*, 160.

21. Meditation 23, *Preparatory Meditations*, First Series. Patterson, *Critical Edition*, 161.

22. Edward Taylor was a Puritan, and the concept of Jesus as the bridegroom of the church and the individual Christian was very central to the thinking and practice of both male and female Puritans in the seventeenth century. For example, in the original covenant of the Puritan church at Dorchester, Massachusetts, established in 1636, the seven male church founders each promised "first, and above all to cleave unto [God] as our chief and only good, and to our Lord Jesus Christ as our only spiritual husband and Lord." *Covenant, and Declaration of Faith*, 22. For more, see Porterfield, *Feminine Spirituality*, 19–50; Winship, "Behold the Bridegroom;" and Hammond, "Bride in Redemptive Time." Similarly, Pope John Paul II (1920–2005), in his Apostolic Letter *On the Dignity and Vocation of Women*, writes, "In the Church every human being—male and female—is the 'Bride,' in that he or she accepts the gift of the love of Christ the Redeemer, and seeks to respond to it with the gift of his or her own person." John Paul II, *Dignity of Women*, 87.

23. Impoverished, distressed.

24. Meditation 1, *Preparatory Meditations*, First Series. Patterson, *Critical Edition*,

such as shock at God's condescending kindness, astonishment at the depth of God's love, and heartfelt passion for Jesus. And, lastly, like the psalms, many of his poems end with a grateful acknowledgment of God's magnificence and grace.

Taylor's poetry falls into the literary style called metaphysical, which was a poetic movement that flourished during Taylor's lifetime and that attempted to explore the depths of emotion associated with love and religion. As a metaphysical poet, Taylor is less interested in smooth-sounding poetry; he desires instead to mine the deep caverns of his heart, and the resulting emotional rawness of his poems connects with modern readers well. Note Taylor's struggle to describe the powerful love he feels for his first wife in a love letter he wrote to her before their marriage:

> I know not how to offer a fitter comparison to set out my love by than to compare it to a golden ball of pure fire rolling up and down my breast, from which there flies now and then a spark like a glorious beam from the body of the flaming sun. But, alas, striving to catch these sparks into a love letter to yourself and to gild it with them as with a sunbeam, [I] find that by [the] time they have fallen through my pen upon my paper, they have lost their shine and fall only like a little smoke thereon instead of gilding them.[25]

Although Taylor exclaims that his love for his fiancée is like "a golden ball of pure fire rolling up and down my breast," he admits that, in his letter, his sentiments appear instead "only like a little smoke." As a writer, Taylor knew both the power and shortcomings of language, and he worked to make each poetic line he wrote convey the true feelings of his heart.

Taylor's poems use heavy-sounding words and sometimes surprising comparisons, which function like powerful word pictures or metaphors to reveal his feelings. For example, Taylor's Meditation 130 below uses the idea of a garden of spices from Song of Songs to explore the relationship between Jesus and his beloved, emphasizing the sweetness of the spices in the garden and how Jesus and his bride share that sweetness through their "Breathings." Taylor asks Jesus at the end of the poem to place him in that garden and "make my sweetened Lungs out sweet Breath send" to

---

127.

25. Perkins, *Old Houses*, 99.

"make my heart thereby more sweet for thee." The speaker and Jesus will then enjoy a "mutual sweetness" as they share the "Garden air."[26]

The best way to read metaphysical poetry like Taylor's is to focus on the main idea in each poem and to read the lines slowly, even out loud, to hear the power and stateliness of the words. Don't expect the poems to sound like current-day speech; even the usual English word order of subject-verb is often adjusted by Taylor so that his writing sometimes sounds a bit like it's coming out of Yoda's mouth in *Star Wars*. Instead of attempting to untangle the exact meaning of every poetic line, look for the overall emotion Taylor is exploring in each poem and expect to find yourself moved by specific lines or phrases.

The four poems I have included here are very personal for Taylor and are part of a collection of 217 poems he wrote as private meditations on his sermon texts for the days his church received communion. Taylor used these poems to prepare his own heart for communion and to apply to his life the biblical passage on which he was preaching. The first poem, Meditation 1, is simply a celebration of Jesus' overwhelming bridal love that overflows heaven and pours into his bride on earth. Taylor asks Jesus to "Enflame" his heart with that same love.

The next three poems are all meditations on passages from Song of Songs. Meditation 23 begins with Taylor's thoughts on the richness of heaven and then highlights the incomprehensibility of Jesus joining himself with humans in a marriage commitment, which for Taylor is as unfathomable as a king marrying a worm or an angel wedding an ant. Taylor ends the poem by asking Jesus to make Taylor's "Wedding Garment" out of his "saving Grace." Meditation 115 emphasizes the beauty and loveliness of Jesus and the speaker's desire to give to his beloved all the love he possesses, saddened if "any drop of love the Heart can hold / Should be held back from thee." As noted above, Meditation 130 celebrates the sweet and mutual enjoyment Jesus and his bride find in sharing the garden of their lives together. I think you will enjoy the emotions and language of this lovesick poet as you ponder the choice you will make to your bridegroom's call to join him upon the flowering hills.

---

26. Meditation 130, *Preparatory Meditations*, Second Series. Patterson, *Critical Edition*, 447–48.

POETRY: PREPARATORY MEDITATIONS BEFORE MY APPROACH TO THE LORD'S SUPPER[27]

MEDITATION 1

What Love is this of thine, that Cannot be
    In thine Infinity, O Lord, Confined,
Unless it in thy very Person See,
    Infinity, and Finity Conjoyn'd?
    What hath thy Godhead, as not Satisfied
    Married our Manhood, making it its Bride?

Oh, Matchless Love! filling Heaven to the brim!
    O'er running it: all running o'er beside
This World! Nay Overflowing Hell; wherein
    For thine Elect, there rose a mighty Tide!
    That there our Veins might through thy Person bleed,
    To quench those flames, that else would on us feed.

Oh! that thy Love might overflow my Heart!
    To fire the Same with Love: for Love I would.
But oh! my straitened Breast! my Lifeless Spark!
    My Fireless Flame! What Chilly Love, and Cold?
    In measure Small! in Manner Chilly! See.
    Lord blow the Coal: Thy Love Enflame in me.

MEDITATION 23. SONG OF SONGS 4:8. MY SPOUSE.

Come with me from Lebanon, my bride; come with me from Lebanon. Depart from the peak of Amana, from the peak of Senir and Hermon, from the dens of lions, from the mountains of leopards.

Would God I in that Golden City were,

---

27. Selections are from Patterson, *Critical Edition*, 127, 159–61, 420–21, 447–48. I have included relevant Bible verses for the reader.

With Jaspers Walled, all garnished, and made Swash[28],
With Precious Stones, whose Gates are Pearls most clear
    And street Pure Gold, like to transparent Glass.[29]
    That my dull Soul, might be inflamed to See
    How Saints and Angels ravished are in Glee.

Were I but there, and could but tell my story,
    'T would rub those Walls of Precious stones more bright:
And glaze those Gates of Pearl, with brighter Glory;
    And pave the golden Street with greater light.
    'T would in fresh Raptures saints, and Angels fling.
    But I poor Snake Crawl here, Scarce mudwalled in.

May my Rough Voice, and my blunt Tongue but Spell
    My Tale (for tune they can't) perhaps there may
Some Angel catch an end of't up, and tell
    In Heaven, when he doth return that way,
    He'll make thy Palace, Lord, all over ring,
    With it in Songs, thy Saint, and Angels Sing.

I know not how to speak't, it is so good:
    Shall Mortal, and Immortal marry? nay,
Man marry God? God be a Match for Mud?
    The King of Glory Wed a Worm? mere Clay?
    This is the Case. The Wonder too in Bliss.
    Thy Maker is thy Husband. Heardst thou this?[30]

My Maker, he my Husband? Oh! Strange joy!
    If Kings wed Worms, and Monarchs Mites[31] wed should,
Glory spouse shame, a Prince a Snake or Fly

---

28. Impressive, decorative.

29. Taylor is referencing the bridal city, the New Jerusalem, described in Rev 21:1—22:5.

30. Taylor is referencing Isa 54:4-6: "Fear not, for you will not be ashamed; be not confounded, for you will not be disgraced; for you will forget the shame of your youth, and the reproach of your widowhood you will remember no more. For your Maker is your husband, the Lord of hosts is his name; and the Holy One of Israel is your Redeemer, the God of the whole earth he is called. For the Lord has called you like a wife deserted and grieved in spirit, like a wife of youth when she is cast off, says your God."

31. A mite is a small arachnid, a class that includes spiders and ticks.

    An Angel court an Ant, all Wonder would.
    Let Such wed Worms, Snakes, Serpents, Devils, Flies.
    Less Wonder than the Wedding in our Eyes.

I am to Christ more base, than to a King
    A Mite, Fly, Worm, Ant, Serpent, Devil is;
Or Can be, being tumbled all in sin,
    And shall I be his Spouse? How good is this?
    It is too good to be declared to thee.
    But not too good to be believed by me.

Yet to this Wonder, this is found in me,
    I am not only base[32] but backward Coy[33],
When Christ doth Woo: and till his spirit be
    His Spokesman to Compel me I deny.
    I am so base and Froward[34] to him, He
    Appears as Wonder's Wonder, wedding me.

Seeing, Dear Lord, it's thus, thy spirit take
    And send thy Spokesman, to my Soul, I pray.
Thy saving Grace my Wedding Garment make:
    Thy spouse's Frame into my soul Convey.
    I then shall be thy Bride Espoused by thee
    And thou my Bridegroom Dear Espoused shalt be.

MEDITATION 115. SONG OF SONGS 5:10. MY BELOVED.

My beloved is radiant and ruddy, distinguished among ten thousand.

What art thou mine? am I espoused to thee?
    What honor's this? it is more bright Renown
I ought to glory more in this sweet glee
    Than if I'd wore great Alexander's Crown.[35]

---

32. Immoral.
33. Shy, reserved.
34. Contrary, difficult.
35. Alexander the Great (356–323 BC), King of Macedonia, famous for his military

Oh! make my Heart loaded with Love ascend,
Up to thyself, its bridegroom, bright, and Friend.

Her whole delight, and her Beloved thou art
    Oh! Lovely thou[36]: Oh! grudge my soul, I say,
Thou straitened stand, locked up to Earth's fine parts
    Course matter truly, yellow earth, Hard Clay.
    Why should these Clay-y faces be the keys
    T'lock, and unlock thy love up as they please?[37]

Lord, make thy Holy Word, the golden Key
    My soul to lock and make its bolt to trig[38]
Before the same, and Oil the same to play
    As thou dost move them off and On to jig.[39]
    The ripest Fruits that my affections bear
    I offer, thee. Oh! my Beloved fair.

Thou standst the brightest object in bright glory
    More shining than the shining sun t'allure.
Unto thyself the purest Love, the Stories
    Within my Soul can hold refined most pure
    In flaming bundles polished all with Grace
    Most sparkingly about thyself t'embrace.

The most refined Love in Grace's mint
    In rapid flames is best bestowed on thee
The brightest: metal with Divinest print
    Thy tribute is, and ever more shall be.[40]

---

conquests.

36. Taylor's use throughout this poem of the word "lovely" to describe Jesus may be a reference to Song 5:16: "His mouth is most sweet: yea, he is altogether lovely. This is my beloved, and this is my friend, O daughters of Jerusalem." (KJV) Bible quotations marked "KJV" are from the King James Version of the Bible, revised in 1769 and in the public domain.

37. The final two lines of this stanza may be a reference to Song 4:9 or Song 6:5 in which the bridegroom admits that his beloved has "captivated" his heart and "overwhelm[ed]" him. Similarly, Taylor wonders how his human, "Clay-y" face can capture or "lock" up the heart of Jesus.

38. To hold firm.

39. To move up and down briskly.

40. A mint produces coins. Taylor references the intensely hot furnaces that are used to soften coins for shaping, the image that is printed or struck onto coins, and the

> The Loving Spouse and thou her Loved sweet
> Make Lovely Joy when she and thee do meet:

Thou art so lovely, pity 'tis indeed
> That any drop of love the Heart can hold
Should be held back from thee, or should proceed
> > To drop on other Objects young, or old.
> > Best things go best together: best agree:
> > But best are badly used, by bad that be.

Thou all o'er Lovely art, Most lovely Thou:
> Thy spouse, the best of Loving Ones; Her Love,
The Best of Love: and this she doth avow
> > Thyself. And thus she doth thyself approve.
> > That object robs thee of thy due that wears
> > Thy spouse's Love. With thee none in it shares.

Lord fill my heart with Grace refining Love.
> Be thou my only Well-Beloved, I pray.
And make my Heart with all its Love right move
> > Unto thyself, and all her Love display.
> > My Love is then right well-bestowed, alone
> > When it obtains thyself her Lovely One.

My Best love then shall on Shoshannim[41] play.
> Like David[42] her sweet Music, and thy praise
Inspire her songs that Glory ever may
> > In sweetest tunes thy Excellency Glaze.
> > And thou shalt be the burden of her song
> > Loaded with Praise that to thyself belong.

---

use of coins to pay "tribute" to a ruler.

    41. Shoshannim is a Hebrew word used in various psalms that means "lilies" and is thought to refer to a musical instrument or popular melody. In Song of Songs, lilies are a symbol of love.

    42. King David of Israel, noted as the author in the titles of many psalms in the Old Testament book of Psalms.

MEDITATION 130. SONG OF SONGS 6:2. MY BELOVED IS GONE DOWN INTO HIS GARDEN, TO THE BEDS OF SPICES.

My sweet-sweet Lord who is it, that e're can
    Define thyself, or Mine affections strong
Unto thyself with ink? Who is the man
    That ever did, or can these riches sum?
    Thy sweetness no description can define
    Nor Pen and Ink can my heart's Love outline.

The Breathings of thy Spice beds' Garden's Spot,
    And of thy Sweet spot o'flowers stowed in the Air
This sweet breath breathed out from thy Garden knot
    Perfume the skies and all their riches fair.
    Thy Garden's Bed thy Civet Box[43] gives vent,
    To th'Gales[44] of Spiced Vapors, Sweetest scent.

Thy Bed of spices in thy Garden Spots,
    Perfumes most sweetly as they are inspired.
With thy rich spirit's breath; thy flower Pots
    Breathe out such sweetness, that's by saints desired
    Ascending up in gracious exercise
    Making these beds of spices thy sweet Joys.

Thou dost delight to visit these, and make
    These spicy beds thy blissful Couches bright
And Visits them even from thy Palace Gate
    And walks their alleys with most sweet delight.
    This sweetness that perfumes bright Glory clear
    Perfumes thy joys, perfumed joys are here.

And all the sweetness of these Beds of Spice
    Doth Spiritually perfume these beds of saints
That they breath in and out perfume, whose price
    Excels all precious jewels, never faints.
    Set me a Lily in thy Bed of Spice,
    With sweetened breath, my Lord e'er to rejoice.

43. A box containing fragrances.
44. Strong winds.

If thou allowest me setting in this Bed,
   Of Spices set in spiritual ranks therein
With Gusts of spiritual Odors over-soared,
   (Oh! Sweet perfume! oh blessed blissful thing)
   I shall suck in and out as sweetened fare[45],
   As ever did perfume the Clear clear air.

Lord, make my sweetened Lungs out sweet Breath send
   'T will make thy spice Beds still more sweet to be.
This Air all sweetened will its sweetness lend,
   And make my heart thereby more sweet for thee.
   I shall breathe sweetness in and out to thee
   And in my spicy Lodge will lodge thee.

The gales of Grace's breath shall rise most sweet
   To thee, my Lord, me sweet with Grace's spice.
A mutual sweetness then shall be the reek[46],
   Thy Garden air that carries there, my voice
   Then shall my tongue thy sweetened praises sing
   In tunes perfumed, thus on airy string.

CHAPTER SUMMARY AND FURTHER READING

Choosing to follow our bridegroom is the second response we hope to make to Jesus because true love requires choice. A lovesick heart gives us the strength to choose and propels us onward in our growth as a bride. Athough the bride in Song of Songs chooses not to join her beloved when he first calls her to deeper intimacy, we can be encouraged by Edward Taylor to press into our bridal relationship with Jesus through any hardships that may come.

    To read more of Edward Taylor's poetry, I would suggest Daniel Patterson's *Edward Taylor's* Gods Determinations *and* Preparatory Meditations: *A Critical Edition*, which includes a very readable introduction to the life and writings of Taylor. Jeffrey A. Hammond's book *Sinful Self, Saintly Self: The Puritan Experience of Poetry* includes four chapters on

---

45. Food.
46. Scent, odor, without the negative connotation.

Taylor and his poetry, and Michael D. Reed's "Edward Taylor's Poetry: Puritan Structure and Form" highlights how Taylor's poems launched a uniquely American Puritan meditative poetical tradition. To see images of Taylor's handwritten manuscripts, visit the online digital collections of the Beinecke Rare Book and Manuscript Library at Yale University.

3

Pursuing Him: Jonathan Edwards
Song of Songs 3:1–5

Night after night I'm tossing and turning on my bed of travail.
Why did I let him go from me?
How my heart now aches for him,
but he is nowhere to be found!
So I must rise in search of him,
looking throughout the city,
seeking until I find him.
Even if I have to roam through every street,
nothing will keep me from my search.
Where is he—my soul's true love?
He is nowhere to be found.[1]

No one enjoys being on the lonely end of a separation. Growing up, I used to hear my mother reminisce about the sadness and longing she felt during the years she was separated from my father during his time as a young man in the military. Even though she had been married to him for decades when recalling those early years, the heartache of their time apart was never completely erased.

1. Song 3:1–2.

As a bride of Jesus, we must recognize the fact that we are not yet permanently and entirely present with our bridegroom. The unity we enjoy with him on earth through the indwelling power of God the Holy Spirit is temporary, incomplete, and, if we're honest, always a bit unsatisfying. There is a natural longing in our hearts for a complete and pure union with our beloved, a union we know cannot be achieved this side of heaven. Thus, we feel his absence. And whether the pain of separation that we experience is due simply to our earthbound existence or to a deliberate choice we have made, being separated from him hurts.

While this pain is real and will never fully disappear until we join him in heaven, its presence in our hearts can be a positive force to motivate us toward the third response we hope to have to our bridegroom—pursuing him. After our hearts have been awakened to his love and we have made the choice to follow him as a bride, we want to begin intentionally pursuing Jesus in a bridal context. But what does this pursuit look like, and what aspects of it are important? In this chapter, we first will examine how the felt absence of Jesus can motivate our hearts to pursue him, and then we will identify the key pieces of the ensuing process of seeking him as a bride.

MISSING OUR BRIDEGROOM

We know from Scripture that Jesus is always present with us through the power of his Holy Spirit dwelling inside us. The final words Jesus speaks on earth before he ascends to heaven assures his disciples, both then and now, of his never-ending presence: "And behold, I am with you always, to the end of the age."[2] Jesus will never, ever leave us. He is always watching us, holding us, guiding us, strengthening us, and loving us. In fact, it's impossible to get away from him! As the prophet Jeremiah reminds us in Jer 23:24, "'Can a man hide himself in secret places so that I cannot see him?' declares the Lord. 'Do I not fill heaven and earth?' declares the Lord."

That said, our *felt* sense of Jesus' presence—our conscious awareness of his nearness to us—can ebb and flow in this life. There are times we simply feel far from him, and those times are hard. In fact, I would argue that it is specifically as our bridegroom that Jesus' absence is the most painfully felt. An absent boss means an employee may be unsure

---

2. Matt 28:20b.

of the next step in a project, an absent teacher means a student may not learn a lesson, and an absent doctor means healing may be delayed. In all of these cases, the pain of absence is real, but the sadness we experience stems from the unfortunate results that may occur because of the absence and not necessarily because the people themselves are missing. In fact, absences like these can be overcome. A boss can send instructions through email, a teacher can record a lecture, and a doctor can call in a prescription.

But when a lover is absent, it is the lover as a person who is missed because the presence of the lover is what counts. In the same way, it is because we are Jesus' bride and not simply his servant or student that we miss *him*, not just what he gives us. I know Jesus is always caring for me, protecting me, teaching me, and keeping his eye on me, even when I don't feel him near. But not feeling him near matters to me. A lot. For a lover, the absence of the beloved is the only thing that does matter.

One of the challenges we face when we feel far from Jesus is how to correctly interpret his felt absence. It is easy and natural for us to jump to certain conclusions at these times based on how distance is often created in human relationships: he doesn't really love me, he's disappointed in me, he's angry with me, he's weary of me, or he's simply distracted or indifferent. Unfortunately, since these actions do not line up with the perfect love Jesus claims to have for us, thinking this way can cause us to question whether Jesus really does love us. How easy it is, then, to begin doubting his intentions, commitment, and care. After all, if he really loves me as a bridegroom, why would he allow me to experience the pain of feeling his absence?

Two problems emerge from this wrong thinking. First, interpreting Jesus' felt absence as indifference or lack of love toward us, while understandable, is simply untrue and unbiblical. While we will not understand all of Jesus' actions and purposes this side of heaven, we know from Scripture that he always loves and cares for us. The apostle John assures us in John 15:13 that Jesus' death on the cross to accomplish our salvation shows beyond any doubt his perfect love: "Greater love has no one than this, that someone lay down his life for his friends." Jesus always loves us with a perfect love that only he can offer. He will never pull back from us out of disappointment, distraction, or weariness, as a human lover might.

Second, believing that Jesus feels far from us because of dislike or disinterest on his part is hurtful to our hearts. Our hearts are wounded when we believe Jesus doesn't truly love us; we feel betrayed, offended, and taken for granted. Jesus does not want us to experience this kind of heart-wounding because he knows it will harm our intimacy with him. Note the warning to protect our hearts in Prov 4:23: "Above all else, guard your heart, for everything you do flows from it."[3] When we entertain the belief that our felt sense of Jesus' absence is because he doesn't really love us, our hearts will be unnecessarily hurt.

To be sure, the Bible is clear that at times our hearts will be wounded in a helpful way by godly sorrow when *we* have chosen to "absent" ourselves from Jesus through deliberate sin or our own disinterest. As Paul explains to the believers of the church in Corinth, "I rejoice, not because you were grieved, but because you were grieved into repenting. For you felt a godly grief, so that you suffered no loss through us. For godly grief produces a repentance that leads to salvation without regret, whereas worldly grief produces death."[4] It is the kindness of God that leads us to turn from our sin so that we can be restored to right fellowship with him, as noted in Rom 2:4. And, thankfully, the moment we repent and turn to Jesus, he forgives and restores us, ending our godly sorrow.

But if our felt experience of Jesus' absence is not caused by his lack of love for us or because we are deliberating turning from him, how should we interpret the times we cannot sense our bridegroom's presence? I would suggest that sometimes Jesus deliberately pulls back our sense of his presence for the purpose of moving us to *greater* love and *deeper* intimacy with him. I know, this sounds at best counterintuitive or at worst like a cruel joke. But, actually, the back-and-forth dynamic of seeking and finding, absence and nearness, longing and consummation is a healthy, necessary feature of all genuine, growing relationships.

For example, a couple's first disagreement can be painful and cause a temporary sense of distance, but it teaches them new insights about each other. Similarly, asking questions of a new friend or trying new experiences with an old friend makes the friendship develop in original ways. Spending time apart can stir up healthy desire in relationships, and facing challenging times together can stretch, strengthen, and expand the bonds of affection. Proverbs 25:2 explains the principle: "It is the glory of God to conceal things, but the glory of kings is to search things out." The apostle James recognizes the same truth when he encourages us to "draw near to God, and he will draw near to you."[5] In other words, all

3. NIV.
4. 2 Cor 7:9–10.
5. Jas 4:8a.

relationships need an organic, synergistic, lively give-and-take to grow and develop and to resist stagnation.

The pain and longing we experience when we feel far from our bridegroom actually provokes our hearts in a healthy, productive, purposeful way to pursue him more passionately. When we feel something is lacking, we chase after it. When we feel far from Jesus, the felt distance motivates us to seek him more fervently. By creating need in our hearts, Jesus is acting in love toward us by gently inviting us to move into a deeper, more intimate connection with him. When we recognize this, the times we long for his nearness, though painful, will not wound our hearts. Instead, we will embrace them, and they will fulfill Jesus' intended purpose of drawing us closer in ardent pursuit.

Perhaps it also might help us to remember that Jesus himself continually longs for us. In fact, our temporary felt separation is much harder on him due to his perfect love! We can sense the painful emotion in Jesus' heart when he utters these words over Jerusalem near the end of his earthly ministry: "O Jerusalem, Jerusalem, the city that kills the prophets and stones those who are sent to it! How often would I have gathered your children together as a hen gathers her brood under her wings, and you were not willing!"[6] Our bridegroom's fierce love for us causes him to long for us ardently, too, expectantly awaiting our eventual union in heaven.

Since we can use our painful longing for Jesus as motivation to pursue him, let's look at some effective ways to chase after our beloved as he draws us to himself. We'll start by examining one way Jesus himself visualizes our pursuit and end with practical steps we can follow as his passionate, pursuing bride.

BRIDAL PREPARATIONS

While on earth, Jesus often used similes and parables to help his listeners understand important principles of the kingdom of God. In the gospels, Jesus shares several ways we can envision a passionate pursuit of him: selling all to buy a field containing a great treasure, purchasing a valuable pearl, refusing to look back while plowing a field, and staying awake while on duty as a doorkeeper.[7] A favorite metaphor of mine that

---

6. Matt 23:37, also recorded in Luke 13:34.
7. Matt 13:33; Matt 13:45; Luke 9:62; Mark 13:34.

Jesus uses to help us visualize the process of pursuing him is that of marriage preparation.

Even if you have never personally prepared for marriage, you have probably been involved in the process in some way as part of the bridal party, family member, or invited friend. Or perhaps you've just seen crazy wedding videos on social media! In any case, most of us know that preparing for a marriage can take significant energy, effort, thought, time, and material resources. The perfect venue must be secured, wedding cakes must be sampled, reception seating must be argued over, flower arrangements must be chosen at the cost of a small fortune, and pre-marriage counseling must strike alternating fear and hope in the hearts of the intended couple. But, on a more serious note, the most important preparation for an engaged couple is to deepen their knowledge of each other. The more they have mutually experienced, discovered about each other, and shared on an intimate level, the more prepared they will be to begin their life together.

Jesus uses marriage preparation to illustrate our pursuit of him in a parable he shares in Matt 25:1–13, part of his final teaching on the kingdom of heaven given just days before his crucifixion. The parable tells the story of ten virgins waiting at a wedding ceremony for a groom who is delayed. Five of the waiting virgins have brought extra oil for their oil lamps, and so they remain at the wedding site throughout the delay, but the other five virgins have not brought extra oil and so must leave the venue to buy some. While the five unprepared virgins are out buying oil, the groom appears and the door to the marriage feast is shut. When the unprepared virgins return, they are not permitted to enter the wedding banquet. Jesus ends the parable with a warning to his bride the church to be prepared for his second coming: "Watch therefore, for you know neither the day nor the hour."[8]

What was Jesus communicating with this wedding parable? Traditionally, the lamp oil is understood as representing the oil of intimacy with Jesus, our eternal bridegroom, whose second coming we are anticipating. The five prepared virgins had invested in "extra" oil for their lamps, meaning that they had pursued Jesus in such a way that their relationship with him was deep enough to sustain them through the challenging delay of his appearing. The unprepared virgins, on the other hand, did not have that reservoir of intimacy with Jesus to draw on, so when the testing time

8. Matt 25:13.

came, they could not sustain their waiting. Thus, Jesus encourages us to passionately pursue intimacy with him as we wait for his return just as a bride eagerly anticipates and prepares for her wedding day.

The metaphor of preparing our hearts to meet our heavenly bridegroom by pursuing him passionately on earth resonates deeply with me. When I see Jesus in heaven and experience the wedding referenced in Rev 21, I want to know the one to whom I will be wed. I want to have studied him, spent time with him, discovered his likes and dislikes, shared experiences with him, opened to him my thoughts and feelings, learned to recognize his voice, and patterned my life after his teachings and commands. I don't want to spend eternity with someone I barely know!

Jesus himself "nourishes and cherishes" his bride the church, according to Paul, so that we will be "holy and without blemish" at the end of time.[9] When God the Father presents to Jesus his bride the church at the beginning of his glorious kingdom, we will be perfect, a flawless eternal companion who will rule and reign with him forever. Thus, our bridegroom inspires us to pursue him on this earth as a bride preparing for her wedding day so our hearts are ready for our final, complete union with him in heaven.

So, what does this bridal pursuit look like on our end? I would like to use the lenses of an adventurer and an entrepreneur to suggest six simple, practical steps for pursuing Jesus as a bride. The bride in Song of Songs and an eighteenth-century pastor and philosopher will help us unpack these helpful suggestions.

AN ADVENTUROUS BRIDE: SONG 3:1–5

Our bride in Song of Songs has come to a difficult pass. Her bridegroom-king has done as she asked in verse seventeen of chapter two and has left her and gone to the mountains alone. Is she surprised? Perhaps. But the bride's experience reveals two realities we must recognize about life with our bridegroom Jesus. First, because we share a real relationship with him, he will take what we say seriously and will respond. In the bride's case, he leaves when she asks him to. Second, he cannot stagnate; he is always moving forward, and so must we as his partner. The Shulamite bride experiences his absence and now misses her bridegroom.

---

9. Eph 5:29, 27.

To pursue and reconnect with him, the bride must become an adventurer and, as such, she reveals four practical steps for pursuing Jesus. First, she must be willing to go to new places. The bride realizes in the first two verses of chapter three that she cannot find her bridegroom in the usual place but must instead leave her home and travel into the city to search: "On my bed by night I sought him whom my soul loves; I sought him, but found him not. I will rise now and go about the city, in the streets and in the squares." As those who pursue Jesus, we must recognize that Jesus is a person, not a concept, and thus he is dynamic, always changing and moving us into deeper relationship with himself. Part of pursuing him as a bride means being open to new discoveries of who he is, unique encounters with him, and unexpected opportunities for growth and connection with him. Stepping into unfamiliar territory can be challenging and scary, but a bride of Jesus must be willing to take a chance on something different when he calls.

My own growth as Jesus' bride has certainly taken me to surprising and sometimes daunting places. I'll share one experience. When I began learning to relate to Jesus more authentically as a bride, I felt led to change several aspects of my personal prayer times with him. One of the first things I believe Jesus desired me to do was to stop kneeling when I prayed and, instead, lie on my back. I was pretty sure kneeling to pray was a time-honored Christian tradition, while lying down to pray seemed a bit irreverent and likely to put me to sleep! But I tried it, and the new physical position actually helped me relax more in his presence. I discovered that I could share my thoughts with him more easily and hear his voice more clearly from that position.

I also felt encouraged to offer Jesus less objective, general praise and thanksgiving and to be more personal and specific in how I expressed my appreciation to him. What did I value about him as an individual, what had I learned about him recently that moved me, in what specific ways had I seen his intimate care for me? This change caused me to really think before I thanked him, pondering his character more deeply and taking time to look for his hand in my life in a distinctly personal way.

Lastly, I began to start praying to Jesus as though he was actually in the room with me. He was there, after all, through the power and presence of the Holy Spirit. I did not attempt to create a mental picture of him; instead, I focused on being intentionally aware of his presence, much as I would a human person sitting near me. This change helped my heart come to rest and made me feel closer to him.

All three of these adjustments to my prayer time seemed weird when I started implementing them, and, honestly, I resisted each of them for a while, I'm sorry to admit. But they ended up making me feel more connected to Jesus and drew my heart out toward him. To grow as a bride, we must always be open to new experiences with our bridegroom, no matter how strange or insignificant they may appear to us. After all, most relationships improve when we try something fresh.

Can you remember a time you started a new hobby with a friend, tried a different hairstyle you thought your spouse would appreciate, or altered your approach to discussing sensitive topics with your supervisor? You probably saw the positive effects of those changes right away. Our relationship with Jesus is no different. Is there something new or different you have been sensing Jesus is desiring that you do? Try it! If you are unsure about it, ask a trusted mentor for confirmation or a close friend for accountability. But begin pursuing Jesus in that new way, and you will be delighted with the growth you will experience in your relationship with him.

The second trait our adventurous bride displays in her pursuit of her bridegroom is persistence. The New Living Translation translates verse two this way: "So I said to myself, 'I will get up and roam the city, searching in all its streets and squares. I will search for the one I love.' So I searched everywhere." The bride in Song of Songs perseveres in her search for her lover, and we hope to demonstrate that same resolve in our pursuit of Jesus. In Rev 12:10–11, the apostle John assures us that we will be conquerors through the blood of Jesus if we persevere:

> And I heard a loud voice in heaven, saying, "Now the salvation and the power and the kingdom of our God and the authority of his Christ have come, for the accuser [the devil] of our brothers [Christians] has been thrown down, who accuses them day and night before our God. And they have conquered him by the blood of the Lamb and by the word of their testimony, for they loved not their lives even unto death.

It's good news for us that we don't have to be the smartest person in the room or the strongest or the most talented; all we need is persistence. Jesus will keep his bride on the path to his heart if we just do not give up.

But an adventurer requires another attribute for the journey and that is self-motivation. Note verses three and four: "The watchmen found me as they went about in the city. 'Have you seen him whom my soul loves?'

Scarcely had I passed them when I found him whom my soul loves." The bride is hopeful that the city patrol will help her find her bridegroom, but, ultimately, she must find him herself.

As believers, we know firsthand the importance in our lives of other people, especially Christians. From others, we receive encouragement, counsel, help, teaching, leadership, support, and other blessings necessary to thrive in life. But when we want to grow in a relationship, no one can make it happen for us. Just as I must personally do the work to deepen my relationships with my husband, children, and friends, so I must personally do the work of growing in intimacy with Jesus, regardless of the advice or encouragement that others may give me. Ultimately, it is up to me.

I love the final words the bride says of her journey to find her beloved at the end of verse four: "I held him, and would not let him go until I had brought him into my mother's house, and into the chamber of her who conceived me." The fourth and final trait of an adventurer is gratitude, and our bride displays this trait when she promises to never let her bridegroom go. She brings him into the deepest, most intimate part of herself with tremendous gratitude because he is so valuable to her. Jesus gives a word picture illustrating this principle in Matt 13:44 when he declares, "The kingdom of heaven is like treasure hidden in a field, which a man found and covered up. Then in his joy he goes and sells all that he has and buys that field." A person will only sell all they own to obtain something of great value, and, likewise, an adventurer will be supremely thankful for the prize they attain at the end of their challenging search.

I'd like to highlight one word from Matt 13:44—*treasure*. Treasures are known and recognized to be of the highest value. And Jesus is the supreme treasure. Read Col 1:15–20 to see the matchless value, overwhelming superiority, peerless preeminence, and spectacular beauty of Christ. As his bride, our hearts and minds must be struck deeply by the unequivocal, profound value of our bridegroom. There is nothing in our lives that should not be joyfully "sold" to obtain him. He is worth everything we have and are. An awareness of and gratitude for this truth must be part of our pursuit of him because it will inspire and encourage us. We are not journeying on the path to bridal love for some mediocre reward; we are chasing the very treasure of heaven. Nothing and no one else can compare.

The bride in Song of Songs has modeled for us four practical steps for pursuing Jesus as an adventurer, but we can find even more suggestions when we add the lens of an entrepreneur. Jonathan Edwards, easily the best-known minister today from colonial America, provides for us the perfect example.

ENTREPRENEURIAL JONATHAN EDWARDS

The grandson of a Puritan pastor who was so influential in New England that he was called the "Pope" of the Connecticut River valley, Jonathan Edwards (1703–58) grew up with serious expectations upon him, most of which he exceeded.[10] Graduated as valedictorian at age seventeen from what would become Yale University, Edwards embarked upon a life that was truly entrepreneurial in nature. Despite his short fifty-five years on earth, Edwards was never afraid to break new ground or take an unpopular position. While he was influential regionally as a pastor, his lifelong commitment to writing expanded his influence to an international level.

Although his grandfather and father were both Congregationalist ministers in New England, Edwards accepted his first job as minister of a Presbyterian church in New York. After a short time there, he became assistant pastor at his grandfather's large, influential church in Northampton, Massachusetts. After his grandfather's death in 1729, Edwards took over the church as sole pastor.

Five years later, Edwards preached a series of sermons highlighting the power and priority of God's grace in salvation, a response to his fellow ministers' more popular emphasis on human choice and free will. Following the sermon series, Edwards's congregation experienced a small revival and increased conversions, prompting Edwards to write an account of the experience that would later be published in book form and become popular in both the American colonies and England.[11] When the transatlantic revival now known as the First Great Awakening erupted in America and Great Britain a few years later in 1739, Edwards was quick to support the movement despite opposition from some of his older, more traditional New England colleagues. His 378-page *Some Thoughts Concerning the Present Revival of Religion in New England* appeared in 1743 and became a standard defense of the movement.

---

10. Jonathan Edwards's maternal grandfather was Solomon Stoddard (1643–1729).

11. *A Faithful Narrative of the Surprising Work of God*, published in London in 1737, and in Boston, with Edwards's corrections, in 1738.

Edwards's next crusade had less favorable results. Against the predominant practice of the time, Edwards decided to ask his church to return to the traditional system of requiring a personal testimony of a salvation experience from congregants who desired to receive communion, thus ensuring that only the truly converted would partake of the Lord's Supper.[12] Subsequently fired by his congregation, the majority of whom were against the idea, Edwards decided to accept an administrative position at a frontier mission for Native Americans. There, he used his free time to write what would become a standard textbook at Yale and other universities for decades on freedom of the will.[13]

Edwards's last great adventure was to become the president in 1757 of a new college founded by those who had favored the First Great Awakening, later known as Princeton University. Sadly, Edwards died soon after his appointment from a failed smallpox vaccination. His entrepreneurial approach to ministry had enabled him to accomplish much both at home and abroad.

Jonathan Edwards became America's first international theologian and philosopher through the more than twenty works he published during his lifetime, but it is his more personal, unpublished writings that reveal a tender heart as well as a disciplined mind. Edwards kept a diary in his younger years and a catalogue of spiritual resolutions, but his "Personal Narrative" most clearly demonstrates his commitment to Jesus and offers us two additional practical suggestions for how to pursue our bridegroom. Probably written when Edwards was in his mid-thirties at the start of the First Great Awakening, his "Personal Narrative" was not published until after Edwards's death by his friend and colleague Samuel Hopkins (1721–1803). The work is a spiritual narrative—Edwards's own retelling of his experiences with God and his spiritual growth over time. We will look at excerpts from the text in two separate sections to highlight the two practical suggestions we learn about pursuing our bridegroom from our entrepreneurial pastor—stirring up our affections and maintaining long-term vision.

---

12. The view that only converted Christians should share in communion is based primarily on 1 Cor 11:27–32.

13. *A Careful and Strict Enquiry into the Modern Prevailing Notions of that Freedom of Will which is supposed to be essential to Moral Agency*, published in Boston in 1754 and in London in 1762.

JONATHAN EDWARDS'S PASSIONATE AFFECTIONS

You may be surprised by the first characteristic of an entrepreneur that I believe correlates to bridal pursuit, but I think I can make a case for powerful, healthy emotions being an important component of our chase after Jesus. No matter how self-disciplined and strong-minded we are, we soon find that as humans, it is difficult to maintain pursuit of any goal without being passionate about what we are seeking, particularly if our path is entrepreneurial in nature. Anyone who has forged a new direction in any field has been zealous for what they are attempting. The spiritual life is the same, for without *feeling* something for our bridegroom, we will struggle to break new ground in our pursuit of him.[14]

Yet, as Christians, we have sometimes been scared away from valuing the role our emotions play in our relationship with God because we know that our emotions, like our minds and our wills, are affected negatively by our sinful nature and can be weakened or deceived. However, just as our minds and wills are transformed to seek God and please him by the power of the Holy Spirit living inside us, so too are our emotions. The Bible consistently highlights the importance of our hearts, encouraging us to love God and obey him wholeheartedly. In Ps 86:11b, David pleads, "Give me an undivided heart, that I may fear your name."[15] Similarly, God promises the Jewish exiles in Babylon in Jer 24:7 that he will give them "a heart to know that I am the LORD, and they shall be my people and I will be their God, for they shall return to me with their whole heart." All relationships are strengthened by a strong, healthy emotional connection, so our relationship with our bridegroom is deepened by our affections of love, gratitude, and reverence toward him.

Practically, how do we stir up our emotions toward Jesus in a positive, effective way? Paul gives us the answer in Col 3:1: "Since, then, you have been raised with Christ, set your hearts on things above, where Christ is, seated at the right hand of God."[16] Choosing to "set [our] hearts on things above" can include memorizing and meditating on Scripture, listening to biblical teaching, sharing testimonies of God's goodness with other believers, and disciplining our thought life so that even our daydreams align with Jesus and his purposes for us.

---

14. For book-length discussions of how to increase your spiritual passion, see Smith, *Godly Character(s)* and Smith, *Hammer & Fire*.

15. NIV.

16. NIV.

I would like to recommend two additional ways I have discovered to provoke affection for our bridegroom. The first practice is engaging with worship songs and hymns that focus on Jesus himself, his actions, his character, and his position as the king and Savior of the universe. Worship music can have varying subjects and purposes. Many worship songs today have believers as their subject and encouragement as their purpose. In these songs, the challenges of life are identified and God's related promises are offered to reassure the listener and increase faith. Like most Christians, I love and need these worship songs because they speak powerfully to me when I am struggling and encourage me to stand strong in faith.

However, these types of songs actually do little to stir up my affections for Jesus, except maybe to be grateful for what he does for me. Instead, I have found that worship music that centers on extoling the person, actions, promises, and prophecies of Jesus moves my heart in a different way. These songs truly arouse my affections for him, and love is awakened to a strong degree in my heart. Some of these songs even highlight Jesus as our bridegroom. Consider noting the subject and purpose of the worship music with which you engage, and perhaps add some songs to your playlists and worship times that have Jesus as their subject and exalting him alone as their purpose to see the effect on your passion toward him.

A second valuable tool in stirring up our affections for Jesus is to spend time alone with him. Although sharing one-on-one time seems like an obvious choice to deepen any relationship, this spiritual practice is often the first to go when life gets busy or demanding. In reality, though, it is nearly impossible to grow in intimacy with Jesus if we do not spend quality time with him. The specifics of what we do in these times are actually less important than following through with the commitment itself. We can praise him with worship music, meditate on Scripture, pray for others, or just rest in silence in his presence. Many excellent resources for how to make this time both profitable and pleasurable exist, so ask your pastor, small group leader, or Christian friend to recommend some. Twenty to thirty minutes a day is a good goal to start with; simply pick a time and place that is comfortable for you and enjoy spending time with your bridegroom. The peace, rest, and love that you experience in these times alone with Jesus will begin to trickle into your everyday life in surprising and wonderful ways and will increase your affections for your beloved.

Jonathan Edwards believed strongly in the necessity of healthy emotions in the life of a Christian. In 1746, he published *A Treatise Concerning Religious Affections*, a three-part examination of the role of emotion in spirituality. In Part I, Edwards argues that emotions are important because they drive our choices. Noting the willingness of believers in the early church to persevere under extreme persecution, Edwards argues, "Their inward spiritual joys were greater than their sufferings, and these supported them and enabled them to suffer with cheerfulness. . . . True religion, in great part, consists in holy affections."[17] For the Christian, then, cultivating affection for our bridegroom will strengthen us in our pursuit to obey him, cherish him, and even suffer for him.

Edwards also prioritized time alone with Jesus in his personal life. In the excerpt below from Edwards's "Personal Narrative," the Massachusetts pastor shares how he prioritizes time alone with Jesus and experiences many emotionally powerful encounters. He reveals how his spiritual passion develops and describes the first time his affections toward Jesus were stirred. Notice how Edwards uses the Bible, especially meditation on Jesus in the Song of Songs, to awaken passion for his bridegroom.[18] Lastly, notice Edwards's commitment to prayer and even singing as key ingredients in his passionate pursuit.

AUTOBIOGRAPHY: "PERSONAL NARRATIVE"[19]

> The first that I remember that ever I found anything of that sort of inward, sweet delight in God and divine things that I have lived much in since was on reading those words, 1 Timothy 1:17: "Now unto the King eternal, immortal, invisible, the only wise God, be honor and glory for ever and ever, Amen." As I read the words, there came into my soul and was, as it were, diffused through it a sense of the glory of the Divine Being—a new sense, quite different from anything I ever experienced before. Never any words of Scripture seemed to me as these words did. I thought with myself, how excellent a Being that was and how happy I should be if I might enjoy that God and be wrapped up

---

17. Edwards, *Religious Affections*, 3.

18. For a sermon by Edwards on Jesus as the bridegroom, see Jonathan Edwards, *The Church's Marriage to her Sons, and to her God* (Boston, 1746).

19. Selections are from Hopkins, *Life and Character*, 25, 26, 27–28, 35–36, 38–39.

to God in heaven and be, as it were, swallowed up in him. I kept saying and, as it were, singing over these words of Scripture to myself and went to prayer to pray to God that I might enjoy him, and prayed in a manner quite different from what I used to do, with a new sort of affection.

From about that time, I began to have a new kind of apprehensions and ideas of Christ, and the work of redemption, and the glorious way of salvation by him. I had an inward, sweet sense of these things that at times came into my heart, and my soul was led away in pleasant views and contemplations of them. And my mind was greatly engaged to spend my time in reading and meditating on Christ, and the beauty and excellency of his Person, and the lovely way of salvation by free grace in him.

I found no books so delightful to me as those that treated of these subjects. Those words, Song of Songs 2:1, used to be abundantly with me: "I am the Rose of Sharon, the Lily of the Valleys." The words seemed to me sweetly to represent the loveliness and beauty of Jesus Christ. The whole book of Song of Songs used to be pleasant to me, and I used to be much in reading it about that time.

And [I] found, from time to time, an inward sweetness that used, as it were, to carry me away in my contemplations, in what I know not how to express otherwise, than by a calm, sweet abstraction of soul from all the concerns of this world and a kind of vision, or fixed ideas and imaginations, of being alone in the mountains, or some solitary wilderness, far from all mankind, sweetly conversing with Christ, and wrapped and swallowed up in God. The sense I had of divine things would often of a sudden, as it were, kindle up a sweet burning in my heart, an ardor of my soul, that I know not how to express.

After this my sense of divine things gradually increased and became more and more lively and had more of that inward sweetness. The appearance of everything was altered; there seemed to be, as it were, a calm, sweet cast, or appearance, of divine glory in almost everything. God's excellency, his wisdom, his purity and love seemed to appear in everything—in the sun, moon, and stars; in the clouds and blue sky; in the grass, flowers, trees; in the water and all nature—which used greatly to [engage] my mind. I often used to sit and view the moon for a long time, and so in the daytime spent much time in viewing the clouds and sky to behold the sweet glory of God in these things, in the meantime, singing forth with a low voice my contemplations of the Creator and Redeemer.

And scarce anything among all the works of nature was so sweet to me as thunder and lightning. Formerly, nothing had been so terrible to me. I used to be a person uncommonly terrified with thunder, and it used to strike me with terror when I saw a thunderstorm rising. But now, on the contrary, it rejoiced me. I felt God at the first appearance of a thunderstorm and used to take the opportunity at such times to fix myself to view the clouds and see the lightnings play and hear the majestic and awful voice of God's thunder, which oftentimes was exceeding entertaining, leading me to sweet contemplations of my great and glorious God. And while I viewed, [I] used to spend my time, as it always seemed natural to me, to sing or chant forth my meditations, to speak my thoughts in soliloquies, and speak with a singing voice.

I felt then great satisfaction as to my good [spiritual state], but that did not content me. I had vehement longings of soul after God and Christ and after more holiness, wherewith my heart seemed to be full and ready to break, which often brought to my mind the words of the psalmist, Psalm 119:28, "My soul breaks for the longing it has." I often felt a mourning and lamenting in my heart that I had not turned to God sooner that I might have had more time to grow in grace.

My mind was greatly fixed on divine things; I was almost perpetually in the contemplation of them. Spent most of my time in thinking of divine things, year after year, and used to spend abundance of my time in walking alone in the woods and solitary places for meditation, soliloquy, and prayer, and converse with God. And it was always my manner, at such times, to sing forth my contemplations and was almost constantly in ejaculatory prayer, wherever I was. Prayer seemed to be natural to me as the breath by which the inward burnings of my heart had vent.

I have sometimes had a sense of the excellent fullness of Christ and his [appropriateness] and suitableness as a Savior, whereby he has appeared to me far above all, the chief of ten thousand.[20] And his blood and atonement has appeared sweet, and his righteousness sweet, which is always accompanied with ardency of spirit, and inward strugglings and breathings and groanings that cannot be uttered to be emptied of myself and swallowed up in Christ.

Once, as I rode out into the woods for my health, in 1737, and having alighted from my horse in a retired place, as my manner commonly has been, to walk for divine contemplation and prayer, I had a view that for me was extraordinary of the glory of the Son of God as Mediator between God and man, and his wonderful, great, full, pure and sweet grace and love, and meek and gentle condescension. This grace, that appeared to me so calm and sweet, appeared great above the heavens. The person of Christ appeared ineffably excellent, with an excellency great enough to swallow up all thought and conception, which continued, as near as I can judge, about an hour, which kept me the bigger part of the time in a flood of tears and weeping aloud.

I felt, [in addition], an ardency of soul to be, what I know not otherwise how to express, than to be emptied and annihilated, to lie in the dust, and to be full of Christ alone; to love him with a holy and pure love, to trust in him, to live upon him, to serve and follow him, and to be totally wrapped up in the fullness of Christ; and to be perfectly sanctified and made pure with a divine and heavenly purity. I have several other times had views very much of the same nature and that have had the same effects.

On one Saturday night in particular, had a particular discovery of the excellency of the gospel of Christ above all other doctrines, so that I could not but say to myself, "This is my chosen light, my chosen doctrine," and of Christ, "This is my chosen Prophet." It appeared to me to be sweet beyond all expression to follow Christ and to be taught and enlightened and instructed by him, to learn of him, and live to him.

---

20. Song 5:10b.

> Another Saturday night, January 1739, had such a sense how sweet and blessed a thing it was to walk in the way of duty, to do that which was right and [suitable] to be done and agreeable to the holy mind of God, that it caused me to break forth into a kind of a loud weeping, which held me some time, so that I was forced to shut myself up and fasten the doors. I could not but, as it were, cry out, "How happy are they which do that which is right in the sight of God! They are blessed indeed; they are the happy ones!" I had, at the same time, a very affecting sense how [appropriate] and suitable it was that God should govern the world and order all things according to his own pleasure, and I rejoiced in it, that God reigned and that his will was done.

JONATHAN EDWARDS'S LONG-TERM VISION

An entrepreneur must also be a visionary, so having long-term vision is the second suggestion for our pursuit of Jesus that we learn from those who break new ground. Every trendsetter must imagine what the future holds and then make a steadfast commitment to pursuing that vision. In the same way, we must commit to our long-term vision as we follow our bridegroom. For the bride of Jesus, this vision consists of both an end-time goal and an intentional commitment.

As Christians, we know our end-time goal: being united with God and other believers in God's perfect, glorious kingdom in heaven. During his ministry on earth, Jesus spoke often of the kingdom of heaven, sharing parables and exhortations to encourage his listeners to prioritize and pursue the kingdom. Knowing that we will spend eternity wedded to our heavenly bridegroom gives us motivation to continue to pursue him on earth.

But pondering our future celestial wedding day and the kingdom of heaven it will inaugurate is not always a popular pastime among Christians. When was the last time you thought about heaven, except maybe when praying for the end-time rapture to deliver you from an upcoming exam, work meeting, or family game night? As humans trapped in an often uncomfortable and painful world, our thoughts of heaven tend to center on its power to deliver us from what we don't like in our current lives and not on the new life we will experience with God for eternity.

But one important aspect of that new eternal life will be our union with our bridegroom, and focusing on that can help us stay motivated in our pursuit of him.

For most of my Christian life, I didn't think often of heaven or eternity, but I found that once I began learning to relate to Jesus as my bridegroom, meditating on and memorizing biblical passages that present Jesus as our end-time, conquering king really helped motivate me to pursue him. For example, Ps 2 beautifully illustrates Jesus' eventual rule over the earth with verses such as seven through nine: "The LORD said to me, 'You are my Son; today I have begotten you. Ask of me, and I will make the nations your heritage, and the ends of the earth your possession. You shall break them with a rod of iron and dash them in pieces like a potter's vessel.'"[21] The well-known passage in Isa 9 about Jesus being born as a child for us includes the promise that "of the increase of his government and of peace there will be no end, on the throne of David and over his kingdom, to establish it and to uphold it with justice and with righteousness from this time forth and forevermore."[22] Revelation presents Jesus the most powerfully in his role as our victorious bridegroom-king. I love meditating on the pictures of Jesus in passages such as Rev 5:6–14, Rev 19:11–16, and Rev 22:12–16.

Reading biblical passages such as these reminds us that our heavenly bridegroom will be established as the supreme ruler of the universe one day, and that promise gives us hope and motivation to continue pursuing him as his bride. The injustices and painful circumstances we suffer on this earth will be righted when Jesus establishes his kingdom—this is our end-time goal as believers.

A second aspect of long-term vision is an intentional commitment. Think of a recent goal you achieved; I bet your success was at least partially based on a determined pledge to accomplish your aspiration. Without a commitment, it is easy to stop trying when faced with difficult challenges. Pursuing our bridegroom takes just such a commitment—a vow to seek him and desire him no matter the cost. But sometimes that's hard to do. As a recovering perfectionist, I've struggled many times with feeling like the worst possible failure when I didn't measure up to a pledge I made to the Lord. At times, I've even hesitated to commit to something he is asking of me simply to avoid the pain of all-too-certain failure.

---

21. Heb 1:5 confirms that this psalm speaks of Jesus.
22. See Isa 9:2–7 for the complete passage.

What I've learned is that the process of evaluating myself and making a commitment to Jesus, failing and receiving his forgiveness, and then recommitting to him is actually the process by which my love for him deepens. When I fail to love Jesus as I desire to, my need for him pushes me to a more intimate, more vulnerable place in our relationship than I would experience if I always did everything perfectly. I am forced to lean on him, and my heart is softened toward him and grateful for his tenderness and love when I struggle, deepening our connection.

The good news is that I am free to commit fully to him, fail, and commit fully again because my standing with him is based on his redemptive work, not my own. He promises me that all of the promises of God "find their Yes in him" and that "it is God who establishes us with you in Christ," so my failures will not derail our relationship or change his affections for me.[23] In fact, it is when I hedge my bets and don't commit fully to him because of potential failure that I lose the opportunity to abandon myself to him without reserve and grow in loving him. Thus, his grace and love allow me to commit to a long-term vision of pursuing him with total abandon despite my own weakness.

Jonathan Edwards understood the importance of long-term vision, writing books that would stand the test of time and investing in institutions such as Princeton University that would last well beyond his own lifetime. Our final excerpt from his "Personal Narrative" includes a "solemn dedication" he made to the Lord when he was only twenty years old, writing down his commitment and dating it. The significance that Edwards attributed to this written dedication is revealed by the fact that he saved it long enough for it to appear in his spiritual narrative almost twenty years later, despite his own self-confessed regret at often failing in his vow. Edwards also shares with us the benefits he receives from meditating on heaven and his ultimate union with Jesus. For Edwards, long-term vision fueled his passionate pursuit of his bridegroom.

AUTOBIOGRAPHY: "PERSONAL NARRATIVE"[24]

On January 12, 1723, I made a solemn dedication of myself to God and wrote it down, giving up myself and all that I had to God, to be for the future in no respect my own, to

---

23. 2 Cor 1:20a, 21a.
24. Selections are from Hopkins, *Life and Character*, 30, 29, 32.

act as one that had no right to himself in any respect. And solemnly vowed to take God for my whole portion and felicity, looking on nothing else as any part of my happiness, nor acting as if it were, and his law for the constant rule of my obedience, engaging to fight with all my might against the world, the flesh, and the devil, to the end of my life. But have reason to be infinitely humbled when I consider how much I have failed of answering my obligation.

The heaven I desired was a heaven of holiness, to be with God, and to spend my eternity in divine love and holy communion with Christ. My mind was very much taken up with contemplations on heaven and the enjoyments of those there, and living there in perfect holiness, humility, and love.

And it used, at that time, to appear a great part of the happiness of heaven that there the saints could express their love to Christ. It appeared to me a great clog and hindrance and burden to me that what I felt within I could not express to God and give vent to as I desired. The inward ardor of my soul seemed to be hindered and pent up and could not freely flame out as it would. I used often to think how in heaven this sweet principle should freely and fully vent and express itself. Heaven appeared to me exceeding delightful as a world of love. It appeared to me that all happiness consisted in living in pure, humble, heavenly, divine love.

After I came home to Windsor, [Connecticut], remained much in a [similar] frame of my mind as I had been in at New York, but only sometimes felt my heart ready to sink with the thoughts of my friends at New York. And my refuge and support was in contemplations on the heavenly state, as I find in my diary of May 1, 1723. It was my comfort to think of that state where there is fullness of joy; where reigns heavenly, sweet, calm and delightful love, without alloy; where there are continually the dearest expressions of this love; where is the enjoyment of the persons loved, without ever parting; where these persons that appear so lovely in this world will really be inexpressibly more lovely and full of love to us. And how sweetly will the mutual lovers join together to sing the praises of God and the Lamb! How full will it fill us with joy to think that this enjoyment, these sweet exercises, will never cease or come to an end, but will last to all eternity!

CHAPTER SUMMARY AND FURTHER READING

Life as Jesus' bride requires us to bear the pain of separation from him, but we can be encouraged that our longing motivates us to pursue him, which is the third response he is hoping for from his bride. If we envision our time on earth as a time of marriage preparation, we will be inspired to prepare ourselves for our heavenly wedding day by investing in a deep, intimate relationship with our bridegroom. Like an adventurer, we will model the choices of the bride in Song of Songs and pursue Jesus to new places, while being persistent, self-motivated, and grateful. And, like an entrepreneur, we will imitate Jonathan Edwards, who stirred up his affections for his bridegroom and maintained a long-term vision in his pursuit of Jesus.

Exceptional works on Jonathan Edwards abound, but background on his writings and thought is easily accessed via *The Jonathan Edwards Encyclopedia*, edited by Harry S. Stout. Yale University Press has published *The Works of Jonathan Edwards*, and you can find everything related to Edwards on the website of the Jonathan Edwards Center at Yale University. George M. Marsden's *Jonathan Edwards: A Life* is a recent, excellent biography of Edwards for those interested in his life and times, while Marsden's *An Infinite Fountain of Light: Jonathan Edwards for the Twenty-First Century* applies key concepts from Edwards's thought to our own culture.

4

Encountering Him: Sarah Edwards
Song of Songs 3:6—5:1a

Look! It is the king's marriage carriage....
Rise up, Zion maidens, brides-to-be!
Come and feast your eyes on this king
as he passes in procession on his way to his wedding.
This is the day filled with overwhelming joy—
the day of his great gladness.[1]

EVERYONE LOVES A WEDDING and for good reason. The longevity, exclusivity, and significance of the marriage commitment is moving and inspiring. No other earthly relationship rivals it, which is exactly why God uses marriage throughout the Bible as a picture of how he loves humanity. Only a commitment as passionate and lasting as marriage can image the unconditional, never-ending, overwhelming love of God for us.

As a bride of Jesus, we have stepped out in faith to awaken our hearts to him, to choose him, and to pursue him. Now, we hope to grow in the fourth and final response to our bridegroom—encountering him. By *encounter*, I mean we learn to experience him, to receive from him, and to allow him to share himself with us. The marriage relationship we share with him enables this encounter.

---

1. Song 3:7a, 11.

BRIDAL ENCOUNTERS

As our bridegroom, Jesus wants to *show* us his love, not just tell us about it. He doesn't want his passion and affection for us to remain intellectual concepts that we hear about in church and worship songs but never actually experience. He wants to share his life with us. Jesus is the repository of all the peace, goodness, love, kindness, health, wisdom, delight, and joy in the universe. Everything that is wonderful dwells in him! What bridegroom doesn't want to share his best with his beloved?

In the same way, Jesus longs to pour himself into us. He wants to meet our needs, calm our fears, wipe away our tears, ease our minds, heal our pain, and draw us near to himself. He is loving and tender, the most kind and gentle-hearted person we will ever know. He is not satisfied with being a concept in our heads; he wants to touch us, share himself with us, and help us receive his goodness.

Jesus wants to pour himself into us because he knows we need him. When we encounter the love and tenderness of Jesus, we are changed. We are healed, strengthened, encouraged, comforted, and made secure in his love. If we are trying to live the Christian life without such experiences with Jesus, we will likely struggle with burnout, confusion, fatigue, or hopelessness. We need to encounter him, in all his fullness.

Relating to Jesus as our bridegroom is the avenue by which we encounter him the most profoundly. When two people are married, the Bible affirms that they become one,[2] and the intimacy, vulnerability, permanence, and depth of our unique oneness with Jesus allows us to experience him in the most deeply special way. It is as our eternal bridegroom, the lover of our souls, that Jesus can draw the closest to us and saturate our life with his.

Do you know how to encounter your bridegroom in this way? Can you still your spirit in his presence, connect with him on a real level, and allow him to pour himself into you? If you struggle in this area, this chapter is for you! We know that fullness of joy and eternal pleasures are in Jesus' presence,[3] and he longs to connect deeply and intimately with us. Let's learn how to encounter our bridegroom in ways that encourage us, heal us, and fill us with joy as his bride.

---

2. See Gen 2:24, Matt 19:4–6a, and Mark 10:6–8.
3. Ps 16:11.

THE MARRIAGE CEREMONY: SONG 3:6–11

The bride in Song of Songs has reached one milestone in her journey: she is ready to wed her bridegroom-king. After awakening her heart, drawing back from following him, experiencing the pain of his absence, choosing and pursuing him, and vowing to never let him go again, she is prepared to encounter him and give herself to him completely. The passage in Song of Songs recounts the wedding ceremony of King Solomon and his bride, as well as the vows they declare to each other. As we examine the ceremony and the vows, we will learn important ways to encounter our passionate bridegroom Jesus.

The passage begins with the marriage ceremony, opening with a stunning description of King Solomon and his royal wedding procession. He arises from the wilderness, fragrant, strong, and alluring. He has come to wed his bride and has prepared a beautiful and elaborate nuptial ceremony. Arriving in a sumptuous carriage made with his own hands, Solomon is surrounded by an entourage that includes sixty warriors, fully-armed experts in the art of war, trained to protect the royal couple from anything that may assail them. The carriage itself is made with the strongest, most superior wood available, and its stunning interior boasts inlaid gold, silver, and purple, all lovingly assembled. The most striking aspect of this ceremony is noted in verse eleven:

> Go out, O daughters of Zion,
>   and look upon King Solomon,
> with the crown with which his mother crowned him
>   on the day of his wedding,
>   on the day of the gladness of his heart.

Solomon's heart is joyous because it is his wedding day, with one translation rendering the final line as "his heart full, bursting with joy!"[4] This is not some ostentatious royal spectacle Solomon is putting on to impress the attendees, a dispassionate civic affair that has little personal meaning for him. No, this ceremony is genuinely beautiful because Solomon's love for his bride is real and deep. His heart is truly delighted because his wedding day has come. All who are present are urged to go to the royal wedding and gaze upon the bridegroom in his kingly majesty and joy.

This verse provides our first clue for how to encounter Jesus: give him our full attention. Just as the verse exhorts the daughters of Jerusalem

---

4. Song 3:11b (MSG).

to "go out . . . and look upon King Solomon," magnificently crowned and arrayed in his royal garments, so we want to turn our focus to Jesus because gazing upon him is where all true encounters begin. Does this sound too simple? Yes, it is simple, but it is also important. If you desire to encounter your bridegroom and experience the love and goodness he longs to share with you, give him your attention.

Jesus is worthy of our attention. All of it. The fact that we have to spend large portions of our time as earth-bound humans working, eating, and sleeping is really quite tragic because *every* moment of our lives, in a perfect world, would be spent contemplating and enjoying the beauty, majesty, and sheer loveliness of our bridegroom. Attending to him is exactly the behavior Jesus honors Mary for in Luke 10 when she chooses to sit at his feet while her sister Martha is focusing on hosting guests. According to Jesus, "One thing is necessary. Mary has chosen the good portion, which will not be taken from her."[5]

Giving our full attention to Jesus simply means we come to him, like Mary did, and deliberately turn our gaze from everything else to focus solely on him. We set aside our questions, our needs, our other interests, and our distractions to simply be with him. Attending to Jesus is the foundation of all true encounters with him because doing so communicates our longing for him and acknowledges his supreme worthiness and primacy of place in our lives and affections. When we come to our bridegroom in this way, the spiritual atmosphere shifts. It moves Jesus' heart immeasurably to be wanted for himself alone and to have our full focus. Our undivided attention is what he is waiting for because it opens a door for him to share his life with us.

I distinctly remember when I first learned this truth as a young adult. I had just graduated from college and desired to deepen my prayer life, so I began reading contemplative writers such as Julian of Norwich, John of the Cross, Thomas Merton, and Richard Foster. These words of Foster's, among others, stunned me: "In its most basic and fundamental expression, Contemplative Prayer is a loving attentiveness to God."[6] Really? Was this true? Was simply attending to Jesus a form of prayer, and was it an important practice?

David's words in Ps 27:4 seemed to suggest it was: "One thing have I asked of the Lord, that will I seek after: that I may dwell in the house of

---

5. Luke 10:42.
6. Foster, *Prayer*, 158.

the LORD all the days of my life, to gaze upon the beauty of the LORD and to inquire in his temple." Similarly, Ps 46:10a recommends we "be still, and know that I am God." Convinced, I started spending time during my private devotions just focusing on Jesus and resting in his presence.

For the first few months, my experiment with attending to Jesus was a spectacular failure. Most days, I either got distracted, fell asleep, or impatiently watched the clock until I could stop! But, slowly, over time, it became easier to quiet my mind and still my spirit in Jesus' presence, and soon he began responding to me in unexpectedly wonderful ways. One day, I would feel surprisingly peaceful when my stress level was at its highest. Another day, I would sense a solution to a problem that had been troubling me or would feel forgiveness rising up in my heart for a friend who had hurt me. Sometimes, I would be moved by an overwhelming sense of Jesus' love for me, or I would realize something new about him.

I was finding that simply turning my attention to my bridegroom placed my heart in a position where I could encounter him and those encounters were amazing! He really had been waiting for me to shift my focus exclusively to him so he could connect with me in the deepest places of my spirit and fill me with himself.

In a practical sense, turning our attention to Jesus is really very simple. Set aside ten or fifteen minutes of your devotional time to stop all activity, bring your mind and body to rest, and turn your full attention to Jesus. I find it helpful to say out loud to him, "Jesus, I am here to be with you because I love you. I am not asking for anything from you; I simply desire to be with you and enjoy you because you are my first love, and I know you love and enjoy me." Then just rest in his presence and center your thoughts on him. Playing soft worship music in the background, recalling a Bible verse, or lighting a candle may help you focus.

It takes time to learn to quiet our continually racing thoughts and train our minds to stop wandering, so if you initially struggle with this practice, don't give up! Everyone struggles for the first few weeks or even months. Simply remember that when you are fully attending to Jesus, you are in exactly the right position to receive from him, and even if you feel nothing, *something* is happening in your spirit. Time spent with your bridegroom is never, ever wasted, regardless of what you experience with your natural senses. With practice and the help of the Holy Spirit, you will begin to encounter Jesus in the deepest parts of your heart, and he will permeate your life with his goodness and love.

If you adopt just one step from this chapter on encountering Jesus, make it this step. Take some moments as often as you can in your times alone with him to stop, rest, and give him your full attention simply because it's *him*, and you love him. This is the single most important step in encountering our bridegroom.

THE BRIDEGROOM'S VOWS: SONG 4:1–15

The wedding vows of the bridegroom and bride in Song of Songs come next in the passage and offer two additional suggestions for encountering Jesus and allowing him to share his life with us. We'll begin with King Solomon and his inspiring vows of love to his bride.

My husband and I did not write our own wedding vows, but if we had, I think even as an English professor I would have been tempted to plagiarize some of the verses from Song 4:1–15 for my vows! The words that Solomon shares on his wedding day with his Shulamite bride are astonishingly beautiful and reveal a heart that is ravished by his beloved with a love that is deep, passionate, and unending. Observe the level of detail in the first seven verses of chapter 4. Solomon opens and closes the passage by pronouncing his bride "beautiful," and then meticulously identifies everything he adores about her eyes, hair, teeth, lips, mouth, cheeks, neck, and breasts. This bridegroom has noticed every detail of his beloved! Notice also his words at the end of his litany of her endowments: "You are altogether beautiful, my love; there is no flaw in you." In Solomon's eyes, his bride is perfect!

The next four verses reveal that Solomon has been forever captivated by his bride. In verse nine, he cries, "You have stolen my heart, my sister, my bride; you have stolen my heart with one glance of your eyes, with one jewel of your necklace."[7] The heart of the most powerful king of his day is in the possession of his beautiful bride. What a statement from Solomon! He declares he is a prisoner of her love.

Solomon's arresting description of the beauty of his bride and his frank admission that his heart has been captured by her reminds us that our bridegroom Jesus sees us in the same way—as his exquisite beloved one who has stolen his heart. Are Solomon's words of love and affirmation to his bride difficult for you to receive as Jesus' words to you? We

---

7. NIV. It was not uncommon for the terms "brother" and "sister" to be used in the ancient love poetry of the Middle East.

all struggle to fathom the extent of Jesus' love toward us, but, like we noticed in verses nine and ten in the first chapter of Song of Songs, our bridegroom truly finds us alluringly beautiful and captivating. We *are* perfect in his eyes.

The final section of Solomon's vows is perhaps the most poetic as the king compares his bride to a garden:

> You are a garden locked up, my sister, my bride;
> > you are a spring enclosed, a sealed fountain.
>
> Your plants are an orchard of pomegranates
> > with choice fruits,
> > with henna and nard,
> > nard and saffron,
> > calamus and cinnamon,
> > with every kind of incense tree,
> > with myrrh and aloes
> > and all the finest spices.
>
> You are a garden fountain,
> > a well of flowing water
> > streaming down from Lebanon.[8]

Why would Solomon compare his bride to a garden? What comes to mind when you imagine a garden? Fruitfulness and harvest, certainly, also beauty and color, serenity and rest, and growth and newness of life.

With this metaphor, Solomon is comparing all the pleasant and pleasurable characteristics of a garden with his bride. She is bountiful and generous; she is beautiful and adorned; she is inviting and restorative. And she is his and his alone. Like a private garden, Solomon's bride is "locked up," "enclosed," and "sealed," not in a custodial or penal fashion, but in a way that denotes exclusivity. She belongs to him and him only, her loving and devoted bridegroom, who finds her absolutely ravishing and flawless. Whew. Solomon certainly knew how to write wedding vows!

It is Solomon's metaphor of his bride as an exquisite private garden that provides our second suggestion for how to encounter our bridegroom Jesus—embracing the unique and equally matched relationship we each have with him. When I first began learning to relate to Jesus as my bridegroom, I was troubled by two questions, the first of which concerned the uniqueness of my relationship with him. Since Jesus is the bridegroom of the church, then he has lots and lots of brides. How special can I really be to him if I'm not his one and only, as he is mine?

---

8. Song 4:12–15 (NIV).

This question bothered me for a long time, and perhaps it has occurred to you as well.

I believe Solomon's comparison of his bride to a garden in Song of Songs helps us answer this question. A garden that is "locked up," "enclosed," and "sealed" belongs to one person only, and it is this exclusivity that helps us understand how Jesus sees each of us as his distinct, unique bride. Just as one child cannot replace another child in a family or one close friend replace another, so no other bride of Jesus can replace us in his eyes. In fact, it is unacceptable to him that we would feel replaceable in any way. The bridal relationship he has with each of us is unique; in a sense, we are each his "favorite" in a way that is possible because he is God. Jesus knows and loves each of us as uniquely and intimately as one knows and loves a perfectly private garden. For Jesus, there is no other but you—you are his own "private paradise."[9]

The garden metaphor also provides the answer to the second question I struggled with, which related to the "equality" or parity of our relationship: since Jesus is perfect and I'm weak and battle endlessly with sin, is it possible for us to share a relationship that is mutually satisfying, one in which both partners receive enjoyment from the other? Surely Jesus gets tired of always being the one to forgive me, answer my questions, rescue and comfort me, and bear with all the irritating things I do? How much fun can such a seemingly one-sided, unequal relationship be?

The garden King Solomon uses to describe his bride, however, is perfectly fruitful and pleasing to him, producing "choice fruits" and "all the finest spices." This garden offers life and abundance of the highest quality, lacking nothing. What makes Solomon's garden so fruitful and satisfying? According to the passage, the garden has within it a "well of flowing water," an internal spring that feeds the garden and is the source of its prosperity. This spring enables the garden to enchant and gratify Solomon with the "finest" fruits and spices.

Like a garden with an underground spring, as the bride of Jesus, we are animated by our bridegroom's life within us. Although we appear to ourselves to be consistently weak and failing, to Jesus, the source of perfect love, we are satisfying and pleasing. Jesus' eternal life and love flow through us back to himself just as an underground spring sustains a garden so it can bear fruit. In this way, we bring Jesus such ultimate joy and contentment that he can exclaim with King Solomon, "How beautiful

---

9. Song 4:12a (TPT).

is your love, my sister, my bride! How much better is your love than wine, and the fragrance of your oils than any spice!"[10] Jesus truly enjoys us and delights in us, recalling God's promise to Israel in Isa 62:4–5:

> You shall no more be termed Forsaken, and your land shall no more be termed Desolate, but you shall be called My Delight Is in Her, and your land Married; for the Lord delights in you, and your land shall be married. For as a young man marries a young woman, so shall your sons marry you, and as the bridegroom rejoices over the bride, so shall your God rejoice over you.

Despite our failings, Jesus is not disappointed in us or angry with us; instead, his every response to us is prompted by his sheer delight in us. Like a garden spring, his perfect love flowing through us makes our relationship with him a partnership of equals, in a sense, each offering the other the exceptional fruits of bridal love.[11]

One of the most wonderful results that I experienced as I grew in accepting how much Jesus delights in me was that my motivation for obeying him changed. The freedom and joy I felt in knowing that I brought pleasure and enjoyment to Jesus made me *want* to make choices that pleased his heart out of gratitude and reciprocal delight in him. No longer did I feel pressure to obey him to avoid his displeasure or judgment. No, I was free from that! His delight in me caused me to enjoy pleasing my beloved bridegroom.

The shift reminded me of how my younger son would give me gifts for my birthday and Christmas when he was small. Every year, I would receive earrings shaped like every animal imaginable as a present from him, and the delight on his face when I opened the packages was indescribable. My son didn't give me those earrings to placate me because he thought I was mad at him or disappointed in him. He gave them because he knew I loved him and he wanted, in turn, to show his love for me and to see the joy on my face when I received the earrings. In the same way, knowing Jesus delights in us and that we share a relationship both partners enjoy frees us to please our beloved with joyful abandon from our secure position as his cherished, dearly loved bride.

Thus, Solomon's wedding vows reveal our second suggestion for encountering Jesus. By meditating on the image of an enchanting, fruitful,

---

10. Song 4:10.

11. In fact, one translation uses the phrase "my equal" in verses nine and ten of Song 4 to denote this parity (TPT).

private garden, we learn to accept that we are each Jesus' unique and equally matched bride, perfectly satisfying and pleasing in his eyes. As this truth makes its way into our hearts, we can encounter our bridegroom without shame and with great confidence, knowing our relationship with him is enlivened and sustained by his perfect, unfailing love.

THE BRIDE'S VOWS: SONG 4:16

In the final verse of Song 4, the bride responds to the wedding vows of the bridegroom with her own vows. The bride's vows continue the garden metaphor begun by King Solomon:

> Awake, north wind,
>   and come, south wind!
> Blow on my garden,
>   that its fragrance may spread everywhere.
> Let my beloved come into his garden
>   and taste its choice fruits.[12]

The bride's vows begin passionately, with many translations including an exclamation point. Her vows seem to practically burst out of her, an authentic and earnest response to her bridegroom's vows to her. The bride's vows actually consist of two requests: that the north and south winds blow on her garden and spread its aroma abroad and that her bridegroom enter and enjoy her garden. In these vows, we will find the third tip for how to encounter our bridegroom Jesus.

It is somewhat surprising that the bride opens her vows with an appeal to the north and south winds to blow on her garden because when we consider what happens when wind blows through a garden, one word comes to mind—disruption. When a gale gusts through a garden, leaves and fruit get shaken off branches, petals are blown off flowers, vines get tangled, water ripples, pollen is whisked off stamens, and various scents comingle and swirl in the air. In short, a mess is made. Why would the bride ask for the north and south winds to cause commotion in her beautiful private garden?

I suspect that the end goal of the bride's request is not commotion or disorder but refinement and growth. When wind rages through a garden, it may appear like chaos on the surface, but much good is accomplished on a deeper level. For example, flowers and fruit that are dead or decaying

---

12. NIV.

are the first to be blown to the ground. The wind thus acts as a pruning mechanism, clearing away all that has already served its purpose and is in decline. In addition, the wind functions as an efficient and effective distribution agent for all that is healthy and productive in the garden, carrying its fruitfulness far beyond its boundaries. Pollen is scattered to fertilize flowers great distances away, moisture is taken up into the air to appear as rain in other locations, and the beautiful fragrances of the garden flowers mix and travel as far as the wind can take them. Thus, the bride is requesting that the winds remove all that is declining and no longer needed in her garden and spread all that is useful and lovely to the world outside.

The bride's request thus provides the third recommendation for encountering our bridegroom Jesus—willingly inviting into our lives his productive disruption. Encounters with Jesus can be disruptive, in every sense of the word. Only three times in the Bible is God compared directly with something: he is "spirit," he is "consuming fire," and he is "love."[13] When you encounter spirit, fire, and love, you will feel the effects. Thankfully, like the north and south winds blowing through the bride's garden, the effects of encounter with Jesus will always remove what is hindering our full potential and maximize the effectiveness of all that is fruitful.

For instance, an encounter with our bridegroom may show us an area in which we are falling short, but we will also experience his forgiveness. We may begin in a place of confusion, but we will end in a place of peace. We may start an encounter in weakness, but we will finish in strength. Jesus longs to meet us where we are, remove what is hurting and holding us back, and lead us into greater love and growth, and encountering us is how he does this. The entire process may take place over multiple encounters with him, but it is a process we know he will complete.

Can this be disruptive to our normal lives? Yes, of course; growth always is. But it is the best path to maturity and a closer connection with our bridegroom, and so the fruit of such encounters is decidedly worth it.

Do you fear you do not have the courage to request such powerful, disruptive encounters with your beloved? You do. Look at how the courage of the bride in Song of Songs has grown over the past two chapters of the narrative. Remember how she failed to follow Solomon when he twice invited her to "arise, my love, my beautiful one, and come away"

---

13. John 4:24; Heb 12:29; 1 John 4:8.

with him in chapter 2?[14] Now, she eagerly embraces a chance to encounter him, even if it challenges her status quo. How has she grown so brave?

Quite simply, the bride has been changed through her courtship with the king. She has experienced the depth of his love for her, ultimately encountering in the marriage ceremony the deepest sentiments of his heart shared through his wedding vows. He has declared to her that he sees her as flawless and beautiful, that his heart is ravished by her, that she is unique to him, and that she is his equal partner. The bridegroom's love has caused in her an identity shift, and she now embraces with confidence her position as Solomon's cherished bride. Truly, "there is no fear in love, but perfect love casts out fear."[15] It is thus within the safety and security of her bridegroom's perfect love for her that she is able to step out with courage and do what she could not do earlier in their relationship—fully encounter him.

In the same way, we have responded to the invitation of our bridegroom Jesus to awaken our hearts to him, to choose him, and to pursue him, and we have grown perhaps imperceptibly into embracing our identity as his bride. Thus, we will begin to long for and invite encounters with him, even if these experiences mean disruption and change and even if we feel less than courageous. We now desire him more than anything else.

The bride ends her vows with a heartfelt invitation to her bridegroom to come to her with the words: "Let my beloved come into his garden and taste its choice fruits." She is eager to encounter Solomon and has, in fact, prepared herself for him. She longs for him to unite with her and enjoy all that she can offer him, all her "choice fruits." This is not the encounter of a student with a teacher, a servant with a master, or a lost soul with a savior. No, this is an intimate encounter of a bride with her bridegroom, the one to whom she has pledged her life and future. This is an invitation to be joined completely. And, guess what? Her bridegroom accepts the invitation!

THE MARRIAGE CONSUMMATION: SONG 5:1A

We find in the first part of Song 5:1 the consummation of the marriage ceremony as King Solomon joins his bride in her private garden:

14. Song 2:10b, 13b.
15. 1 John 4:18a.

> I have come into my garden, my sister, my bride;
> I have gathered my myrrh with my spice.
> I have eaten my honeycomb and my honey;
> I have drunk my wine and my milk.[16]

Solomon and his Shulamite bride have joined themselves in marriage and thus experience the deepest encounter two people can enjoy—"the day of his great gladness." They have committed themselves to each other forever and will now reap the fruits of their eternal nuptial bond.

As our bridegroom, Jesus has joined himself to us with a permanent, unbreakable vow. As Paul declares in 1 Cor 6:16b–17, "For, as it is written, 'The two will become one flesh.' But he who is joined to the Lord becomes one spirit with him." In Revelation, we see that Jesus' role as our bridegroom-king will be his primary identity in eternity as he establishes his everlasting kingdom and celebrates his wedding with his bride the church. And while he loves to be our teacher, master, and friend while we live in time and space, those roles do not come with a permanent vow as does that of bridegroom. Thus, we can embrace our marriage bond with Jesus as his loved and cherished bride, encountering him as our treasured bridegroom on earth and looking in expectation toward our future perfect union with him in heaven.

We have covered a lot in this chapter, so let's turn our attention to a helpful illustration of these ideas. Through a mutual friend, we have access to a compelling encounter one eighteenth-century woman experienced with her loving bridegroom.

SARAH EDWARDS: WIFE, MOTHER, SPIRITUAL LEADER

Perhaps calling Jonathan Edwards our friend is a bit of a stretch, but reading his spiritual narrative in chapter 3 of this book certainly helped us get to know him. Now, we will enjoy an inside look at a powerful, intimate encounter his wife, Sarah Edwards (1710–58), had with Jesus.

Sarah and Jonathan met when he was a student at Yale and she was living with her family in New Haven, Connecticut, where her father was a minister. Jonathan's well-known description of Sarah when they first became acquainted highlights her deep relationship with God:

> They say there is a young lady in [New Haven] who is beloved of
> that Great Being who made and rules the world, and that there

16. NIV.

are certain seasons in which this Great Being, in some way or other invisible, comes to her and fills her mind with exceeding sweet delight, and that she hardly cares for anything except to meditate on him—that she expects after a while to be received up where he is, to be raised up out of the world and caught up into heaven, being assured that he loves her too well to let her remain at a distance from him always. There she is to dwell with him and to be ravished with his love and delight forever.[17]

Sarah and Jonathan married in 1727 and had eleven children, all of whom survived to adulthood.

Sarah Edwards was well-known and respected in her town, entertained guests and seminary students, traveled for business, managed the household and children, and counseled many spiritually. When the religious revival now known as the First Great Awakening erupted in New England in 1739, Edwards was at the forefront. She hosted many revivalist preachers in her home, offered spiritual counsel into the night after revival meetings ended, and shared the gospel with her neighbors. One young minister who stayed with Edwards later recalled how she had encouraged him when he was battling doubts by praying for him and assuring him of the important ministry she believed he would have.[18] But Edwards was also human, struggling with depression at times and the challenges of being the wife of the town's leading pastor. Like most of us, she experienced highs and lows in both her life and relationship with God.

The end of Edwards's life shows not only her challenges but also her close relationship with Jesus. When their daughter Esther Edwards Burr lost her husband, the Reverend Aaron Burr, to smallpox in the fall of 1757, Jonathan traveled to Newark, New Jersey, to comfort Esther and to replace her husband as president of the College of New Jersey in Princeton. Sadly, Jonathan died just a few months later after receiving a smallpox vaccination. Brokenhearted, Sarah wrote to Esther, encouraging her to trust God and stay close to him through the difficult time:

> What shall I say.... The Lord has done it. He has made me adore his goodness that we had [Jonathan] so long. But my God lives, and he has my heart. Oh, what a legacy my husband, and your father, has left us! We are all given to God, and there I am and love to be.[19]

17. Dwight, *Life of President Edwards*, 114.
18. Hopkins, *Works of Hopkins*, 1:19.
19. Dwight, *Works of President Edwards*, 580–81.

Tragically, Esther died within a month of Jonathan, and Sarah traveled to New Jersey to bring Esther and Aaron's two small children back with her to live. She never completed the journey home, as she died in Philadelphia of dysentery, probably from the strain of bereavement and travel. Sarah had lived her life for Jesus, and she went to him at the young age of forty-nine.

SARAH EDWARDS'S BRIDAL ENCOUNTER

In January 1742, while the First Great Awakening was in full swing, Sarah Edwards had an encounter with God that overwhelmed and changed her. She had been feeling uneasy in her spirit for several weeks, struggling with concerns over her reputation in the town and feeling resentment and jealousy toward visiting ministers who were more positively received by the town than was her husband.

One morning, Edwards was struck by the reality of God's forgiveness in Jesus Christ, and she retired to her bedroom to spend time with God. Over the next two weeks, Edwards had a series of powerful encounters with God in which she experienced his intense love for her, at times overwhelming her physically. Often during those weeks, she remained awake through the night, enjoying the presence of Jesus. Edwards managed sporadically to continue with her household and ministry duties, attend revival meetings, and converse with guests, but she was forced often to retire to her bedroom when the encounters were the strongest.

Edwards's husband Jonathan was traveling during the weeks of her encounters, but he was so moved by her description of the experience that he encouraged her to write an account. He later included a summarized, anonymous version of her narrative in his written defense of the revival published the next year, *Some Thoughts Concerning the Present Revival of Religion in New England*. In the work, Jonathan asserts that his wife's testimony proves the importance and appropriateness of experiential encounters with God and refutes challengers who claim such experiences are caused by emotional disorders or a weak mind: "Now if such things are enthusiasm and the offspring of a distempered brain, let my brain be possessed evermore of that happy distemper! If this be distraction, I pray God that the world of mankind may all be seized with this benign, meek, beneficent, beatific, glorious distraction!"[20]

---

20. Dwight, *Works of President Edwards*, 188–89.

Edwards's encounters with Jesus changed her. She records that she was released from concern over her reputation and that she began to sincerely desire the success of the visiting ministers. The promises of God in the Bible became real to her, and she became more secure in God's love for her. Her experiences with Jesus were so affecting that Edwards struggles to describe them, not having the words to fully explain her encounters and reaching for earthly comparisons to help the reader understand what she felt. At one point, she observes:

> At the same time, my heart and soul all flowed out in love to Christ so that there seemed to be a constant flowing and reflowing of heavenly and divine love from Christ's heart to mine. . . . So far as I am capable of making a comparison, I think that what I felt each minute during the continuance of the whole time was worth more than all the outward comfort and pleasure which I had enjoyed in my whole life put together.[21]

Wow! What a testimony of the absolutely incalculable pleasure of encountering our bridegroom!

We find in Edwards's narrative one individual's experience with encountering Jesus and how it affected her. We also can see how she applied many of the ideas discussed in this chapter. For example, despite being very busy hosting traveling ministers in her home along with her regular duties, Edwards still prioritizes being with Jesus, giving him her full attention. She willingly embraces the productive disruption that he brings into her heart and life, rejoicing in the growth and refinement she experiences. Lastly, Edwards becomes securely established in her identity as Jesus' beloved, remarking, "It seemed as if nothing that could be said of me or done to me could touch my heart or disturb my enjoyment."[22]

I hope you enjoy this sneak peek into one woman's powerful encounter with our bridegroom. Every time I read Sarah Edwards's account, my heart is encouraged and my desire is strengthened to seek and expect encounters with Jesus for myself!

---

21. Dwight, *Works of President Edwards*, 178–79.
22. Dwight, *Works of President Edwards*, 183.

TESTIMONY: SARAH EDWARDS'S ACCOUNT[23]

On Tuesday night, January 19, 1742, I felt very uneasy and unhappy at my being so low in grace. I thought I very much needed help from God and found a spirit of earnestness to seek help of him that I might have more holiness. When I had for a time been earnestly wrestling with God for it, I felt within myself great quietness of spirit, unusual submission to God, and willingness to wait upon him with respect to the time and manner in which he should help me, and wished that he should take his own time and his own way to do it.

While Mr. Reynolds[24] was at prayer in the family this morning, I felt an earnest desire that in calling on God, he should say, *Father*, or that he should address the Almighty under that appellation, on which the thought turned in my mind: Why can I say *Father*? Can I now at this time, with the confidence of a child and without the least misgiving of heart, call God my Father? This brought to my mind two lines of Mr. Erskine's sonnet:

I see him lay his vengeance by,
And smile in Jesus' face.[25]

I was thus deeply sensible that my sins did loudly call for vengeance, but I then by faith saw God "lay his vengeance by, and smile in Jesus' face." It appeared to be real and certain that he did so. I had not the least doubt that he then sweetly smiled upon me with the look of forgiveness and love, having laid aside all his displeasure towards me for Jesus' sake, which made me feel very weak and somewhat faint.

23. Selections are from Dwight, *Works of President Edwards*, 171, 172–74, 177, 178–79.

24. Peter Reynolds (1700–68) was a minister in Enfield, Connecticut, from 1724 until his death.

25. Ralph Erskine (1685–1752) was a Scottish minister whose *Gospel Sonnets; or, Spiritual Songs*, originally published in Edinburgh, Scotland, in 1720, was published in its first American edition by Benjamin Franklin in 1740. The six-part poem, extremely popular during the First Great Awakening and subsequent revivals, uses bridal language and imagery throughout to encourage the Christian to seek divorce from the law and marriage with Christ. The sonnet Edwards refers to here is titled "The Valour and Victories of Faith" and is found in Part VI: The Believer's Principles, Chapter IV, Section 4. See Roberts, "Calvinist Couplet," 412–31, for more on Erskine's *Gospel Sonnets*.

In consequence of this, I felt a strong desire to be alone with God, to go to him, without having anyone to interrupt the silent and soft communion which I earnestly desired between God and my own soul, and accordingly withdrew to my chamber. It should have been mentioned that before I retired, while Mr. Reynolds was praying, these words in Romans 8:34 came into my mind: "Who is he that condemns; it is Christ that died, yea rather that is risen again, who is even at the right hand of God, who also makes intercession for us," as well as the following words, "Who shall separate us from the love of Christ,"[26] etc., which occasioned great sweetness and delight in my soul.

But when I was alone, the words came to my mind with far greater power and sweetness, upon which I took the Bible and read the words to the end of the chapter, when they were impressed on my heart with vastly greater power and sweetness still. They appeared to me with undoubted certainty as the words of God and as words which God did pronounce concerning me. I had no more doubt of it than I had of my being. I seemed, as it were, to hear the great God proclaiming thus to the world concerning me: "Who shall lay anything to your charge,"[27] and had it strongly impressed on me how impossible it was for anything in heaven or earth, in this world or the future, ever to separate me from the love of God which was in Christ Jesus.[28] I cannot find language to express how *certain* this appeared—the everlasting mountains and hills were but shadows to it. My safety and happiness and eternal enjoyment of God's immutable love seemed as durable and unchangeable as God himself.

Melted and overcome by the sweetness of this assurance, I fell into a great flow of tears and could not forbear weeping aloud. It appeared certain to me that God was my Father, and Christ my Lord and Savior, that he was mine and I his.[29] Under a delightful sense of the immediate presence and love of God, these words seemed to come over

---

26. Rom 8:35a.
27. Rom 8:33a.
28. A reference to Rom 8:38–39.
29. Song 2:16a.

and over in my mind, "My God, my all; my God, my all." The presence of God was so near and so real that I seemed scarcely conscious of anything else.

God the Father and the Lord Jesus Christ seemed as distinct persons, both manifesting their inconceivable loveliness and mildness and gentleness, and their great and immutable love to me. I seemed to be taken under the care and charge of my God and Savior in an inexpressibly endearing manner, and Christ appeared to me as a mighty Savior, under the character of the Lion of the Tribe of Judah,[30] taking my heart, with all its corruptions, under his care and putting it at his feet. In all things which concerned me, I felt myself safe under the protection of the Father and the Savior, who appeared with supreme kindness to keep a record of everything that I did and of everything that was done to me, purely for my good.

The peace and happiness which I hereupon felt was altogether inexpressible. It seemed to be that which came from heaven, to be eternal and unchangeable. I seemed to be lifted above earth and hell, out of the reach of everything here below, so that I could look on all the rage and enmity of men or devils with a kind of holy indifference and an undisturbed tranquility.

At the same time, I felt compassion and love for all mankind and a deep abasement of soul under a sense of my own unworthiness. I thought of the ministers who were in the house and felt willing to undergo any labor and self-denial if they would but come to the help of the Lord. I also felt myself more perfectly weaned from all things here below than ever before. The whole world, with all its enjoyments and all its troubles, seemed to be nothing. My God was my all, my only portion. No possible suffering appeared to be worth regarding; all persecutions and torments were a mere nothing. I seemed to dwell on high and the place of defense to be the munition of rocks.[31]

---

30. In Rev 5:5, Jesus is referred to by one of the elders in heaven as the "Lion of the tribe of Judah."

31. Isa 33:16a.

About 11 o'clock, as I accidentally went into the room where Mr. Buell[32] was conversing with some of the people, I heard him say, "Oh, that we who are the children of God should be cold and lifeless in religion!" and I felt such a sense of the deep ingratitude manifested by the children of God in such coldness and deadness that my strength was immediately taken away, and I sunk down on the spot. Those who were near raised me and placed me in a chair, and from the fullness of my heart, I expressed to them in a very earnest manner the deep sense I had of the wonderful grace of Christ towards me, of the assurance I had of his having saved me from hell, of my happiness running parallel with eternity, of the duty of giving up all to God, and of the peace and joy inspired by an entire dependence on his mercy and grace.

Mr. Buell then read a melting hymn of Dr. Watts[33] concerning the loveliness of Christ, the enjoyments and employments of heaven, and the Christian's earnest desire of heavenly things, and the truth and reality of the things mentioned in the hymn made so strong an impression on my mind, and my soul was drawn so powerfully towards Christ and heaven, that I leaped unconsciously from my chair. I seemed to be drawn upwards, soul and body, from the earth towards heaven, and it appeared to me that I must naturally and necessarily ascend thither.

These feelings continued while the hymn was reading and during the prayer of Mr. Christophers[34] which followed. After the prayer, Mr. Buell read two other hymns on the glories of heaven, which moved me so exceedingly and drew me so strongly heavenward that it seemed, as it were, to draw my body upwards, and I felt as if I must necessarily ascend thither. At length, my strength failed me, and I sunk down, when they took me up and laid me on the bed,

---

32. Samuel Buell (1716–98) traveled as a popular revivalist preacher from 1741–45, until he was settled as a minister in Long Island, New York, in 1746.

33. Isaac Watts (1674–1748) was an English minister and popular hymn writer. Sereno Dwight suggests this hymn may have been "The Glory of Christ in Heaven," from Book II, Hymn 91, of Watts's *Hymns and Spiritual Songs* (London, 1707).

34. This may be Christopher Christophers (1717–75), a merchant in New London, Connecticut, who was a strong supporter of the First Great Awakening.

where I lay for a considerable time, faint with joy, while contemplating the glories of the heavenly world.

I continued in a sweet and lively sense of divine things until I retired to rest. That night, which was Thursday night, January 28, was the sweetest night I ever had in my life. I never before, for so long a time together, enjoyed so much of the light and rest and sweetness of heaven in my soul, but without the least agitation of body during the whole time.

The great part of the night I lay awake, sometimes asleep, and sometimes between sleeping and waking. But all night I continued in a constant, clear, and lively sense of the heavenly sweetness of Christ's excellent and transcendent love, of his nearness to me, and of my dearness to him, with an inexpressibly sweet calmness of soul in an entire rest in him.

I seemed to myself to perceive a glow of divine love come down from the heart of Christ in heaven into my heart in a constant stream, like a stream or pencil of sweet light. At the same time, my heart and soul all flowed out in love to Christ, so that there seemed to be a constant flowing and reflowing of heavenly and divine love from Christ's heart to mine, and I appeared to myself to float or swim in these bright, sweet beams of the love of Christ, like the motes swimming in the beams of the sun or the streams of his light which come in at the window.

My soul remained in a kind of heavenly Elysium.[35] So far as I am capable of making a comparison, I think that what I felt each minute during the continuance of the whole time was worth more than all the outward comfort and pleasure which I had enjoyed in my whole life put together. It was a pure delight, which fed and satisfied the soul. It was pleasure, without the least sting or any interruption. It was a sweetness which my soul was lost in. It seemed to be all that my feeble frame could sustain of that fullness of joy which is felt by those who behold the face of Christ and share his love in the heavenly world. There was but little difference whether I was asleep or awake, so deep was the impression made on my soul, but if there was any difference, the

---

35. Edwards is referring to the afterlife paradise in classical mythology to make the point that what she experienced felt like heaven.

sweetness was greatest and most uninterrupted while I was asleep.

As I awoke early the next morning, which was Friday, I was led to think of Mr. Williams of Hadley[36] preaching that day in the town, as had been appointed, and to examine my heart, whether I was willing that he, who was a neighboring minister, should be extraordinarily blessed and made a greater instrument of good in the town than Mr. Edwards, and was enabled to say with respect to that matter, "Amen, Lord Jesus!" and to be entirely willing, if God pleased, that he should be the instrument of converting every soul in the town. My soul acquiesced fully in the will of God as to the instrument, if his work of renewing grace did but go on.

This lively sense of the beauty and excellency of divine things continued during the morning, accompanied with peculiar sweetness and delight. To my own imagination, my soul seemed to be gone out of me to God and Christ in heaven and to have very little relation to my body. God and Christ were so present to me and so near me that I seemed removed from myself. The spiritual beauty of the Father and the Savior seemed to engross my whole mind, and it was the instinctive feeling of my heart, "Thou art, and there is none beside thee."[37]

I never felt such an entire emptiness of self-love or any regard to any private, selfish interest of my own. It seemed to me that I had entirely done with myself. I felt that the opinions of the world concerning me were nothing and that I had no more to do with any outward interest of my own than with that of a person whom I never saw. The glory of God seemed to be all and in all and to swallow up every wish and desire of my heart.

Mr. Sheldon[38] came into the house about 10 o'clock and said to me as he came in, "The Sun of righteousness arose

---

36. Chester Williams (1718–53) was a minister in Hadley, Massachusetts, from 1740 until his death. On January 20, 1742, one day before Edwards's encounter with God began, Edwards notes that she was admonished by her husband Jonathan because "he thought I had failed in some measure in point of prudence in some conversation I had with Mr. Williams of Hadley the day before." Dwight, *Works of President Edwards*, 172.

37. Possibly a reference to 1 Sam 2:2 or 2 Sam 7:22.

38. This could be Jonathan Sheldon Jr. (1711–60), a citizen of nearby Suffield, Connecticut, and a strong revival supporter.

on my soul this morning before day,"[39] upon which I said to him in reply, "That Sun has not set upon my soul all this night. I have dwelt on high in the heavenly mansions, the light of divine love has surrounded me, my soul has been lost in God and has almost left the body."

CHAPTER SUMMARY AND FURTHER READING

As our bridegroom, Jesus desires to share his life and love with us, so encountering him is the fourth response we want to have as his beloved bride. In the marriage ceremony in Song of Songs, the bridegroom shares his vows of love and commitment with his bride, and she responds by embracing her identity as his beloved partner and inviting him into her private garden. As a bride of Jesus, we learn from the bride in Song of Songs to give Jesus our full attention, to embrace our role as his unique and equal partner, and to invite his productive disruption into our lives to change us and help us grow. As Sarah Edwards discovered, encounters with Jesus are the most pleasurable and transformative experiences we can have in this lifetime for there is no one like him.

We do not know of additional extant works written by Sarah Edwards, but several books have chapters devoted to her and her religious experience. The most complete treatment of Edwards and her two-week encounter with God is *The Silent and Soft Communion: The Spiritual Narratives of Sarah Pierrepont Edwards and Sarah Prince Gill* by Sue Lane McCulley and Dorothy Z. Baker. This work reprints and explicates Edwards's complete testimony and includes biographical background. George M. Marsden's chapter titled "Heavenly Elysium" in his biography of Jonathan Edwards discusses the main events of Sarah Edwards's life, focusing on her two-week encounter with God. For the first short biography of Sarah Edwards written just after her death, see Appendix 2, pages 92–98, of Samuel Hopkins's *The Life and Character of the Late Reverend Mr. Jonathan Edwards*. Another modern reprinting of Edwards's full narrative along with related texts and devotional commentary is *In Love with Christ: The Narrative of Sarah Edwards*, edited and annotated by Jennifer Adams.

---

39. Mal 4:2.

Ministering with Our Bridegroom

Introduction
Song of Songs 5:1b

Come, all my friends—
feast upon my bride, all you revelers of my palace.
Feast on her, my lovers!
Drink and drink, and drink again,
until you can take no more.
Drink the wine of her love.
Take all you desire, you priests.
My life within her will become your feast.[1]

OUR JOURNEY TO BECOME the bride of Jesus has focused thus far on our responses to Jesus' courtship of us. Like a true bridegroom, he draws us to himself with love and tenderness, creating in our hearts a lovesick desire for him. We respond by awakening our hearts to him, choosing him, pursuing him, and encountering him.

All these responses to Jesus' overtures of love propel us toward embracing our true identity as his bride and relating to him consistently in that way. Embracing our identity as his bride does not mean we still don't have room to grow or that we never fail. Instead, it means that our position as Jesus' marriage partner is now a central component of how we see ourselves and relating to him as our bridegroom is a priority for us. We

1. Song 5:1b.

join the bride in Song of Songs in affirming, "I am my beloved's and my beloved is mine"![2]

Having responded to Jesus and established our identity as his bride, we now want to turn our attention to maturing in our love for him. Courtship love can be passionate and hopeful, but mature married love is powerful and unshakable in ways that courtship love is not. Mature love is selfless, not easily offended or hurt, generous, patient, and tender. The apostle Paul's exposition on love in 1 Cor 13 is often read at weddings, but, truthfully, the passage should be saved for fifty-year wedding anniversaries because it is a description of mature married love.

There are many ways to mature and deepen our love for our bridegroom, but an important one is ministering with him. Ministering with Jesus simply means joining him in caring for others and blessing them. We minister with Jesus when we assist an elderly parent, serve at a local food bank, donate money to a charity, teach a children's Bible class, or comfort a friend who is hurting. When we join with Jesus in ways like these, we are ministering with our bridegroom as he brings the values, hope, and peace of his kingdom of love to the earth.

Partnering with Jesus in ministry helps mature our love for him by compelling us to look beyond our own relationship with our bridegroom to the needy world he loves and cares for. As Jesus' bride, we have received and responded to his irresistible, life-altering bridal love, and we rejoice in that. But the deepest desire of Jesus' heart is that *everyone* he has created will come to salvation in him and know him as their bridegroom. This is his greatest longing. When we join him in pursuing the advancement of his kingdom by loving and blessing others with him, we help him fulfill his chief passion.

Perhaps the most amazing aspect of ministry with our bridegroom is that he *wants* us to join him in blessing the world. At the beginning of this section, notice the very first words the bridegroom in Song of Songs speaks after entering the garden of his bride to consummate their marriage: "Come, all my friends—feast upon my bride, all you revelers of my palace. Feast on her, my lovers! Drink and drink, and drink again, until you can take no more. Drink the wine of her love." These are surprising words to speak directly after becoming one with your beloved bride. Most of us would be focused on our own newly minted marriage union. But our eternal lover has an eternal agenda on his mind—gathering and

---

2. Song 6:3a.

perfecting his bride the church for her triumphant end-time union with himself. Thus, once we have responded to Jesus' love and embraced our identity as his bride, he desires that we join him in ministering to the world.

But this shift from enjoying Jesus' bridal love to ministering with him to a hurting world can be scary. If we're honest, most of us would rather stay in the bridal suite and enjoy the caresses of our beloved than engage with a difficult, troubled world. We've all experienced the very real and often unjust suffering and pain that can accompany genuinely trying to help someone. After all, the sentiment that "no good deed goes unpunished" is a staple concern in popular works ranging from the Broadway musical *Wicked* to the *Star Trek* universe.[3]

Joining Jesus in bringing his kingdom to earth can be challenging, as we recognize that serving, blessing, teaching, encouraging, and sharing our lives with those God loves will require selflessness and sacrifice. But we also know that we do not minister with Jesus from our own strength, resources, or abilities. Instead, our ministry flows directly out of our intimate bridal relationship with him, and this strengthens and encourages us in ministry.

This reality is reflected in the words of the bridegroom in Song of Songs at the end of the passage quoted above: "Take all you desire, you priests. My life within her will become your feast." As the cherished bride of Jesus, his own private garden, we are continually nourished by his eternal love for us, and his life and love within us radiate out as we minister with him. A passage from 2 Corinthians helps us picture this reality: "But thanks be to God, who in Christ always leads us in triumphal procession, and through us spreads the fragrance of the knowledge of him everywhere. For we are the aroma of Christ to God among those who are being saved and among those who are perishing."[4] The beautiful and alluring "fragrance" of our beloved's life inside us attracts those whom our bridegroom desires to bless, and thus we offer fruit that becomes a satisfying, unending "feast" for the ones he loves. The love we share with our bridegroom encourages and strengthens us for ministry with him.

The second half of this book thus shifts from *responding* to our bridegroom to *ministering* with our bridegroom. The four chapters in this section discuss interceding for others, encouraging others, loving

---

3. Schwartz, *Wicked*; Aarniokoski, *Star Trek: Picard*.
4. 2 Cor 2:14–15.

our bridegroom, and bearing his authority. As we look outward to offer the blessings of Jesus to others, we find the bridal love we share with him maturing, deepening, and expanding.

5

Interceding for Others: Dorothy Ripley
Song of Songs 5:2—6:3

After this I let my devotion slumber,
but my heart for him stayed awake.
I had a dream.
I dreamed of my beloved—
he was coming to me in the darkness of night.
The melody of the man I love awakened me.
I heard his knock at my heart's door
as he pleaded with me.[1]

AS A BRIDE OF Jesus, we desire our love for him to deepen and grow into mature love. One way this happens is by ministering with him to the ones he loves. As the verse above reveals, Jesus is quick to come to our hearts and call us out to minister with him. In this chapter, we will examine the first ministry we can do with our bridegroom—intercessory prayer.

Intercessory prayer, or intercession, as it is sometimes called, is lifting before God in prayer the needs and concerns of others. When we pray for our neighbor to find a job, our daughter to have wisdom in her career choices, our supervisor's wife to be healed from cancer, or our friend to come to know and follow Jesus, we are ministering in intercession. Intercession presents the concerns of others to God and asks him to use

1. Song 5:2a.

his power and kindness on their behalf. When we intercede, we step in between the person and God and, in a sense, represent them and their needs before our gracious and loving Father. Praying for others is our privilege as Christians and is founded on God's perfect love for humanity.

Intercessory prayer can sometimes be a struggle, however, because we don't always know how to pray for the ones we love. In our hearts, we recognize that intercession is more than just showing up and telling God what we think he should do in people's lives. Authentic, effective intercession happens when we discover what *God* wants to do in the lives of those we love, and then we partner with him by asking him to move in those exact ways. The Father's plans for his children are always good, loving, and for our best, so our goal in intercessory prayer is to bring our hearts and minds in line with God's so our requests echo his goals. But what is the most effective way to align our prayers with God's desires?

I believe the deep intimacy we share with Jesus as his bride positions us perfectly to pray according to the will of the Father for the needs of others because our bridegroom is the perfect intercessor. As Heb 7:25 assures us, "Therefore [Jesus] is able to save completely those who come to God through him, because he always lives to intercede for them."[2] Jesus knows the Father's heart and intercedes perfectly according to the Father's will. Thus, our nearness to our bridegroom conforms our hearts more and more to his, making us increasingly receptive to the Father's desires for his people. We begin to pray more in line with God's will for the ones he loves as we grow in our intimacy with Jesus.

Jesus modeled for us two important choices that produce effective intercession: identification and sacrifice. When Jesus came to earth to provide the ultimate act of intercession for humankind by placing himself between God's righteous judgment and humanity's sin, he accomplished our salvation by taking upon himself the judgment of God for our wrongdoing through his brutal death on the cross. To do that, Jesus had to both *identify* with us by becoming human and *sacrifice* himself on the cross for our sins. Romans 8:34b makes explicit the connection between Jesus' sacrificial death and his perpetual intercession for us: "Christ Jesus is the one who died—more than that, who was raised—who is at the right hand of God, who indeed is interceding for us."

As Jesus' bride, we also can choose to identify with others and sacrifice ourselves for them. We identify with the ones for whom we pray

---

2. NIV.

by getting to know them, joining with them in their pain and need, and serving them. We sacrifice for them when we give of our time, energy, resources, and peace of mind to help meet their needs and to bring their concerns before the Father. Paul uses the word picture of "being poured out as a drink offering" to image how his personal energy and resources are being expended for others.[3]

Another way to think of intercession is as burden-bearing, like Paul exhorts in Gal 6:2 when he advises, "Bear one another's burdens, and so fulfill the law of Christ." When we intercede for another, we "carry" in our heart their burden, thinking of them, spending time praying for them, and often forfeiting our own equanimity as we bear within us some small portion of the trials and struggles they are facing. The choice to identify with and sacrifice for another tenderizes our hearts and enables us to feel the Father's compassion and love for them, remember his promises to them, and discern his desires for them.

When we join our bridegroom in interceding for the ones he loves, we are thus working with him to bring the blessings of his kingdom of love into the lives of others. What a privilege to intercede with Jesus, our perfect intercessor![4]

MATURING OUR LOVE THROUGH INTERCESSION

How can we expect partnering with Jesus in his ministry of intercession to deepen and mature our love for him? I would suggest that we grow in loving our bridegroom in two important ways when we minister with him in intercession.

First, our love for Jesus matures as the priorities of his heart become our own. In any healthy marriage, each partner prioritizes the deepest concerns of the other. My husband and I share work issues with each other, talk and pray together for our children, and help each other with our elderly parents. He has always enjoyed camping, so I learned to camp. I played tennis when we met, so he learned to play, too, although I quickly

---

3. 2 Tim 4:6a.

4. The topic of intercessory prayer is too vast and complex to be covered in one chapter of a book, so if intercession is of interest to you, you may want to find a text devoted to the topic. Four books that have helped me over the years to understand and practice intercessory prayer are Foster, *Celebration of Discipline*; Simmons and Simmons, *Throne Room Prayer*; Smith, *Beyond the Veil*; and Wiens, *Bridal Intercession*.

put a stop to our tennis dates once he started beating me! Big or small, the priorities of one partner matter to the other.

When we intercede with Jesus, we learn what is on his heart, and our bridegroom is searching for a bride who desires to know his heart. During his last night on earth, through his anguish of soul in the garden of Gethsemane, Jesus asked his Father for unity with his followers both then and now, requesting, "I in them and you in me, that they may become perfectly one."[5] At this pivotal moment in his earthly journey, he invites his closest friends to intercede with him: "Then he said to them, 'My soul is very sorrowful, even to death; remain here, and watch with me.'"[6]

As Jesus' cherished bride, we are his friends, so his call to intercession reverberates within us as well. Our personal experience with our bridegroom's profound and unconditional bridal love naturally motivates us to join him in interceding with the Father for those he desires to reach with that same passionate love. Thus, when we partner with Jesus in intercessory prayer, our love for him matures as we adopt his priorities and help him fulfill the chief passions of his heart.

Second, intercession matures our love for Jesus because we learn to see the ones he loves through his eyes. As we intercede for the Father's good will to come to pass in people's lives, we begin to adopt Jesus' lens of unconditional love and tenderness, and we long for God's goodness to manifest in the lives of others. A friend of mine shared a story with me recently of a time she felt called by God to intercede specifically over the course of several months for her husband. Over weeks of prayer, she began to see her husband as Jesus saw him, but she was surprised to find that she began to see everyone else she met through Jesus' eyes as well. In her words to me, she was from that time forward "literally unable to *not* see others as precious, loved children of God." That shift in her thinking, accomplished as she drew near to her bridegroom in intercessory prayer, changed her perspective forever on the ones God brings into her life.

Jesus is well aware that joining him in intercession matures our love for him. When the Jewish religious leaders ask him why his disciples do not engage in the religious fasts from food that other Jews do, Jesus answers, "Can the wedding guests mourn as long as the bridegroom is with them? The days will come when the bridegroom is taken away from them, and then they will fast."[7] Jesus knows that we will enjoy times of

5. John 17:23a.
6. Matt 26:38.
7. Matt 9:15. The same statement appears in Mark 2:19 and Luke 5:34–35.

sweet intimacy with him as his bride, but he also knows that this same intimacy will drive us to pray and fast as we plead for the Father's good will to be accomplished in the lives of those our bridegroom cherishes. Our growing partnership with Jesus in intercession both reflects and deepens our intimacy with our beloved.

Let's turn our discussion now to some practical ways we can join our bridegroom in intercession. The bride in Song of Songs and a traveling evangelist named Dorothy Ripley (1767–1831) will show us how.

A SECOND INVITATION: SONG 5:2-7

The bridegroom and bride in Song of Songs have joined themselves in marriage and embarked upon their life together. Their married life, however, begins with a startling encounter. The bride is asleep, her heart still open and responsive to her bridegroom. Suddenly, he appears at her door, but not as the strong, magnificent suitor to which she is accustomed. Instead, he is in pain, his head drenched with the dew of the night: "Open to me, my sister, my love, my dove, my perfect one, for my head is wet with dew, my locks with the drops of the night."[8] The Passion Translation expands the verse to make its meaning more explicit:

> Arise, my love.
> Open your heart, my darling, deeper still to me.
> Will you receive me this dark night?
> There is no one else but you, my friend, my equal.
> I need you this night to arise and come be with me.
> You are my pure, loyal dove, a perfect partner for me.
> My flawless one, will you arise?
> For my heaviness and tears are more than I can bear.
> I have spent myself for you throughout the dark night.

The bride is surprised to see her lover in this state of suffering, and she hesitates to join him when he asks her to open the door to him, rationalizing in the next verse, "I had put off my garment; how could I put it on? I had bathed my feet; how could I soil them?" At this rejection, her bridegroom touches the door handle, causing the bride to arise and open the door, but when she does, he is gone.

Distraught, the bride searches the city for her lover, much like she did at the end of chapter 2 of Song of Songs. But this time, her pursuit

---

8. Song 5:2b.

is more difficult. Instead of simply ignoring her like they did during her first search, during this search, the city watchmen beat, bruise, and rob the bride.[9] She finally collapses, unable to sustain the chase.

How are we to understand the bride's experience here? Is this the same as the first invitation she receives from her bridegroom in chapter 2 when he asks her to join him on the mountains of deeper intimacy? As you may recall, in the first instance, the bridegroom appears to his bride as a powerful, alluring suitor, calling her to follow him upon the hills of greater love. Afraid, she refuses, asking him to go on without her, and he does. Her bridegroom gone, the bride immediately realizes her deep need of him and becomes motivated to find him no matter the cost. When she does find him, she vows to never let him go again, having learned his value to her.

I would suggest that the bridegroom's second invitation in chapter 5 is different from his first invitation in chapter 2 in two important ways. First, in the second invitation, the bridegroom comes to his beloved not in strength, as he did in the first, but in weakness and suffering. Why is he suffering? He is suffering for the ones he loves, the ones he wants to bless and bring into his kingdom of love. He has been awake throughout the night, carrying the heavy burdens of his beloved ones, shedding tears over their needs and pain, pouring himself into interceding for them. He thus comes to his bride at his most vulnerable, revealing to her his heart that is breaking for the ones he loves, pleading with her to join him in interceding for the lost and needy. This is a very different bridegroom than the one who courted the bride, and she is understandably startled at the change.

Second, what the bridegroom is requesting of the bride this time is very different as well. In the first invitation, he calls his beloved to the hills of greater lovesickness, longing to bring her deeper into a committed relationship with himself. But by the second invitation in chapter 5, the bride has already established her commitment to her lover, having invited him into her garden to consummate their marriage and having asked the north and south winds to blow on her garden in Song 4:16.

---

9. Some biblical commentators interpret the watchmen and their actions in this passage as representing spiritual leaders who, despite their positions of power and influence in the body of Christ, do not appreciate the sincere believer's spiritual struggles or do not themselves have personal experience with deep intimacy with Christ and so cannot help those who are seeking to draw closer to Jesus. In fact, a believer's intense pursuit of Christ may even challenge and anger these types of leaders. See, for example, Henry, *Commentary*, 3:1082–83.

The bridegroom knows this, so he now invites his devoted bride to move deeper into mature love, developed by joining him in his intercessory ministry. This is an invitation to sacrifice and suffer for others as he himself does. But, sadly, the bride does not do it. She does not join her bridegroom in his intercession for the world.

This picture of the bridegroom as vulnerable and suffering is sad and troubling for all of us who love and follow Jesus. Reading the description in Song of Songs, his head "wet with dew, [his] locks with the drops of the night," do we not recall our anguished bridegroom in the garden of Gethsemane on the night of his betrayal by one of his closest companions? Can we not see in this biblical narrative a heartbreaking image of our beloved in the darkness, his body and soul exhausted as he pours out his heart to his Father, awaiting the imminent onset of his long, excruciating journey to the cross? How painful is this image of our bridegroom!

Like the bride in Song of Songs, we would much rather see him as the commanding, captivating suitor who won our heart than as the suffering intercessor who has "spent [himself] for [us] throughout the dark night." But Jesus is both. And just as he invited us to respond to his courtship of love, he now asks us to join him in his ministry of intercession. How will we respond?

Despite her faltering start, the bride eventually overcomes her initial hesitation, finds her lover, and joins him in his ministry of suffering. As she does this, she shows us two key steps to joining our bridegroom in his intercession for the world.

RELEASING CONTROL AND SHIFTING FOCUS: SONG 5:8—6:3

The bride has collapsed in her search for her bridegroom, wounded and discouraged. Surely her vow in Song 2 to never let him go again after she finds him comes back to mock her. She has, in fact, broken her vow and let him go, refusing his invitation to join him in his ministry of intercession. Not nearly so confident or successful in her second search, she gives up and instead asks her friends to deliver to her bridegroom the message that she is lovesick for him: "I adjure you, O daughters of Jerusalem, if you find my beloved, that you tell him I am sick with love."[10]

---

10. Song 5:8.

With these words, probably uttered with her last ounce of strength, the bride demonstrates the first important step in finding her bridegroom and joining him in his ministry of intercession: releasing control. The bride's willingness to release control is revealed most clearly at this crucial juncture by what she does *not* do. She does not complain to her bridegroom about his absence. She does not accuse her friends of not helping her. She does not scream angrily at the city watchmen and blame them for her failed search. She does not shake her fist at a world that is spitefully arrayed against her. She does not even pity or condemn herself.

Instead, she simply reaches out to her bridegroom in the only way she can and offers him the message that he is still the one she loves, the one she desires, the one she is seeking. She asks him for help, trusts him, and gives up control, despite being in great physical pain and sorrow. She now willingly embraces the position of weakness and suffering modeled by her bridegroom at her bedroom door.

Likewise, when we yield control to our bridegroom Jesus, we take the first necessary step in learning how to intercede with him. Accepting our dependence on our eternal lover helps our intimacy with him grow as well as our effectiveness in intercession. Praying for others works best when we leave the results in God's hands, and Jesus is the premier example of this. During his time of intercession in the garden of Gethsemane, Jesus prayed three times in great sorrow of spirit as he looked toward his crucifixion, ending each time of prayer with the words "your will be done," releasing control of his life and destiny and the future of his followers to his Father.[11] So, we too can learn from Jesus' example of submission and cede control to God, partnering effectively with our beloved in interceding for those he loves because our hearts will be open to coming into alignment with the Father's will.

In Song of Songs, the bride's friends are surprised at her words and ask, "How is your beloved better than others, that you so charge us?"[12] They cannot understand why the bride won't just find someone else to replace her lover. With this question, her friends prompt the bride to make a second helpful choice in learning to intercede with her bridegroom: shifting her focus from her problem to her beloved.

In answer to her friends' question, the bride begins a passionate description of the strikingly desirable qualities of her bridegroom that runs

11. Matt 26:36–46.
12. Song 5:9b (NIV).

seven verses and culminates with the words, "His mouth is sweetness itself; he is altogether lovely. This is my beloved, this is my friend, daughters of Jerusalem."[13] The bride's depiction of her bridegroom reminds us of Solomon's wedding vows—they are flattering and specific in detailing the physical beauty of her beloved, mentioning his head, hair, eyes, cheeks, lips, arms, body, legs, and mouth. Her friends are so affected by her description of her lover that they offer to seek him with her![14]

But guess what? No seeking is necessary after all because now that she has shifted her focus to her bridegroom and rehearsed his admirable qualities, the bride remembers where to find him! She announces, "My beloved has gone down to his garden to the beds of spices, to graze in the gardens and to gather lilies. I am my beloved's and my beloved is mine; he grazes among the lilies."[15]

Unlike her first search, in which she has to practically run into Solomon to find him, and unlike her opening interaction with him in chapter 1 in which she has to ask him where he grazes his flock, she now knows exactly where to find her lover because they are one—"I am my beloved's and my beloved is mine." *She* is, in fact, the garden in which he resides and gathers lilies, as the bridegroom himself declares in Song 5:1. They are together forever through the eternal bond of marriage and are one in spirit. Thus, she will always know where to find her beloved. Shifting her focus from her problem to her bridegroom allows the bride to receive the revelation that he is always with her through their consummated love.

How does deciding to focus on our bridegroom Jesus instead of our problems and concerns help us with intercession? Quite simply, when our minds are captured by the negative, painful realities of life, it is more difficult for us to hear God's voice and connect with his heart. However, when we turn our minds and hearts to the beauty of Jesus, his kindness to us, his perfect power and authority, and his love for those he has created, we open our spirits to hearing the Father's desires for those for whom we are interceding. Notice the promise in Ps 50:23: "Those who sacrifice thank offerings honor me, and to the blameless I will show my salvation."[16] Like the bride, we suddenly remember that Jesus loves us and that we are his. We know what to pray for those we love because we reconnect with God's heart.

13. Song 5:10–16 (NIV).
14. Song 6:1.
15. Song 6:2–3.
16. NIV.

To shift our focus in this way in intercession requires an intentional choice on our part. After sharing our pain with God honestly and openly, we can choose to remain in that place, or we can shift to remembering Jesus and allowing him to heal our hearts and direct our prayers. Some ways to shift our minds and hearts include singing along to worship music, reading a psalm of praise, or sharing with Jesus what we love about him, as the bride in Song of Songs does. These simple acts will move our spirits in a direction of thanksgiving and praise that will lead to more effective intercession aligned with God's plans and purposes. We will find that we have greater clarity on how to pray for the ones we love as we praise and intercede with our beautiful bridegroom.

FRIENDS OF THE BRIDE

To close this section of our discussion, let's take a quick look at a group of people in Song of Songs whom we have not yet mentioned: the friends of the bride. In the narrative, the friends function similarly to the chorus in Greek theater, reflecting and commenting on the main action of the story. Until now, their input has been mostly commentary, but beginning in chapter 5, their interactions with the bride take on more meaning, as we have already seen. The friends are the ones who ask the bride why she simply does not find another lover when hers is gone, providing her with an opportunity to share the qualities of the bridegroom that she admires. They are also the ones who proclaim their desire to search for him with the bride after hearing her description of his remarkable beauty.

The friends in the bridal narrative can be viewed as representing, in a way, the ones to whom the bridegroom and his bride are ministering. There is no indication in the text that the friends know the bridegroom personally or are at all interested in him initially. They appear briefly in chapter 1, but, in most translations, they do not speak at all in chapters 2 through 4, so they may not be privy to all the aspects of the developing relationship between the bride and the bridegroom. Perhaps that is why when the bride collapses in her search for Solomon, they counsel her to forget him and seek another. They do not see in Solomon anything unique or special.

However, a shift happens when the friends hear the bride's description of her beloved. They are captivated by the desirability and beauty of the bridegroom as expressed by the bride and decide they will join her in her search for him, asking, "Where has your beloved gone, O most beautiful among women? Where has your beloved turned, that we may seek him with you?"[17] Their question is the catalyst that causes the bride to realize where she can find her beloved. Now that the friends have their own interest in the bridegroom, they appear regularly throughout the rest of the narrative, obviously having kept their promise to join the bride in seeking her bridegroom.

It is through the friends that we see how far the Shulamite bride has come in her relationship with Solomon. After being unsure of where to even search for him in chapter 1, she now is mature enough to recount his loveliness to others so accurately and winsomely that their hearts are stirred to seek him for themselves. She also knows how to advise them in finding him—he comes intimately as a husband to the one he loves, making them his own private, spring-fed garden. As the story progresses and we continue in subsequent chapters to discuss ministering and maturing in love with our bridegroom Jesus, we will watch the bride and Solomon draw her friends into their own relationships with the king.

RADICAL DOROTHY RIPLEY

We have learned from the bride in Song of Songs two steps we can take to join Jesus in his ministry of suffering intercession: releasing control to him and shifting our focus from our problems to our bridegroom. Now, we will look at an unconventional female evangelist to learn two additional tips for effective intercession with Jesus.

Dorothy Ripley can, without a doubt, be accurately labeled a radical. Born in England, she felt called by God to travel to America as an itinerant evangelist. She crossed the Atlantic at least ten times to minister in America, was the first woman to preach to the US Congress, had a private meeting with President Thomas Jefferson, and was ultimately buried in Virginia upon her death.

Although she ministered to all denominations, races, and status of people, she focused specifically on the marginalized and disenfranchised, serving and advocating for prisoners and sex workers in cities, enslaved people in America, and the poor and sick in workhouses and hospitals. Even more radical was her approach to ministry: to keep her ministry options open, Ripley did not associate herself officially with any religious

---

17. Song 6:1.

organization, although she was connected informally with the Quakers and the Methodists, and she traveled alone, something women seldom did at the time. Finally, Ripley traveled without money, trusting God to provide for her.[18]

Ripley faced significant challenges as a female itinerant minister. Many churches refused to open their pulpits to her, and she was ridiculed in both public and print for choosing to leave the domestic sphere thought most proper for women and "expose" herself in a public way to preach. One of the most difficult trials for Ripley was the criticism often leveled against her that she was sexually promiscuous due to her willingness to travel alone and speak in public, a charge commonly made against female preachers of the time. Throughout her travels, Ripley was propositioned by men and endured rumors of "lewdness," despite her choice to dress in the extremely modest clothing of a Quaker.[19]

In addition, she was sometimes disparaged for her enthusiasm for God and evangelism, noting during her first trip to America, "Some bring a charge against me, saying, 'I am too zealous and run too fast.' Alas for me! I am always behindhand with my work, having a desire if possible to please both God and man."[20]

Ripley was born into a devout Christian family in England, her father a lay Methodist preacher, and she felt called by God at an early age to pursue ministry. After her father's death, when Ripley was twenty-one years old, her mother lost all her property in a natural disaster, probably an earthquake, and Ripley committed herself to life as a single woman; in her words, "I bid adieu to all finite things; that is, I determined to take my Maker for my husband and seek to build up a spiritual house for him henceforward," a reference to Isa 54:5.

At the age of thirty, Ripley was knocked to the floor of her bedroom by the power of God, "covered with his glorious majesty, beholding as through his Spirit the riches of his kingdom." Believing God was calling her to public ministry, she spent the next sixteen months reading the Bible and waiting before the Lord for four hours a day in her bedroom, often committing whole nights to seeking God in prayer and worship.

---

18. For details on Ripley's life as an itinerant minister, see Everson, "'Little Labour of Love.'"

19. For instances of Ripley's challenges with unwanted propositions from men and unfounded rumors of sexual promiscuity, see Ripley, *Extraordinary Conversion*, 61–62, 68, 77–78, 98–99, 131–32.

20. Ripley, *Extraordinary Conversion*, 73.

After four additional years of waiting on God and attending Quaker meetings for instruction and fellowship, Ripley heard God direct her to "go ten thousand miles" to preach and minister to those persons enslaved in America, for whom she had been praying for twelve years.[21]

Thus, Ripley embarked on her first missionary journey to America in February 1802, leaving behind her mother and two sisters and taking little money with her, deciding to live and travel solely on faith. In April 1802, Ripley landed in New York and spent the next fourteen months traveling along the eastern seaboard, preaching to those enslaved and free, meeting with Quaker and Methodist communities, and sharing the gospel wherever she went. She published the story of her experience in 1810 as *The Extraordinary Conversion, and Religious Experience of Dorothy Ripley, with Her First Voyage and Travels in America.*

THE HARD WORK OF INTERCESSION

Although Dorothy Ripley's international travel and ministerial exploits provide the most arresting headlines, she considered her most important ministry to be intercessory prayer, especially during her first trip to America. According to Ripley, God placed upon her heart at a young age the burden of those persons enslaved in America, and thus her first journey to America centered there.

As she passed through America, especially the states with large enslaved populations, her heart was grieved at the deplorable conditions of those in bondage, and she cried out to God for both their earthly freedom and spiritual salvation. While Ripley notes in her record of the trip the various challenges she endures with traveling, rejection, and criticism, it is the prayer burden she feels for the enslaved that is the most exhausting for her. As she remarks during her travels through Richmond, Virginia, Jesus sent her to "groan in secret for the poor Africans, for whom my spirit is pressed this day."[22]

Ripley's intercessory burden for those persons enslaved in America highlights for us a third point about interceding for others—it is hard work! Sometimes we are surprised by the fatigue, frustration, pain, and even hopelessness we may experience when interceding for others. It is challenging to help carry others' burdens, especially when time and

---

21. Ripley, *Extraordinary Conversion*, 15–22, 38.
22. Ripley, *Extraordinary Conversion*, 92.

setbacks seem more frequent than victories. There is an element of suffering when we minister in intercession, and we can be caught by surprise at the demands of prayer ministry.

Dorothy Ripley experienced these challenges as well, but she found a way forward through the pain and exhaustion of intercession—turning to her bridegroom. Leaning on Jesus and trusting him, Ripley knew she did not have to carry her burdens alone:

> The intolerable burden which I have been pressured with must contribute to prepare me for the vineyard of my God,[23] and I rejoice to say, my soul hangs upon him as a suckling does upon the breast of its mother. For I have no dependence separate from him, neither can I find any other to throw my insupportable load upon except on him who gives this gracious invitation, "Come unto me, all you that labor and are heavy-laden, and I will give you rest."[24] I find his rest sweet to my troubled spirit, which is measurably purified since I entered into the state of Virginia to sympathize with the poor blacks, whom I now commit as a heavy burden to Jesus Christ, the Maker of them and the world.[25]

Ripley rests in the assurance that Jesus hears the cries of his beloved partner, and she confidently declares, "I cannot give up hoping at times that my sighs will be succeeded with acclamations of great joy. Why should I labor in my spirit in vain, for faith is able to accomplish every glorious design of the wise Creator's unto every nation which he has made."[26] Knowing her favored position as Jesus' bride strengthens Ripley to continue with her ministry of intercession for those persons trapped in enslavement.

Like Ripley, we can rest in our position as Jesus' beloved and receive strength from him as we intercede for others. We are not a stranger to him, and he is not some distant, uninterested deity whose attention and help we must frantically attempt to attract. We are his bride, the one with whom he will spend eternity. We are his delight, his true love, his perfect spouse, his intimate partner, the one whose voice he loves to hear, as Song 2:14 reminds us. We are the one with whom he shares his heart.

---

23. Possibly a reference to Matt 20:1–16, a parable shared by Jesus about workers in a vineyard.

24. Matt 11:28.

25. Ripley, *Extraordinary Conversion*, 100.

26. Ripley, *Extraordinary Conversion*, 125.

As Jesus himself assures us, "No longer do I call you servants, for the servant does not know what his master is doing; but I have called you friends, for all that I have heard from my Father I have made known to you. You did not choose me, but I chose you and appointed you that you should go and bear fruit and that your fruit should abide, so that whatever you ask the Father in my name, he may give it to you."[27] As Jesus' bride, we are privileged to know the desires of his heart and can look to him for strength and hope when our intercessory burdens seem too much to bear. From our place of favored intimacy, we pray with our bridegroom, trusting he will hear and respond to us, his beloved bride.

NEXT-LEVEL INTERCESSION

The fourth and final key to fruitful intercessory ministry with Jesus that Dorothy Ripley models for us is that we must be willing to take our prayers to the next level. Ripley was not only eager to pray for those persons enslaved in America; she was prepared to go to them across an ocean, by herself, without money, multiple times in her lifetime, pouring herself out for the ones Jesus had placed on her heart. One of her prayers recorded during her first journey shows her commitment to joining sacrificial, fervent action to her private prayers:

> You have given me an ardent solicitude for the oppression [of slavery] to cease and have filled my soul with tenderness to all who are degraded by the tyrannical power of man. And why am I concerned thus for the wretched situation of your creatures if you will not aid me with ability to show my hatred to sin and strife, which are contrary to you, a God of purity and love? I know you are well pleased with my compassionate regard for your workmanship, who are despised and [treated as worthless] through the reigning power of individuals;[28] therefore, follow with your blessing my earnest prayers for the speedy deliverance of such as you have made me groan in spirit for from my childhood.[29]

Many would, and did, think Ripley was too extreme in her choice to travel as an itinerant preacher to those enslaved on another continent. Indeed,

---

27. John 15:15–16.
28. The enslaved, a reference to Eph 2:10a.
29. Ripley, *Extraordinary Conversion*, 42–43.

she admits that "I am humbled by others who . . . affirm my life madness and my end to be without honor."[30] Yet, Ripley persevered, choosing to offer to God and others her strength and resources along with her intercession.

We, too, may have occasions when we are led by Jesus to join action to intercession. Our prayers for overseas missionaries may lead us to join a short-term mission team. Our intercession for the needs of orphaned children may motivate us to foster or adopt. Our requests to God for the concerns of our elderly neighbor may prompt us to prune her flowers or bring her dinner.

In this way, we follow in the footsteps of our bridegroom, who gave both himself and his prayers to accomplish our salvation. As Heb 5:7–9 declares, "During the days of Jesus' life on earth, he offered up prayers and petitions with fervent cries and tears to the one who could save him from death, and he was heard because of his reverent submission. Son though he was, he learned obedience from what he suffered and, once made perfect, he became the source of eternal salvation for all who obey him."[31] As his bride, we desire to imitate Jesus by being willing to join action to prayer when the need arises. As Ripley asks in her text, "When I consider that the Redeemer of the world died for me, I ask, what can I do for so virtuous an action as has brought into my soul eternal life?"[32]

The excerpt that follows is from Dorothy Ripley's account of her conversion and first ministry trip to America. Note as you read how this radical woman of God embraced her intimate position as Jesus' bride and joined her bridegroom in interceding for and ministering to those whom he had placed on her heart.

---

30. Ripley, *Extraordinary Conversion*, 127. Ripley references Wisdom of Solomon 5:4, a deuterocanonical book that was included in the 1611 King James Version of the Bible, which included the Apocrypha.

31. NIV.

32. Ripley, *Extraordinary Conversion*, 25.

AUTOBIOGRAPHY: THE EXTRAORDINARY CONVERSION, AND RELIGIOUS EXPERIENCE OF DOROTHY RIPLEY, WITH HER FIRST VOYAGE AND TRAVELS IN AMERICA[33]

A Calling from God

When I was in my twenty-first year, my mother lost all the property which she had by a shock in the ground, which rent the foundation of the houses where we lived and blasted all my hopes on earth, so that I had the enjoyment of God to comfort me, which, if I had not sought for in early life, I should have been miserably poor. But thanks be ascribed to God, who enabled me to kneel down and adopt the language of Job: "Naked came I out of my mother's womb, and naked shall I return. The Lord gave, and the Lord has taken away; blessed be the name of the Lord."[34]

Rising from the ground, I encouraged myself with an eternal foundation, which would bear the shock of nature when the mountains shall melt as wax before the fire[35] and all earthly things pass away.[36] Strong in the faith of Jesus Christ I appeared, having a hope of immortality through the Redeemer's merit, so that I bid adieu to all finite things; that is, I determined to take my Maker for my husband[37] and seek to build up a spiritual house for him henceforward.

On February 28, 1797, entering my room to worship God, the power of God felled me to the earth, where I lay as covered with his glorious majesty, beholding as through his Spirit the riches of his kingdom "which God has prepared for them that love him."[38] For some hours, I lay on the ground viewing the glory of the city, where the Spirit assured me I should dwell forever in bliss unutterable, which

---

33. Selections are from Ripley, *Extraordinary Conversion*, 15–16, 19, 21, 24–25, 37–39, 50–51, 56–57, 75–76, 81, 91–93, 100, 126–27, 129, 157.

34. Job 1:21.

35. Mic 1:4.

36. Possibly a reference to Rev 21:1.

37. Isa 54:5.

38. 1 Cor 2:9.

then I participated through the overshadowing glory of this visitation, which filled me with rapturous joy and surprising awe so that I was lost in wonder, love, and praise.[39]

The Lord commanded me to "go ten thousand miles," to "provide neither gold nor silver, neither two coats, neither shoes, nor yet a staff,"[40] the omnipotent arm of Jehovah being my support, leaning on no arm of flesh. Ethiopia's, or Africa's, children by oppressors were brought to till the ground for many of the American planters. Therefore was I led thither by the unsearchable wisdom of their Creator and mine to exhort them with tears to "stretch out their hand unto the Lord"[41] that they might find redress from a gracious God whose compassion fails not to any of the children of men. Ah, the solitary path that I took! Who but a God of everlasting strength could have brought me safe through? Yes, who but Abraham's God could have delivered me from Satan's power?

No words can express the eternal union which has taken place on earth, my heaven being already begun, and knowing I shall delight myself through millions of ages. Yes, and the excellent God will delight himself with the least of his saints who love him through choice and not of necessity. It is my choice to serve the eternal I AM[42] because he is infinitely good and gracious, full of wisdom, and full of compassion to all nations, without respect of persons, if I believe "Jesus Christ tasted death for every man."[43] And surely I must believe this if I believe he died at all or died for me, the chief of sinners...."[44] Man, as man, cannot arrive to perfection in righteousness, but God in man can effect wonderful works of purity in every age of the world to testify the power of the Highest, using either male or female

---

39. Probably a reference to the final line in the fourth stanza of the popular hymn "Love Divine, All Loves Excelling" by Charles Wesley (1707–88), published in 1747.

40. In Matt 10:5–15, Jesus sends his twelve disciples out on a preaching journey with these words.

41. Ps 68:31b.

42. A reference to Exod 3:14–15.

43. Heb 2:9.

44. 1 Tim 1:15.

for his own glory, that the church, the bride, the Lamb's wife, may be complete.

In the morning, I arose with a humbling sense of divine favor resting upon me and at ten went to [church] to worship God with my spirit. . . . The tears I shed and the bitterness of spirit which I felt for the African race and [non-Christians] at large God only knows, and it sufficed me to believe that he will soon cause the oppressors to cease their oppression and reward with peace such who travail in spirit for the spread of the gospel of our Lord Jesus Christ. . . . I told the company my movement was not a hasty one, for it had been contemplated by me from a child and that I had seen it necessary to give up to the same for the last twelve years that my peace might be secured, knowing that the Lord required of me to instruct the [non-Christians], or the African race, which I was willing to comply with to promote their happiness if I lay aside my own ease and present comfort. When those friends had proved my concern by the light of the Lord, they sympathized with me.

I read the law of my God by his Spirit and understand his mind, or will, concerning those things which he requires of me and can say with one of old time, "Your law is my delight,"[45] for I meditate therein day and night.[46] All other objects are nothing to me when compared with Christ, my spiritual Bridegroom, whom I apply to for strength in the time of weakness, for riches in poverty, health in sickness, and find in him all I want either for myself or others, whom I am bold to ask for, through faith, trusting in his merit. To his honor, I can testify this is the truth.

A Ministry of Intercession

April 6, 1802. Our passage [to America] is now finished through the goodness of the Almighty, and we are come to our destined port, which I feel unfeignedly thankful for, having been accommodated with every necessary blessing.

---

45. Ps 119:77.
46. Josh 1:8.

So, we set off from Stafford [Virginia] and passed through Fredericksburg [Virginia]. On this side of [the city] were four hundred and thirty-two acres of standing corn just in flower, which was beautiful to the eye, and opposite it on the other side of the road were a number reaping wheat, well-clothed, who appeared to have a good master. I counted thirty men and women who were all black. As we were riding along the road this morning, I felt very sorrowful in contemplating how many thousands of the poor Africans were sorely oppressed in those southern states, and while I was weeping and silently groaning in spirit, my mind was covered with awe, and I was fully persuaded of God that in due time they should become possessors of this state where I am now sowing tears in abundance. I was also cheered by this, and a hope was given me to believe that many in the midst of their afflictions would seek help at the hand of the Lord, there being some in every city praying to a gracious God in their behalf.

Many young Baptists were present when I supplicated the throne of mercy, and they also were melted into tears and wept much that they were born in a land of oppression, fearing the blood of their fathers would be on their heads as their parents were slaveholders. They all vowed in my presence that when they came to inherit their property of slaves that they would free them, that they might free themselves from the curse of their fathers, or as they expressed it, "Their blood which was upon their fathers' heads." I desired to retire a little that I might render thanks to God in silently waiting upon him in my own soul.

Alas for them [enslavers] if the truth does not humble them in time, does not break their stiff-necked wills by the Stone which will grind to powder all the disobedient,[47] all the stubborn who are in nature unlike Jesus Christ, who was meek and lowly in heart. I mourn, I sigh, and water my pillow night by night while I pass along this desert land where thousands are toiling to support luxury and haughtiness of spirit. What a favor that I was not born in a land where the souls and bodies of men are prized and bought

---

47. Possibly a reference to Matt 21:44 and Luke 20:18.

and sold like so many cattle who are driven by the whip.[48] God only knows why my days should be lingered out in thus groaning for them, but certain I am that those tears I sow here shall water the seed sown by some whom God appointed to preach the gospel before I was a resident among mortals.

Well, let it suffice me then that my labors shall not be in vain, and let me also remember how many years of sorrow my Lord and Savior Jesus Christ endured before he opened his gospel mission and proclaimed liberty to the captive souls. Oh, that my faith may increase for this purpose! That my love to the indigent may not be suppressed, neither a weariness in the spirit or in the flesh impede the work of salvation that is even now completing by the eternal Spirit, who is secretly working in me and many others whom he appoints to work in this land for the redemption of his creatures.

August 2. The Spirit of Christ sings this song in my soul: "Glory to God in the highest, and on earth peace, good will to men."[49] My spirit also joins in the divine anthem and is invigorated thereby with the heavenly harmony so that I am ready to break out with the ecstatic joy, but restrain for a short moment among men, believing it best to worship God alone in my spirit. And so [I] fly to my pen to bless the day which gave me existence among mortals that I might sound forth his love abroad and testify to the truth of the living oracles wherein I read of his ancient love and the powerful effects of faith that produced many signs and wonders wrought in different ages by the Spirit in his prepared instruments, who all gave glory to him that lives forever to receive praise and adoration of all such as yield obedience to serve him.

I am a free woman by the authority of our Lord Jesus Christ, who sends me where and when he pleases and who has sent me here at this time. . . . Some will abuse me for

---

48. Although England participated in the African slave trade for decades, few of those enslaved came to England itself but were instead primarily transported to England's land holdings in the Caribbean. Buying and selling enslaved people was outlawed across the British Empire in 1807, and the institution of slavery was completely abolished in 1833.

49. Luke 2:14.

speaking the truth, I know, and others will love me for it, but as I am called to give up every tender endearment, I will hazard my life in the cause for the rights of the African nation, for whom I have mourned secretly twenty years and could no more avoid it than I could cease to breathe, unless I made use of improper means to stop the natural functions of life. The Spirit of the Lord has laid a necessity upon me to cry mightily to the Lord God, that he may arise and make bare his omnipotent arm in defending them and freeing them from the thralldom which they are in. But, above all, that he would unveil his glory to them as a nation, that they might believe in Jesus Christ as their Redeemer from the cruel bondage of sin and the tyranny of Satan by whom they have long been captivated to their shame.

Now if the Lord requires me to spend my little strength for the promotion of his righteousness among them, I must obey the great and mighty God herein, not consulting whether it will please or offend individuals whose interest it is to keep them in bondage for to answer their desires, which may be either carnal or lucrative. I shall, therefore, by the help of God, proclaim to them that this is the day which David saw when he prophetically cried, "Ethiopia shall soon stretch out her hand to the Lord."[50]

Many have already tried to suppress and damp the ardor of my soul by withholding help from me, but Jesus' sweet voice whispers, "Peace on earth and good will towards men," and assures me his strength shall be equal to my day, and says that he will maintain his own right and his Father's glory. And his Spirit shall arise in me and aid every endeavor with his blessing, so that I shall cease to mourn on their account and have as much joy as I have had sorrow, as much prosperity as I have endured poverty for them, yes, friends as numerous as my foes have been. How good is God to encourage me thus, lifting me above all the fear of man and making my faith and love stronger each trial I pass through in their cause.

In leaving Richmond [Virginia] on August 28, my [intercessory] weight fell off, and I have enjoyed my ride this day to my friends.

---

50. Ps 68:31b.

A Committed Life

This is my birthday, and I am thirty-six years old, if I make a true calculation, but it seems as if all my work was to do yet for the great Master, which makes it a gloomy return to me.... In these dry seasons, where there are no productions, I labor to live by faith, but find it hard work to the mind that has been accustomed to gather large grapes from its own vine planted in its own vineyard. A hope does arise in me this moment that faith which has been in daily exercise shall be lost in sight when a full reliance is obtained on him who says, "I am the bread of life."[51] May I yield up myself to the exercise of faith and wait with patience until the end designed is fully accomplished by the sanctifying Spirit of truth, which is preparing me for himself, that glory may arise at last to the Father, Son, and Holy Ghost.

I know that there is a Spirit in man which reveals the mind of the Most High to his lowly pilgrims who are his burden-bearers in this our day; therefore, such must declare his will whatever it be, whether it be for or against those whom it concerns.... The world has banished me from her to enjoy peace in my God, which is more desirable than my daily food that I receive to sustain my body. The love of the world and the love of the creature are now each turned into the proper channel, and each fixed on my God, my everlasting inheritance, whence all my hopes of permanent peace are derived.

For, alas, there are on earth continual vicissitudes to damp the true spirit of joy and prevent the soul's rest in her beloved Bridegroom unless she can "in everything give thanks." Now the blessing of "praying without ceasing" God has conferred upon me, which leads me to expect that I shall "rejoice evermore" when the Lord is pleased to give me my heart's desire upon the children on earth or cause me to cease travailing in spirit for the redemption of the sons of Adam.[52]

May my pen testify your unalterable goodness by a uniform life of holiness crowned with the salvation of poor

---

51. John 6:35.
52. 1 Thess 5:16-18.

sinners, which are dear to me by the sprinkling blood of Jesus my eternal Bridegroom, whose interest I seek on earth that we may be one forever.

CHAPTER SUMMARY AND FURTHER READING

This chapter opens the second half of the book, the subject of which is maturing our love for our bridegroom by ministering with him. Our first area of ministry with Jesus, joining him in intercessory prayer, requires us to connect with the Father's heart for people and to identify with and sacrifice for the ones for whom we pray. Partnering with Jesus in intercession matures our love for him because through intercession, we take upon our own hearts the burdens of our bridegroom and learn to see the world through his eyes. Practically, we seek to release control to Jesus, shift our focus from our problems to our bridegroom, turn to our beloved to strengthen us through the challenges of intercession, and unite action to prayer when the need arises. In this way, we join our bridegroom in seeking the Father's will for those he has created and loves.

For courageous readers who would like to learn more about Dorothy Ripley, Elisa Ann Everson's 650-page doctoral dissertation, "'A Little Labour of Love': The Extraordinary Career of Dorothy Ripley, Female Evangelist in Early America," provides the most complete treatment I am familiar with of the evangelist. Excerpts from the second edition of Ripley's *Extraordinary Conversion* also appear with a short biographical introduction in Paul Wesley Chilcote's *Her Own Story: Autobiographical Portraits of Early Methodist Women*. For those interested in female preachers in pre-Civil War America, see Catherine A. Brekus, *Strangers and Pilgrims: Female Preaching in America, 1740–1845*. Lastly, the complete text of Ripley's *Extraordinary Conversion*, both the 1810 New York edition and the 1817 London edition, can be found in the digital collections of many university libraries and some larger public libraries and historical societies.

6

Encouraging Others: Sarah Osborn and Susanna Anthony

Song of Songs 6:4—7:13

Come away, my lover.
Come with me to the faraway fields.
We will run away together to the forgotten places
and show them redeeming love.
Let us arise and run to the vineyards of your people
and see if the budding vines of love are now in full bloom.
We will discover if their passion is awakened.
There I will display my love for you.[1]

ENCOURAGEMENT HAS ALWAYS BEEN important to humans and their communities. Sports teams, dance studios, classrooms, activist groups, food networks, book clubs, work teams, neighborhoods, and religious organizations all seek to strengthen and unify their members through encouragement. Writing groups push struggling scribblers through writer's block, running clubs refuse to let joggers stop halfway up hills, parenting cliques assure new moms and dads they'll eventually sleep through the night again, and emotional support groups point heartbroken comrades

---

1. Song 7:11–12.

to the light at the end of the tunnel. It's in our nature as humans to need encouragement and to respond positively to it.

As a college professor, I've seen firsthand just how powerful encouragement can be in the classroom. The students who show up at the four-year residential college where I teach have already experienced eighteen years of the heartaches and joys that life brings. I've taught students who have endured homelessness, battled cancer, grieved the death of a parent or sibling, experienced the suicide of a close friend, lost their homes in fires, struggled spiritually, and survived lengthy debilitating illnesses. I've also taught students who have enjoyed loving families, supportive friends, academic success, athletic accomplishments, financial security, and a godly spiritual heritage. What unites them all is that each and every one craves and responds to encouragement. When I speak encouraging words of hope into a student's life, that student grows and is strengthened, regardless of their past or current life circumstances.

I've learned that authentic, effective encouragement is personalized. I once taught a student in a first-year writing course who was the least prepared student for college writing that I had ever encountered in all my years of teaching. I had serious doubts that she would be able to pass my class. Surprisingly, I felt the Holy Spirit leading me to tell her my thoughts directly, but also promise to help her grow as a writer. While I was a bit worried that honesty was not the best policy in this case, I followed what I believed was the guidance of the Spirit and told her my concerns candidly, offering my assistance if she wanted to improve. Almost immediately, a spark came into her eyes, and she said yes, she would like to work on improving.

To this day, I have never seen a student work harder in one of my classes than this student did, and she grew tremendously as a writer, beyond what I honestly thought possible in one semester. At the close of the course, she told me how my straight talk had encouraged her, noting that she always did her best when she knew the challenge ahead and could face it squarely. How thankful I was that I had followed the leading of the Holy Spirit instead of my own judgment! God knew exactly how to encourage the student in a personalized way that she would receive and respond to.

The same semester, I had another student in a different writing course who was already an excellent writer. Eager to learn even more, she sat near the front of class, took copious notes on my lectures, and turned in beautifully composed assignments. One day while I was teaching, I noticed that she didn't have her textbook, so I made a joke about her not being prepared for class. Immediately, her face fell, and she refused to make eye contact with me for the remainder of the class. Really, I thought? One little joke and she gets her feelings hurt? Typical Generation Z!

Not long after class ended that day, God and I had a little chat, and he revealed to me how my comment had worked perfectly to *discourage* the student since she took her classes very seriously and valued her professors' opinions highly. I felt terrible. When I asked the Holy Spirit for a better way forward, I felt assured that the relationship could be restored, but that it would require time and effort, and, in fact, that was what happened. It took weeks of me going out of my way to connect with the student and encourage her directly to bring her back around to enjoying the class and learning from me. We each are unique when it comes to encouragement, and its effectiveness for everyone when personalized cannot be underestimated.

ENCOURAGEMENT RESTORES HOPE

Encouragement motivates and moves us forward because it offers hope and a vision for the future. When I tell a student that I see a positive outlook for them, either in the area of academic success, professional advancement, or spiritual growth, I am creating a hopeful, positive picture they can focus on and believe is achievable. It's like showing writing students examples of excellent writing at the start of an assignment. Being able to envision the final, successful product generates hope and motivation to move toward the goal.

Recently, an upper-level student related to me how his two most recent history courses had impacted him in strikingly different ways. The first course had been so difficult, he simply gave up trying, but the second course had made success appear so reachable that he poured himself into the class and learned more than he ever imagined he could. As he remarked to me, "Success in the second class seemed within reach, so it made me want to try!" As God reminds us in Prov 29:18a, "Where there is no vision, the people perish."[2]

Jesus understands the power of encouragement—his very first miracle did not heal the sick or cast out a demon but encouraged a bridegroom! In John 2:1–12, we read of how Jesus and his newly called

2. KJV.

disciples attend a wedding at Cana in Galilee along with Jesus' mother. Sadly, the bridegroom runs out of wine during the festivities, a very significant social blunder in ancient Jewish culture. Responding to his mother's prompting, Jesus directs the servants to fill six large stone jars with water and take some to the master of ceremonies. When the master of ceremonies tastes the water, it has miraculously turned into wine, and he pulls the bridegroom aside to compliment him: "Everyone serves the good wine first, and when people have drunk freely, then the poor wine. But you have kept the good wine until now." How encouraged the bridegroom must have been to find his wedding celebration and reputation saved and his guests blessed with excellent wine! Jesus' first miracle, performed at a wedding, brought great encouragement to a bridegroom and the wedding guests, inaugurating his earthly ministry of restoration and hope.

Jesus desires to give us his personalized, loving encouragement through his closeness to us as our bridegroom. The intimate connection we share enables him to work out his plans for our lives and to draw near to our hearts, whispering words of love and blessing and reassuring us with his tender affection. His encouragement strengthens us, motivating us to trust him, helping us persevere and grow through both good times and bad. He loves to point us to the bright, hopeful future we have as his beloved bride.

It is then our privilege to encourage others as we ourselves have been encouraged. Following the lead of our bridegroom, we offer personalized messages of inspiration that strike the hearts of the weary with blessing and hope. We speak to them of Jesus and his love for them, his good plans for their lives, and his commitment to drawing ever nearer to their hearts. The overflow of the love and encouragement we have received from our beloved thus blesses and encourages the ones he loves.

Both of these experiences, receiving Jesus' encouragement and encouraging others, matures and deepens our love for our bridegroom. As our hearts are strengthened and made secure in Jesus' love and encouragement, our love and gratitude for him increases, and we are motivated to look outside ourselves to inspire others. As the bride in Song of Songs learns to receive and share her bridegroom's encouragement, she models for us how to minister in this way with our bridegroom Jesus.

THE BRIDE RECEIVES ENCOURAGEMENT: SONG 6:4–9; 7:1–9A

From the beginning of her relationship with King Solomon, the bride in Song of Songs has enjoyed his encouragement. His first words in Song 1:9 reveal his esteem for her: "I compare you, my love, to a mare among Pharaoh's chariots." The king's beautiful wedding vows in Song 4:1–15 also praise the desirable attributes of the bride.

Now, we encounter two additional instances in the narrative in which the bridegroom tells the bride all that he loves about her. Divided between chapters 6 and 7 of Song of Songs, these fifteen verses encourage the bride as Solomon extols her loveliness. In the first section of verses, he proclaims the beauty of her hair, teeth, and cheeks, and in the second section of verses, he admires her feet, thighs, navel, belly, breasts, neck, eyes, nose, head, and hair. In addition, like in his wedding vows, the bridegroom also declares the powerful effect the bride's beauty has on him. He pleads in Song 6:5, "Turn away your eyes from me, for they overwhelm me," and he acknowledges in Song 7:5, "A king is held captive in the tresses [of hair]."

We see by this quick glance at Solomon's encouragement of his bride how very personalized his words of praise are. He honors her as an individual, even including this powerful affirmation in Song 6:9a: "My dove, my perfect one, is unique, the only daughter of her mother, the favorite of the one who bore her."[3] Solomon's delight in his beloved bride reveals itself as he encourages and celebrates her.

The bride chooses to receive her lover's encouragement, and while this may seem like an obvious response, I would suggest that it might be more surprising than we initially think. If I were in the bride's shoes, I could see myself feeling a bit self-conscious about all the praise and struggling to accept my bridegroom's passionate words of affirmation. I suspect I might interrupt him a few times by protesting that I'm not really that amazing, that I'm not actually as attractive as the maiden down the street, or that I really should look into updating my wardrobe. The bride, on the other hand, simply listens to her bridegroom's words and receives them. She allows her beloved to share his heart of love with her, and she is encouraged by his declaration of passion and esteem.

The bride has learned to receive King Solomon's encouragement over time. In the beginning of the narrative, she struggles to receive his words

---

3. NIV.

of praise, apologizing for her lack of preparation to meet him.[4] Now, having experienced her bridegroom's loving encouragement throughout the course of their relationship, she is able to receive it and be blessed by it.

How comfortable are you with receiving encouragement from your bridegroom Jesus? Do you allow him to share with you his affection? Do you listen to and receive his affirmations of your beauty? Do you believe he is overwhelmed by one glance from your eyes?[5] Personally, I often struggle with believing Jesus loves me as passionately as he claims to in the Bible. Years of living in a fallen world, encountering my own sinfulness and failures, and enduring others' criticisms and rejection have caused me to build protective walls around my heart that resist Jesus' tender declarations of affection. When I read many of the passages in Song of Songs, I find myself tensing, refusing to accept that such words of passion and love could possibly be indicative of Jesus' feelings for me.

But I can't escape the fact that the Bible declares that Jesus loves me this way, and that he chose to lay aside his divinity, adopt the flesh of a man, and die a violent death to bring me to himself. *I am the joy that was set before him*, motivating him to despise the shame of the cross, as Heb 12:2 reminds me. *I am the individual he cares for and desires to know intimately and personally*, as Ps 56:8 and Matt 10:29–31 teach. *I am the partner with whom he will spend eternity*, ruling and reigning in his end-time kingdom of love, as I read in 2 Tim 2:12 and Rev 5:10. This is my reality, and yours as well. We truly are the beloved, cherished, eternal bride of Jesus, and he absolutely loves telling us how much he adores us.

If you struggle like I do with receiving Jesus' encouragement, adopt the response the bride in Song of Songs learned. Choose to set your heart at rest in his presence, remain silent, and allow your bridegroom to share his feelings of love for you without interrupting, diminishing, or rejecting his words. Just sit with him, letting his passionate love and desire for you wash over your heart.

If you struggle to hear Jesus' words of encouragement, use the words he has already shared with us in the Bible. After all, the Bible is God's love letter to us! Passages such as Song 6:4–9 and 7:1–9, Isa 43:1–7, and Zeph 3:17 speak of Jesus' affections for us. Read verses such as these out loud over yourself and receive them as the true sentiments of your bridegroom for you. Over time, your heart will become receptive to receiving

---

4. Song 1:6.
5. Song 4:9.

encouragement from your beloved, and you will grow in hearing his still, small voice in your spirit encouraging you personally.

THE BRIDE SHARES ENCOURAGEMENT: SONG 6:11–13; 7:9B–13

After receiving her bridegroom's admiring words, the bride in Song of Songs is motivated to reach out and encourage others. In chapter 6, the bride decides to go to the valley to see if the trees are blossoming: "I went down to the nut orchard to look at the blossoms of the valley, to see whether the vines had budded, whether the pomegranates were in bloom."[6] The bride decides to focus outward, looking for signs of growth and newness of life in the world around her. We can understand this symbolically to mean that the bride is searching throughout the kingdom for signs of interest in the king among the villagers, hoping others are becoming intrigued about Solomon like the friends do in the beginning of chapter 6, when they offer to join her in searching for him. The Passion Translation expands the verse:

> I decided to go down to the valley streams
> where the orchards of the king grow and mature.
> I longed to know if hearts were opening.
> Are the budding vines blooming with new growth?
> Has their springtime of passionate love arrived?

The bride is yearning to find and encourage others to seek her bridegroom and enjoy his love and affirmation as she does.

Similarly, after the bridegroom's encouragement in chapter 7, the bride is again motivated to seek out others who might be longing for the love of her bridegroom. But, this time, she asks the king to join her as she strives to encourage others to pursue him:

> Come, my beloved,
>   let us go out into the fields
>   and lodge in the villages;
>   let us go out early to the vineyards
>   and see whether the vines have budded,
>   whether the grape blossoms have opened

---

6. Song 6:11. The NIV translation identifies the speaker of this verse as the male in the narrative, but most other translations, including the KJV, ESV, and TPT, identify the speaker as the female.

and the pomegranates are in bloom.
There I will give you my love.
The mandrakes give forth fragrance,
    and beside our doors are all choice fruits,
new as well as old,
    which I have laid up for you, O my beloved.[7]

The picture here is that of the bride and bridegroom traveling together to the villages and expressing their mutual love in the presence of the people. As the villagers see the surpassing love the bride has for her devoted bridegroom, symbolized by the fragrant "choice fruits" that are in the home of Solomon and his bride, they will be encouraged to seek the love of the bridegroom for themselves. The bridegroom's encouragement of the bride thus motivates her to travel with him to the villages to share the wonders of his love.

Several aspects of the bride's encouragement to the villagers stand out to me. First, her effort to inspire them to seek Solomon is very natural and authentic. The bride comes to where the people are and displays her love for the king there so that all can see the mutual delight they have in each other. She doesn't preach at the villagers, criticize their way of life, or shame them into pursuing the king. She simply allows them to see the love she and Solomon enjoy, knowing their hearts will be stirred to pursue such enchanting love for themselves. Even the friends are enticed, demanding, "Return, return, O Shulamite, return, return, that we may look upon you" in Song 6:13. The bridegroom's encouraging words to the bride thus move her very naturally into encouraging others in a way that blesses them.

Second, the bride is quick to notice and encourage the villagers in personalized ways, noting where each one is in their understanding of and desire for the bridegroom. She looks to see if the vines have "budded," if the grape blossoms have "opened," or if the pomegranates are "in bloom." Encouraging others effectively requires us to recognize where they are in their own spiritual journey. For some, we will need to encourage what we see in them in the "bud" stage, speaking words of hope to their potential, noticing the work God is doing in their lives that may only be present in nascent form. For others, their hearts may already be "opened" to what God is doing, and so they can receive and appreciate more direct, even challenging, encouragement. Lastly, we may be privileged to join with

---

7. Song 7:11–13.

ones who are "in bloom" and experiencing the fruit that comes from maturity in an area of their lives or ministry. We can celebrate with them all that God is doing and further inspire their gratitude toward our loving bridegroom. Recognizing where each individual is on their journey enables us to offer personalized, effective encouragement as modeled for us by the bride.

A third notable aspect of the bride's encouragement of the villagers is who she is ministering to. The villagers she seeks to inspire may very well be some of the same people who didn't bother to help her on her first search for her bridegroom in Song 3:3 or even the ones who beat her and stole her cloak during her second search in Song 5:7. How incredibly transformed is the bride by her bridegroom's love and encouragement! She now rushes to the very people who hurt and ignored her to encourage them toward her beloved.

The bride has thus grown and matured in her bridal love, learning to receive and enjoy the encouragement of her bridegroom as well as to look beyond herself, even to those who have hurt her, to encourage them organically and engagingly to pursue her king. Hopefully, we are inspired to do the same in the places we live, work, and play. But, sometimes, our bridegroom leads us to encourage others within a narrower scope, perhaps even just one person—a friend, coworker, family member, or neighbor. Below, two women from colonial Rhode Island reveal for us how bridal encouragement works within the context of meaningful, lifelong friendship.

SARAH OSBORN AND SUSANNA ANTHONY: A SURPRISING, SUSTAINED FRIENDSHIP

Sarah Osborn (1714–96) and Susanna Anthony (1726–91) both lived in the town of Newport, Rhode Island; attended the same church and small group; and shared many mutual friends and acquaintances. Their friendship of fifty years stands as a testimony to the unique and enduring power of encouragement. Their pastor, Samuel Hopkins of the First Congregational Church in Newport, shared this about their connection: "They were truly, and in a distinguished degree, of one heart and one soul, and during the whole time loved each other with a pure heart, fervently."[8]

---

8. Hopkins, *Memoirs of Osborn*, 350.

Osborn and Anthony's long friendship reveals for us two important aspects of encouragement: it can occur in surprising situations, and it can remain effective over the long haul. Osborn and Anthony were in many respects unlikely friends, differing in age by more than a decade and experiencing vastly different lives. Yes, despite their dissimilarities, the women forged a bond through passionate pursuit of their bridegroom Jesus that enabled them to support each other through challenging times and rejoice with each other in times of blessing.

And, remarkably, they sustained their relationship and the mutual encouragement it provided through five decades, first meeting when Osborn was in her mid-twenties and Anthony was just fourteen.[9] Over the years, they came together for times of fasting and prayer; helped each other with tasks such as house-sitting; ministered together; and supported each other through illness, grief, and loss. Who were these two brides of Jesus who encouraged each other so effectively through their surprising, sustained fifty years of friendship?

S & S 4 EVER

Sarah Osborn lived an ever-changing and challenging life. Born in England, she moved to the American colonies with her family when she was nine years old, settling in Rhode Island in her early teens. After eloping with a sailor at eighteen, Osborn was widowed by age twenty with a son under two years of age. Osborn took up work as a schoolteacher, committing her life to Jesus soon after. Receiving communion in church the first Sunday after her conversion, Osborn rejoices as she contemplates her forgiving and beautiful bridegroom:

> Oh, when I considered how often and how long [Jesus] had stood knocking, but could have no entrance into my hardened heart, I was astonished at myself, that I could possibly be so cruel, and astonished at free grace and redeeming love, that I was spared to see that happy day. Oh, then I begged that the everlasting doors of my soul might be lifted up that the King of glory might enter in and take full possession. Oh, how gladly did I embrace a Savior upon his own terms, as my Prophet, Priest, and King!

---

9. Osborn and Anthony, *Familiar Letters*, 2. The editor of the letters notes that Osborn and Anthony began corresponding in 1740.

He appeared lovely, the chief among ten thousand, and was ten thousand times welcome to me.[10]

In her late twenties, Osborn married a widower with three sons, but the family struggled with poverty and debt because her husband's emotional and physical ailments often made him unable to work. Osborn ran a boarding school and worked as a seamstress to support the family financially.[11]

Osborn was very committed to ministry in her church, functioning as a church leader by hosting numerous prayer meetings throughout the week in her home. Beginning in 1741, she led a weekly female "religious society" for fifty years until her death, with members totaling as many as sixty at times.[12] She also hosted additional meetings for instruction and prayer, rotating groups of people through her home on different evenings of the week—boys, men, women, girls, and even "heads of families." Osborn had a particular ministry to African American members of Newport, both enslaved and free, hosting gatherings for them as well.

Osborn's role at all these events varied from reading Christian books out loud, to praying and offering spiritual counsel, to providing religious instruction. She notes in her diary that during some months, hundreds literally came to her house each week, with the winter of 1767 seeing that number rise to more than five hundred people as a local revival swept through her region.[13] As her pastor records in a memoir, "Her house was indeed, and in an eminent sense, *a house of prayer*."[14]

Osborn's meetings caused their share of controversy. Her leadership as a woman and the throngs of people who attended her meetings made some question whether Osborn had gone "beyond her line."[15] But Osborn was not deterred. She continued the meetings until age and illness prevented her, and she also shared her spiritual counsel and experiences through her writing, penning thousands of pages of unpublished diaries and letters that circulated among Christians near and far as devotional

---

10. Hopkins, *Memoirs of Osborn*, 28–29. In this quotation, Osborn references Rev 3:20, Ps 24:9, Song 5:16, and Song 5:10.

11. Hopkins, *Memoirs of Osborn*, 5, 16, 18, 20, 52.

12. Hopkins, *Memoirs of Osborn*, 50, 70–74.

13. Hopkins, *Memoirs of Osborn*, 75–83.

14. Hopkins, *Memoirs of Osborn*, 83. Hopkins's biblical reference is to Isa 56:7; italics are present in the original.

15. The quotation is from the Rev. Joseph Fish (1705–1781), a close friend of Osborn's, quoted in Brekus, *Sarah Osborn's Collected Writings*, 241.

literature. Osborn even received unsolicited donations for her ministry from supporters in Canada and the Caribbean.[16]

Susanna Anthony, on the other hand, led a much quieter life. The daughter of Quaker Christians, she was introduced early to Jesus and as a child committed to following him. She never married, lived in her family home, and supported herself with needlework and, at times, teaching school. When she was sixteen, Anthony made the decision to leave the Quaker denomination and join the First Congregational Church in Newport, a choice her parents ultimately supported. She also joined Osborn's female religious society around that time.[17] Her local church held a special place in her heart, and she was grieved when she could not attend Sunday services because of her intermittent poor health. Notes her pastor in a memoir, Anthony's "grateful affection to God and the Redeemer united her heart to the disciples of Christ and his church with peculiar and strong affection."[18]

Anthony's ministry, unlike Osborn's, was predominantly private. At seventeen, she committed herself to a life of solitary personal prayer, years later recalling her resolution:

> After I had publicly given myself up to God and commenced a member of Zion, I felt some disposition to study what I should render to the Lord for all his benefits and how I could in my low and private capacity best promote his interest and serve the church of Christ. Prayer and supplication appeared the only or chief way, as good in that way might come more pure and unsullied. Accordingly, I devoted myself to the service of the sanctuary in this way, if God would but accept and assist me herein, though I should be but as a burden-bearer.[19]

Like Osborn, Anthony pursued her ministry with regularity and zeal, having set times and days to pray specifically for ministers and missionaries, the advancement of Christ's kingdom throughout the world, the conversion of Jews and gentiles, and the Holy Spirit to be poured out upon God's people "until he makes Jerusalem a praise in the whole earth."[20] Other times of fasting and prayer were "kept more especially for

---

16. Brekus, *Sarah Osborn's Collected Writings*, xv.
17. Hopkins, *Memoirs of Anthony*, 14.
18. Hopkins, *Memoirs of Anthony*, 237.
19. Hopkins, *Memoirs of Anthony*, 18–19. Anthony references Ps 116:12 and possibly Luke 2:36-38.
20. Hopkins, *Memoirs of Anthony*, 16. Anthony quotes here from Isa 62:6-7, a

my own soul," writes Anthony. She records many instances of answered prayer in her diary, eagerly following news of the progress of Christ's kingdom both domestically and internationally.[21]

Anthony utilized her prayer gifting corporately as well, particularly as a member of Osborn's female religious society. Society members noted that, on occasion, Anthony would lead the gathering by praying herself for more than ninety minutes at one time, and the members attested that words could not describe the fervency and beauty of her prayer: "A full description of the holy fervor, the clear view of invisible things, and that nearness to God while she poured out her heart before him, which she discovered, cannot be made by any narration of them."[22] Similarly, Sarah Osborn observes in a letter to a pastor friend, "And, oh, could you, sir, but be in a corner and hear our dear Susa when wrestling for the outpourings of God's Spirit for the conversion of sinners; for strengthening, sanctifying grace, that God may be glorified in his children; and for gospel ministers, I believe you would, with me, be constrained to say you never heard anything to exceed if even to equal."[23]

Despite their very different lives and ministries, Osborn and Anthony each made such an impression on their pastor, Samuel Hopkins, that upon their deaths, he published memoirs of both women that offer biographical information, commentary on their characters, excerpts from their journals, and letters they wrote to each other and to other correspondents.[24] Both works reached second editions, encouraging readers beyond their town of Newport to emulate the remarkable lives and friendship of these two brides of Jesus.

---

passage encouraging intercessory prayer: "I have posted watchmen on your walls, Jerusalem; they will never be silent day or night. You who call on the Lord, give yourselves no rest, and give him no rest till he establishes Jerusalem and makes her the praise of the earth" (NIV).

21. Hopkins, *Memoirs of Anthony*, 15–16.
22. Hopkins, *Memoirs of Anthony*, 14–15.
23. Brekus, *Sarah Osborn's Collected Writings*, 209.
24. The first editions are Samuel Hopkins, *Memoirs of the Life of Mrs. Sarah Osborn* (Worcester, MA, 1799) and Samuel Hopkins, *Life and Character of Miss Susanna Anthony* (Worcester, MA, 1796). I am quoting from the second editions of both works in this chapter.

LETTERS FROM THE PAST

Today, we learn about Osborn and Anthony's friendship primarily through the letters they exchanged. Letter writing was an important part of eighteenth-century men's and women's lives; many literate Americans maintained frequent correspondence with numerous friends, relatives, and business associates, both nationally and internationally. Even colonial women, who were seldom involved in business, were expected to be proficient in letter writing. So important was letter writing that penmanship and letter-writing manuals were published to encourage improvement in the skill. A letter-writing manual from 1793 offers this advice:

> When you write to a friend, your letter should be a true picture of your heart—the style loose and irregular, the thoughts themselves should appear naked and not dressed in the borrowed robes of rhetoric. For a friend will be more pleased with that part of a letter which flows from the heart than with that which is the product of the mind.[25]

As the primary means of nonverbal communication at the time, letters give us a unique window into relationships of the past like Osborn and Anthony's.

Osborn and Anthony exchanged many, many letters over their years of friendship during times when they could not see each other in person because of travel, illness, or just the busyness of life. The correspondence was very important and meaningful for both women; as Anthony writes in the opening to one of her letters to Osborn, "Into your breast, I have often poured out the joys and sorrows of my soul and as often have found compassion, tenderness, and sympathy there; and now, though I cannot see your face, yet let me reach your pity and prayers by a few lines."[26]

In 1807, ten years after both Osborn and Anthony had died, a collection of their letters was published, possibly edited by Elizabeth West Hopkins, wife of Samuel Hopkins, titled *Familiar Letters, Written by Mrs. Sarah Osborn, and Miss Susanna Anthony, Late of Newport, Rhode Island*.[27] The advertisement for the collection notes the goal of the publication: "[The letters] expect not the attention of the learned nor the notice of the gay. If they obtain the approbation of the pious and, in any degree,

---

25. *American Letter-Writer*, 3.
26. Osborn and Anthony, *Familiar Letters*, 27.
27. Brekus, *Sarah Osborn's Collected Writings*, 349n3.

promote the Redeemer's interest, the end of their publication will be answered."[28] Through the collection, Osborn and Anthony's friendship became a means to encourage even more Christians beyond the confines of their colonial town.

Below are several letters from the collection that reveal how Osborn and Anthony supported and encouraged each other. Through their writings, they rejoice with each other in blessing, join together in prayer and fasting, and inspire each other to pursue their eternal lover and friend. In the final letter, Anthony encourages Osborn during the extreme trial of the death of her only biological child, her eleven-year-old son who was working as an apprentice about thirty miles from home.[29] I hope you are encouraged as you read these intimate writings between two women who enjoyed the encouragement of their bridegroom and sought to share that blessing with each other.

LETTERS: FAMILIAR LETTERS, WRITTEN BY MRS. SARAH OSBORN, AND MISS SUSANNA ANTHONY, LATE OF NEWPORT, RHODE ISLAND[30]

Rejoicing with Each Other

My very dear and lovely friend,

As I cannot pay you a personal visit, I must beg your acceptance of a short one from my pen just to tell you my heart is with you and also to call upon you to praise God with and for me. God has graciously appeared for me this day in his house and at his table,[31] notwithstanding all my unbelieving fears! Oh, my friend, trust, love, and live upon this good and faithful God and pray for me that I may constantly do so, too.

I long to know how you do in this trying time. I hope your precious soul is swallowed up in the God of ordinances[32]

---

28. Osborn and Anthony, *Familiar Letters*, 2.

29. Brekus, *Sarah Osborn's Collected Writings*, 68.

30. Selections are from Osborn and Anthony, *Familiar Letters*, Letters I (3), II (4–5, 7), V (10–12), XVII (31–32), XVIII (32–35), XL (86–90), XLVIII (106–8), XXXIX (83–85).

31. By God's "house," Osborn means the worship service at her church, and by "table," she means communion.

32. An ordinance is a religious ritual like baptism or communion.

while, for wise and holy ends, you are at present detained from God's house! The Lord preserve you from any murmurings and enable you patiently to submit to his blessed will at all times. If you are able, let me hear from you by a line or two, which will be very grateful to,

Your sincere friend,
S. Osborn

My very dear friend,

[Your letter] I last night received, which was like cold water to a thirsty soul! It did refresh my soul to think that I, unworthy I, was in your thoughts and on your heart when you were taken near your God! I trust it has raised my love to my Redeemer, that he was pleased to manifest himself to you.

Oh, my friend, surely I love and honor my glorious Savior for any displays of his power and grace, though they be not directly made to me; yet, if Jesus be glorified in his saints, I rejoice and thereby am made a partaker of their joys! Oh, let my infinitely glorious God be magnified and exalted, and I am delighted, yes, even ravished! It is well, infinitely well, though I was denied the happy privilege of meeting God in his house and at his table.

My spirits sunk within me while, in thought, I viewed the table spread, the guests invited, and a happy few permitted to lean on the breast of Jesus while at supper and hear him saying to them, "Eat, oh friends, drink, yes, drink abundantly, oh beloved,"[33] but I, shut out, not [allowed] to taste the children's bread![34] My soul melted into heaviness! I had prayed, waited, and hoped there to meet my God, and the denial was, and still is, affecting and afflicting, but I forbear! God is just and holy; I am sinful and unworthy!

Yet, I rejoice for you, and more, that the divine perfections are gloriously displayed! But, oh, my dear, were you thus highly favored by the King of kings, the eternal Jehovah! Did this pure, this holy Being permit you to draw near to him and even take you near him! Oh, why? Lord, what is man, that you are mindful of him![35] Verily, the contemplation and enjoyment of God

---

33. A reference to the Last Supper and Song 5:1b.
34. A reference to the story in Matt 15:21–28 and Mark 7:24–30.
35. Ps 8:4.

is the highest dignity of human capacity! Oh, here my thoughts are lost in wonder, love, and adoration! . . .

    Yours, affectionate,

    S. Anthony

Joining Together in Prayer and Fasting

My very dear and constant friend,

When the bridegroom is absent, shall not the children of the bride-chamber fast as well as pray?[36] A passage in your prayer on Friday—that we were now called to this—struck me and has continued with me. I once could practice this without going from home, but it is otherwise with me now for want of room.

It has been suggested to my mind to propose one thing to you, but the fear of [pressuring] you has prevented me! I will, however, just mention it. I know you will be as forward as I if your circumstances will admit. It is this: to set apart one whole day for solemn fasting and prayer and let the whole society join.[37] I wish you to consider of it until Wednesday evening, that if you approve, and providence permit, it may be on Friday next, and thus begin the New Year. I do not desire to crowd upon you, but do not let Satan cast difficulties in your way as he does in mine. For who knows, but our God will be with us and yet cause us to glorify him and thus avenge us of our adversaries!

Oh, may we seek the Lord, who hides himself from the house of Jacob! And if we gain no more than an encouragement to hold on seeking him, we shall surely find our account in it, for he will come and will not tarry. Oh, it is a time of great discouragement, and who can tell whether we are come to the darkest time of the night! I fear not, nor do we know how long the night will last! I know the day will come, but faith and patience will be necessary to wait for the dawn![38]

    36. These words appear in Matt 9:15, Mark 2:19–20, and Luke 5:34–35.

    37. This is probably a reference to the female religious society that met in Osborn's home.

    38. Anthony's mention of a "time of great discouragement" may be a reference to the French and Indian War (1756–63), which caused food shortages, trade disruption, and fear in the colonies. Two of Osborn's stepsons enlisted to fight in the conflict.

Yours, in the firmest bonds,
S. A.

Observation. Blessed be thou of the Lord and blessed be your advice! This was before the beginning of our solemn fast, January 1, 1762. S. O.

Remaining Faithful

Dear S[usanna],

By every letter I receive from you, I think something more of my own heart is discovered to me. In your last, you have showed me how much more the hateful principle of self-love reigns in me than love to God! This I did not discern when I wrote my last [letter]. You are right, my dear, the glory of God, the exalting of Jesus, ought to be the object of our pursuit rather than our own ease. The Lord humble me for the narrowness of my heart!

Well, blessed be God, I have had a discovery of the fullness, sufficiency, willingness, truth, and faithfulness of the great Redeemer the week past in conversing with one who is in great distress for her soul, one who thinks her day is past, her sins too great to be forgiven! And, verily, I believe there is not anything that will stir up the zeal and courage of a poor, faint-hearted Christian like meeting with those who distrust the Savior. For, if we are not quite senseless, it constrains us to speak for him whom we trust has broken through such opposition and caused his grace to triumph over and subdue such rebels! Oh, if he has conquered me, surely nothing can be too hard for him! I would gladly add, but time will not permit.

Let us press forward, dear friend; we shall find God's grace sufficient to perfect that which he has begun in us![39] Then we will adore and praise forever, without any of these breaks and pauses. The Lord be with you. Pray hard for your affectionate,
S. O.

Brekus, *Sarah Osborn's Collected Writings*, 120.
39. Phil 1:6.

Dear Mrs. O.,

Notwithstanding my purpose of writing to you, yet my backward heart would have deferred it did I not hope it might, by the blessing of God, be a means of reviving our souls. I wish we may reap a double crop, namely, in writing and receiving. Oh, may we again take sweet counsel together and walk in the light of God's countenance!

Oh, my friend, I long for the freedom and familiarity we once enjoyed when we were brought near to our God and to each other! How did we then share each other's joys and sorrows! Jesus was known to us by the lovely name Emmanuel! Was he not with us, and did not our hearts burn within us while we conversed with and of him![40] *How sweet was it to hear and tell in what manner the blessed God had revealed himself to us, either in his providences or ordinances! Surely his ways were pleasant and all his paths peace!*[41] *Come then, my friend, let us join heart and hand in pursuing religion as the only object worthy our esteem!*

I think while I am writing to so dear a friend, I am only conversing with my own soul and may use the utmost freedom.... When I hear profane wretches speak lightly of Christ, it is then, with renewed vigor, faith, and love, I embrace him as the only portion of my soul. Here, have I said to my soul, take up your rest forever, even in your God! Oh, it is sweet, resting our souls and all their concerns on a faithful covenant God and Father through our dear Redeemer.

Oh, my friend, I have renewed my choice, and now, I think, I am as happy as I can be here. I have enough; I ask no more! Nothing, but what flows from union and communion with the blessed God! Oh, this is enough, were I stripped of all the delights of the universe! I am happy now, but, oh, what does yet remain! Rivers of pleasure, yet unfathomed by us, even the open vision and full fruition of our God, for which I long!

Your constant,
S. A.

---

40. Luke 24:32.
41. Prov 3:17.

Encouraging Pursuit of the Bridegroom

Dear Mrs. O.,

. . . Blessed be God, I am renewedly established in the firm belief of salvation only through faith in Christ Jesus. A faith which unites to, rests on, and receives Christ as a whole Savior. A faith which purifies the heart, works by love, and influences the whole man to a life of universal obedience. Surely this must be most worthy of God and most safe for wretched, miserable man, who is without strength or will to help himself!

Oh, glory to God for Jesus Christ! In him I will glory forever! Though the cross of Christ be to the Jews a stumbling block and to the Greeks foolishness, yet to all those who are saved it was, is, and ever shall be the power of God and the wisdom of God! . . .[42]

I abhor a contradictory, censorious temper, I trust you know, and I think I could bear anything easier than to have my dear, my ever-glorious Redeemer set low and degraded! Well, he is still more precious to me, and I renew my flight to him. If others can do without him, I cannot. Oh, glory to this dearest God-man Mediator, this sovereign God who can bring light out of darkness [and] can establish my faith in Christ . . . and cause me renewedly to renounce all hope in any other name.

Verily, I see such a display of the divine character and perfections in the way of salvation by Jesus Christ that I am assured it must be of God! Oh, the depths of the riches, both of the wisdom and knowledge of God![43] *Oh, the infinite goodness and love of Jehovah!*

Let us, my dear, show our love and gratitude to God by making great use of this Savior, and let us do it with a view to the glory of God and not merely for our own ease! We should certainly find more comfort and pleasure by looking more to Christ, but we should seek the glory of God, even in this, *rather than our own enjoyment.*

Let us set the crown on the head of King Jesus, saying, reign, glorious Emmanuel! Reign, Almighty Redeemer,

---

42. 1 Cor 1:23–24.
43. Rom 11:33.

display *your glory and cause those who see neither form nor comeliness in you to cry out, "You are all fair, there is no spot in you, the chief among ten thousand, yes, altogether lovely!"*[44] *And those who have such faint views of you, as I have, let them be even swallowed up in the open vision and full fruition of your glory!*

Oh, let me see your face, let me taste your love, oh, my God, my everlasting all! When, oh, when shall I be with you where you are, to behold your glory! To be changed into your image! There it shall be the glory of our glory to glorify and exalt you! Till then, my soul can never be completely at rest.

Oh, waste me near your feet; let me dwell but where I long to, and I shall be what you would have me be and what I wish to be! This I dare promise, yes, because God has promised it. There, oh, there, my exalted Redeemer shall reign gloriously, and none of the blessed inhabitants disdain his regal scepter! There no discord will have place, for the redeemed of the Lord shall all *sing redeeming love to all eternity! Oh, I think I long to join their acclamations and extol Jesus the Savior before men and angels!*

God has now, I trust, been showing me my utter inability to do anything acceptable to him of myself and the necessity I am under of constantly looking to Christ for righteousness and strength! Now is Christ precious, and I now long to yield a universal and perfect obedience to all his commands, for true faith does not hinder, but promotes, obedience. Oh, let me now show this by a more holy life and conversation.

Your real friend,
S. A.

My dear friend,
I would gladly write you some suitable answer to your letter, but know not how to do it. I seem, in some sense, to be like the inquiring, wandering daughters of Jerusalem when the spouse was seeking her Beloved, Song of Songs, [chapter 5], verse 9: "What is your beloved more than another beloved, O thou fairest among women, that you do so charge us?"

---

44. In this sentence, Anthony combines phrases from Isa 53:2, Song 4:7, Song 5:10, and Song 5:16.

Alas, I have lost those transforming views of his glorious perfections which so animate and inflame your soul, and the language of my practice is, "There is no form nor comeliness in him, wherefore I should desire him."[45] Yet, I believe "he is the altogether lovely one, the chief among ten thousand!"[46] But, oh, I cannot get near to him, and this cannot, I plainly see, is my stubborn will! Oh, if that were but bowed to the scepter of King Jesus, I should soon find better times.

I have been for some time past rambling out among means and creatures in a wilderness. And I am sure I shall not find rest till I return and stay myself upon God. But I cannot find the way back again! Yet, I think I hear Christ speaking to me in his word, "I am the way, the truth, and the life."[47] Oh, if I could but clasp my Savior in the arms of a strong and lively faith, I should do well, though a thousand things were against me. But, without him, I can do nothing.

I know I have too often tried your patience with my fruitless complaints, yet if I write at all, I must write as I feel. "Out of the abundance of the heart, the mouth speaks."[48] The Lord be with you and make you exceeding glad with the light of his countenance. If God gives you a heart to pray, pray hard for
Your friend,
S. O.

Trusting God During a Severe Trial

Friday morning, September 22, 1744.[49] On Thursday afternoon, the sixth day of this month, I had the sorrowful news that my only son was sick unto death. God in his providence provided presently for me: my dear Susa Anthony to keep my house, a horse for my husband and myself to ride, and all other things comfortable. And on my way God gave me such a sense of his goodness to me in a thousand

---

45. Isa 53:2.
46. Song 5:16; 5:10.
47. John 14:6.
48. Matt 12:34; the same sentiment is expressed in Luke 6:45.
49. This is a short excerpt from Sarah Osborn's journal. Brekus, *Sarah Osborn's Collected Writings*, 68–69.

instances, that instead of sinking under my sorrow, my mind was employed in attention to and blessing God for my mercies....

On Friday morning we got to Rehoboth [Massachusetts], where I found my son much swelled with a dropsy and pined to a mere skeleton with the jaundice, scurvy, and consumption, all combining.[50] He rattled in his throat like a dying person, laboring for every breath. He was given over by the doctors and all friends, who lamented him and did the best for him in their power as to the body. But, alas! My great concern was for that precious jewel, his immortal soul. I endeavored to improve every opportunity to discourse with him, and read to him such portions of scripture as I thought suitable, with passages out of Mr. Alleine's *Alarm*, etc.[51] And I was enabled to pray all the day by ejaculatory breathings, and sometimes to plead and wrestle with God on his behalf, though, alas, God was pleased to hide his dealings with him altogether. For I could discern no evidence of a work of grace wrought on his soul, for which I did plead from day to day.... On Thursday, September 13, the day before he died, I was just ready to give up and sit down discouraged. My heart even almost died with fear of what would become of him. But just in this juncture, God in his providence ordered it so that I received a letter from my dear Susa [see letter below], which was a cordial to my drooping spirits.

My dear friend,

I am deeply affected with your affliction and tenderly sympathize with you in your sorrow. I think I could be willing to put my shoulder to yours and bear part of the burden, yes, the whole of it, rather than you should be crushed under it! But what shall I say? Has your God and Father put this cup into your hand? Then drink it, my dear, with submission, love, and fear; forget the cup, while you behold the hand which gives it to you. It is not from my hand. No, nor from the nearest friend on earth; if so, you might fear some poison with the gall.

---

50. Consumption is now called tuberculosis.
51. Joseph Alleine, *Alarm to Unconverted Sinners* (London, 1671).

Oh, that I could tell you, or rather that God would show you from whose hand it is. Is it not from the hand of your God and Father—your Redeemer—Savior—head and husband—and has he not said you are as the apple of his eye,[52] and will he hurt that? No! Surely, he will not! Oh, arise, and by faith cast your child upon Christ—tell him he is your only son, and you want a pardon for him—and will not he, who is an inexhaustible fountain, a boundless ocean of infinite fullness, be as ready to pity the soul of your son as he was to pity the bodies of those who came to him for healing in the days of his flesh? Verily, the promises are to believers and their children.[53]

But however God may deal with you as to giving comfortable evidence of his being born again, study and seek a resigned will. Oh, do not fall out with your Father! Kiss the hand, though it has a rod in it—it is the hand of your God still. Oh, my dear, you and I may, yes, must love him, because he is a sovereign God! Set your King on his holy hill, Zion[54], and not only [allow], but entreat him to be sovereign still.

And now, my dear, once and again I commit you and yours, both living and dying, into the hands of the Father of mercies, the God and Father of our Lord Jesus Christ! Bury not living mercies with dead sorrows, but still adore your God in adversity! If your child yet lives, tell him from me not to delay one moment longer, but fly to the blessed Jesus! Tell him I have prayed and by God's leave that I will still pray for him, and I beg he would pray for himself. And now, farewell, my friend; bless the Lord, for he is good. I long to see you, but must say, "Father, your will be done!"

Yours,
S. A.

CHAPTER SUMMARY AND FURTHER READING

Encouragement, particularly when it is personalized, is a powerful tool for inspiring hearts toward a hopeful vision of the future. As Jesus' bride,

52. Ps 17:8.
53. Acts 2:39.
54. Ps 2:6.

we desire to grow in receiving his tender affirmation and affection toward us without minimizing or resisting. As we are inspired and transformed by Jesus' passion for us, our love for our bridegroom matures, and we are motivated to step outside our comfort zone and encourage others. As the bride in Song of Songs and Sarah Osborn and Susanna Anthony show us, encouragement can happen on a large scale or within an intimate friendship. In every situation, our hearts are inspired by loving encouragement.

To read all of Sarah Osborn and Susanna Anthony's published letters, including some written to other correspondents, a copy of *Familiar Letters* may be obtained digitally through a university library or large public library. The second edition of Sarah Osborn's memoir is available via Google Books, and Susanna Anthony's memoir can be obtained through a university library.

Catherine A. Brekus has done significant research on Sarah Osborn, publishing a study of how Osborn's writings connect with the eighteenth-century rise of evangelicalism titled *Sarah Osborn's World: The Rise of Evangelical Christianity in Early America*. Brekus has also published a collection of Osborn's writings with informative and interesting biographical and historical context titled *Sarah Osborn's Collected Writings*.

7

Loving our Bridegroom: Sarah Jones
Song of Songs 8:1–7

If only I could show everyone
this passionate desire I have for you.
If only I could express it fully,
no matter who was watching me,
without shame or embarrassment.
I long to bring you to my innermost chamber—
this holy sanctuary you have formed within me.
O that I might carry you within me.
I would give you the spiced wine of my love,
this full cup of bliss that we share.[1]

DOES THE TITLE OF this chapter surprise you? It might seem unusual to see Jesus included in a section of a book that focuses on looking outward to minister to others. After all, Jesus is the one who ministers to us! The bride's words above from Song 8, however, should make us pause and reconsider the idea of ministering to Jesus. *Can* we minister to him? *Should* we? And how would we do it?

Ministering to the Lord is a practice established and valued by God himself. Under the old covenant, Aaron and his descendants ministered

---

1. Song 8:1–2a.

to God in the tabernacle as priests while the rest of the tribe of Levi supported and protected them: "Then [David] appointed some of the Levites as ministers before the ark of the LORD, to invoke, to thank, and to praise the LORD, the God of Israel. . . . So David left Asaph and his brothers there before the ark of the covenant of the LORD to minister regularly before the ark as each day required."[2]

Under the new covenant, all believers are called to minister to the Lord, as Peter encourages us in 1 Pet 2:5: "You yourselves like living stones are being built up as a spiritual house, to be a holy priesthood, to offer spiritual sacrifices acceptable to God through Jesus Christ." Even in the eternal kingdom of God, believers will minister to the Lord, as one of the twenty-four elders assures John in Rev 7:15: "Therefore they are before the throne of God, and serve him day and night in his temple; and he who sits on the throne will shelter them with his presence."

But what does it mean to minister to the Lord? We commonly think of ministry as meeting needs—we offer counsel, financial support, or comfort, among other things, to those who are lacking. Jesus, however, does not experience lack. As Ps 24:1a reminds us, "The earth is the LORD's and the fullness thereof," so we do not need to offer him anything tangible.

Instead, when we minister to Jesus, like the Levites of old, we are presenting to him our love, and all the worship, honor, gratitude, and acclaim that accompanies that love. Love is what God wants most passionately from us. As 1 John 4:8 assures us, God *is* love. Jesus adopted the body of a man, came to earth, and suffered and died for our sins just so he could have a people with whom to share his love. As he entreated his disciples before his crucifixion, "As the Father has loved me, so have I loved you. Abide in my love."[3] We are the fulfillment of his greatest desire for a relationship of love.

So important is a ministry of love to Jesus that he does not hesitate to rebuke those who forsake it. In Rev 1:12–17, Jesus stands among seven golden lampstands, blazing out from his person such glory, power, and magnificence that John falls to the ground like a dead man. Jesus then pronounces both judgments and praise upon the seven first-century churches to whom the book of Revelation was sent. His very first words to the very first church, the church at Ephesus, are these:

---

2. 1 Chr 16:4, 37.
3. John 15:9.

> I know your works, your toil and your patient endurance, and how you cannot bear with those who are evil, but have tested those who call themselves apostles and are not, and found them to be false. I know you are enduring patiently and bearing up for my name's sake, and you have not grown weary. But I have this against you, that you have abandoned the love you had at first.[4]

Wow. Despite performing godly deeds, persevering in the faith, testing the spirits, and withstanding adversity for the sake of the gospel, the church at Ephesus is faulted for failing to love Jesus. This is a sobering judgment, and one that reveals the importance of ministering in love to our bridegroom.

Thankfully, our identity as Jesus' bride is the absolute best position from which to minister to Jesus in pure, deep love. Love is, after all, the defining characteristic of marriage. In my own marriage, my husband and I share parenting duties, home responsibilities, leisure activities, and family vacations. These activities, however, are not the heart of our marriage; our love for each other is at the center. Likewise, as a bride of Jesus, serving with him, studying his word, and sharing the good news of his salvation are not at the heart of our relationship. Love is. Thus, love flows to our bridegroom most powerfully from our position as his beloved bride.

As a bonus, we will find our love for Jesus maturing as we minister to him. This maturing happens naturally because to draw near to Jesus in ministering love requires that we value and pursue personal purity. Throughout the Bible, God requires holiness from those who draw near to minister to him. In the Old Testament, God announces strict and explicit instructions for priests to preserve their purity, commanding Aaron, "You are to distinguish between the holy and the common, and between the unclean and the clean, and you are to teach the people of Israel all the statutes that the Lord has spoken to them by Moses."[5]

In the New Testament, after proclaiming that God "has made us sufficient to be ministers of a new covenant," Paul admonishes us that "having this ministry by the mercy of God, we do not lose heart. But we have renounced disgraceful, underhanded ways."[6] Peter, too, after assuring us that we are "a chosen race, a royal priesthood, a holy nation," immediately warns us to "abstain from the passions of the flesh, which wage

---

4. Rev 2:2–4.
5. Lev 10:10–11.
6. 2 Cor 3:6a, 4:1–2a.

war against your soul."[7] James explicitly associates purity with drawing near to God: "Draw near to God, and he will draw near to you. Cleanse your hands, you sinners, and purify your hearts, you double-minded."[8] Ministering in love to Jesus thus matures our love for him by requiring us to become more like him, growing in holiness and self-denial as we draw ever closer to the lover of our souls.

To learn more about how to minister bridal love to Jesus, we will return to the bride in Song of Songs. In chapter 7, the bride and her bridegroom Solomon have been ministering to the people in the villages, but, in chapter 8, a shift occurs in the narrative. The bride turns her attention to her bridegroom, sharing with him how she desires to love him. We do not learn explicit *actions* associated with ministering to Jesus from this passage because the specifics of how each of us ministers to our bridegroom is a personal journey led by the Holy Spirit. We can, however, draw three important conclusions about ministering in love to Jesus from the bride's words to her bridegroom.

THE SECRET PLACE: SONG 8:1

The first reality the bride recognizes about ministering to her bridegroom is that it is done in secret, away from the public eye. Although she and Solomon display their mutual love in the presence of the villagers in chapter 7, she admits in Song 8:1 that she cannot reveal her deepest feelings for him openly like she can with a sibling: "Oh that you were like a brother to me who nursed at my mother's breasts! If I found you outside, I would kiss you, and none would despise me." The fullest expression of her love for her bridegroom is not appropriate for a public setting as it is the fruit of their exclusive, committed relationship.

In marriage, only the married couple themselves know the most intensely personal aspects of their relationship. The ways they express their love, their physical intimacy, their most vulnerable moments—all these are shared only with each other, not the outside world. That is why we are often shocked to hear of divorces among people we thought were happily married. Only a husband and wife know and experience the true depth of their marriage in an authentic, comprehensive way.

---

7. 1 Pet 2:9, 11.
8. Jas 4:8.

As a bride of Jesus, we share our love for him publicly at times when we talk about him with others, testify to his goodness and beauty, worship him corporately, or serve others in his name. However, the deepest expressions of our bridal love for him will only happen in the secret place, the place we share with him alone. We will never be able to fully describe to anyone else the details and depth of the unique relationship we have with our beloved.

This reality has two consequences for us as Jesus' bride. First, ministering bridal love to Jesus will always, in a significant way, be a solitary endeavor. If we are hoping that we can minister our purest, most profound love to our bridegroom consistently with other people, we are mistaken. A commitment to the secret place we share with Jesus is non-negotiable because the most genuine, intimate connection only happens when we are alone with him.

Second, we must accept that ministering bridal love to Jesus will seldom be acknowledged by others. The effort, time, and passion we pour into ministering to our bridegroom will receive few pats on the back from other Christians and understandably so, as it is performed in private. Our motivation to continue to minister to Jesus must come from within ourselves through the grace of the Holy Spirit.

If the solitary nature of ministering to Jesus provokes in your heart a fear of isolation, let me reassure you that Jesus will provide for you select friends who are pursuing him in the same way and can understand your commitment and desire to minister love to your bridegroom. You may have to be intentional in cultivating connections with those who appreciate the importance of ministering to Jesus, but those friends are always available to be found. And we who love Jesus as a bride will bond on a deeply satisfying level because of our shared pursuit of our eternal lover.

VULNERABILITY AND OPENNESS: SONG 8:2

In Song 8:2, the bride acknowledges a second truth about ministering to her beloved—it happens in the place of complete vulnerability and openness. In the bride's words, she desires to bring Solomon into "the house of my mother." The Passion Translation presents the bride as drawing her lover into "my innermost chamber—the holy sanctuary you have formed within me." The "house of my mother" connotes the bride's place of origin, and the "innermost chamber" suggests the most private space in which she dwells. Taken together, these locations suggest that the bride is drawing her bridegroom into the most profound, most intimate part of who she is, her truest self. In this special place, all her pretenses are gone, and she connects with her lover in the most authentic, vulnerable way. She cannot hide any part of herself from the one she has invited into her "innermost chamber."

For us as well, ministering love to our bridegroom requires a commitment to absolute honesty and openness with him because he desires all of us. Jesus' ultimate goal is to possess our whole heart for he has given us his whole heart, holding nothing back. He knows that connecting with us in the most open and vulnerable way possible produces the greatest degree of intimacy. He will never be content until we are fully his, completely open and responsive to him, our heart completely joined with his in perfect bridal love.

Allowing Jesus into the deepest places of our heart can be challenging, however, because when we do so, shame very often rears its ugly head. In light of Jesus' perfection, we may be ashamed of our weaknesses and failings, and this causes us to step back and close ourselves off, pretend to be something we're not, or distract ourselves with other interests. It can be difficult for us to expose ourselves completely to our bridegroom, especially if we have previously experienced rejection, scorn, or judgment from others when we have been vulnerable.

Thankfully, Jesus does not despise our frailties or shortcomings. Instead, he longs to bring us into the place of total exposure to his bridal love so he can heal, restore, and strengthen the parts of us that are broken and hurting. Our position as his cherished bride provides the perfect opportunity for us to reject shame and guilt and embrace vulnerability.

Jesus' unconditional bridal love creates a place of safety and tenderness that invites and enables us to open to him the deepest parts of our heart, regardless of what he finds there. The welcoming, sheltering love of our bridegroom creates an environment in which we can be fully ourselves, unafraid for him to see all of us and touch the parts of us that need healing and restoration. As we are made whole and strong in his love, our connection with him deepens even more. He is perfectly safe, so we can open ourselves to him without fear or shame and enjoy the powerful intimacy that vulnerability creates.

When I started learning to connect intentionally with Jesus as my bridegroom, I was surprised at the unsettling thoughts that started to come up in my mind. Forgotten hurts, unfulfilled dreams, unanswered questions, shameful failings—these memories began to rise in my mind often as I drew closer to Jesus as a bride. I soon realized that the Holy Spirit was reminding me of these experiences because Jesus wanted to deal with them. He was not content for me to suffer the pain associated with these memories, even subconsciously, and he was determined that we would work through them together.

Most of the issues he brought up surprised me; I had buried them so deeply, I didn't even really believe they were still challenging for me. However, as I learned to embrace Jesus' love as a bridegroom, I began to feel safe and accepted enough that I became willing to face these past hurts and disappointments squarely. With great love and tenderness, Jesus led me through processing each of my issues as he healed and restored my heart. My position as his beloved bride gave me the courage to deal with my past and taught me that Jesus is not content unless I am always pursuing complete openness and honesty with him, unafraid to be vulnerable about my areas of greatest weakness, failure, and pain.

Remember that ministering love to Jesus means giving all of yourself to him, even the parts you would rather hide. Your bridegroom's perfect love is in no way diminished by your weaknesses, shortcomings, or even outright resistance. In fact, it is the areas of your greatest frailty and failing that Jesus pursues with the most passion, longing to release you from the pain and shame associated with them. You are free to be completely open and vulnerable as you minister love to your bridegroom Jesus, and you will encounter his accepting, restorative love in return.

LOVE IS ENOUGH: SONG 8:3–4

Third, the bride affirms that a ministry of love to her bridegroom is sufficient as an end in and of itself. In Song 8:3–4, she remarks, "His left hand is under my head, and his right hand embraces me! I adjure you, O daughters of Jerusalem, that you not stir up or awaken love until it pleases." The bride is completely at peace in her lover's embrace. Nothing else is needed. The Passion Translation ends verse three with the bride's words, "We are at rest in this love." The bride knows the value of loving her bridegroom, and she does not seek anything else outside of it. In addition, she will not permit others to disturb her time with her lover.

As Jesus' bride, we also must be firmly established in our conviction that ministering love to our bridegroom is a valid ministry and is enough. It is enough for Jesus, and it is enough for us. Nothing else is needed to "validate" the ministry of loving Jesus.

Our confidence in the value of loving Jesus is important in light of two temptations that can assail us as we minister to our bridegroom. First, we may be tempted to view the ministry of expressing love to Jesus in the secret place as not quite "real" ministry at the level of serving, teaching, counseling, and sharing the gospel. We may worry that spending time loving Jesus is selfish or immature or not as valid as spiritual works that bless people. We may even feel pressured to reduce our time of ministry to Jesus so that we can spend more time ministering to people.

This is a very serious mistake. Ministering to our beloved, the treasure of heaven, is just as valid as any other ministry. In the Old Testament, King David employed thousands of singers and musicians to minister to God in the temple unceasingly throughout the day and night.[9] In the New Testament, the prophetess Anna spent her long life ministering continually to the Lord, never leaving the temple in Jerusalem.[10] We should never give in to pressure to reduce our time expressing love to our bridegroom in order to engage in other ministries.

The second temptation we may encounter is to subconsciously attempt to leverage ministry to Jesus as a way to produce blessings in other areas of our lives. For example, we may believe that if we spend time ministering to Jesus, he will be more likely to answer our prayers or bless our other ministries with fruitfulness. If I'm being honest, I make this same mistake in my own marriage, assuming my husband will be more willing to drag the trash cans down to the street for pickup if I remind him that I just made dinner. But just as my husband deserves better treatment, so does our bridegroom Jesus. Ministry to our beloved should never be viewed as a means to generate his blessings or approval. He loves us and loves to bless us. We don't need to try to curry his favor by offering our love.

Unquestionably, the supreme worthiness of our bridegroom means that loving him is enough. Consider how Paul presents Jesus in Col 1:15–20:

> He is the image of the invisible God, the firstborn of all creation. For by him all things were created, in heaven and on earth, visible and invisible, whether thrones or dominions or rulers or

---

9. See 1 Chr 6:31–47; 15–16; 23:1–5; 25.
10. Luke 2:36–38.

authorities—all things were created through him and for him. And he is before all things, and in him all things hold together. And he is the head of the body, the church. He is the beginning, the firstborn from the dead, that in everything he might be preeminent. For in him all the fullness of God was pleased to dwell, and through him to reconcile to himself all things, whether on earth or in heaven, making peace by the blood of his cross.

This is not someone who should be shortchanged so we can minister elsewhere or who should be viewed as valuable only when we see blessings in other endeavors. No, Jesus is absolutely priceless and worthy of our ministry of love to him. In fact, ministering to Jesus just might be the most important ministry we do in our time on earth! And our position as his bride perfectly facilitates our expression of this ministry of love. We never need to apologize for time and energy spent in ministering to our beloved. He is worthy of absolutely all that we can give him.

A COMPLETE BRIDE: SONG 8:5A

The result of the bride's ministry of love to her bridegroom is revealed in verse five of the chapter. The friends of the bride make an observation about her in the form of a question: "Who is that coming up from the wilderness, leaning on her beloved?"

This description calls to mind a similar one made of Solomon as he arrives for the marriage ceremony in chapter 3: "Who is this coming up from the wilderness like a column of smoke, perfumed with myrrh and incense made from all the spices of the merchant?"[11] Before their wedding, Solomon emerges from the wilderness, fragrant with myrrh, a burial spice, and incense made from all the other spices that can be purchased. His splendor, power, and majesty are revealed as well as his victory over the wilderness.

Now, after ministering to her bridegroom, the bride herself arises from the wilderness, leaning on her lover. What an incredible picture of how far the bride has come in her relationship with Solomon! Through her ministry of love, she has learned to fully trust and lean on her bridegroom and his strength, enabling her to conquer the wilderness just as he did.

11. Song 3:6 (NIV).

The description of the bride emerging from the wilderness supported by her bridegroom is not the only statement in this passage that reminds us of earlier moments in the narrative. In previous verses, we have read phrases regarding public affection, the bride's mother's house, spiced wine, resting in each other's arms, and the admonition not to disturb love before it is ready.[12] The fact that the bride refers back to these previous moments in her relationship with Solomon at this point in the narrative further attests to how her love for him has matured. Many of their shared moments have reached a culmination in this passage in which she ministers love to him as a complete, secure bride.

As Jesus' cherished bridal partner, we can receive this picture of the bride as also being true of us. We are made complete and secure in our bridegroom as we minister to him, and our love for him matures as we embrace him fully, leaning on him and his perfect strength.

The closing section of the passage in Song of Songs reveals for us two additional keys in understanding and embracing our ministry of love to Jesus. In the powerful words spoken by Solomon, we discover both the source and the nature of their mutual bridal love.

THE SOURCE OF LOVE: SONG 8:5B-6A

With his opening words in this passage, King Solomon shares a surprising bit of information with his bride: "Under the apple tree I awakened you. There your mother was in labor with you; there she who bore you was in labor." Wait, what? The bride just wished earlier in the passage that she could bring her beloved into her mother's house, desiring to show him her love in the place of her origin. But, apparently, her bridegroom has already been to this most private place. In fact, *he* awakened *her* while in her mother's house! What does this startling disclosure mean?

The bride learns an important lesson from her bridegroom's words: the source of the love she releases in ministry to him is his own perfect love for her. He was the one who found her under the apple tree, and he was the one who roused her. Just as he declared his bride to be a locked garden fed and sustained by his living water within her in his wedding vows in Song 4:12–15, so he now declares that he himself initiated their bridal relationship by awakening her while she was still in her mother's house, blissfully unaware of his existence and certainly not troubling

---

12. See Song 2:6, 7; 3:4, 5; 7:9, 12.

herself to discover or search for him. He originated their love, igniting in her heart the spark of passion that would grow and intensify, ultimately driving her to seek him and find him, content only when she became his spouse, his beloved bride that leans upon him to conquer the wilderness. Their bridal love affair was his idea all along, and she can feel his joy and satisfaction as he recalls his initiation of their courtship.

We, too, should recognize that the source of the love with which we minister to Jesus is his everlasting love for us. When we draw near to our bridegroom and release our love to him, we are not ministering to him out of a love that we ourselves produce. Instead, we are stepping into the flow of his eternal love that pours into us, through us, and back into his own heart. We are loving Jesus with his own perfect love, a love that is worthy of him and delights him. Our ministry of love to our bridegroom is created and sustained by our beloved himself!

This realization should stir many emotions in us. Thankfulness, certainly, for such a precious gift. Relief that we do not have to personally produce love worthy of our ravishing bridegroom. And excitement at the thought of stepping into the flow of an eternal love so magnificent it carries along with it any and all who desire to join themselves to Jesus, its true source. What a glorious ministry we participate in through the kindness and generosity of our lover!

However, although the bride in Song of Songs is not the source of the love she has for Solomon, she does have a crucial role to play in her ministry to him. She must choose to step into and embrace the current of his everlasting love that flows between them. Notice Solomon's request in his very next words: "Set me as a seal upon your heart, as a seal upon your arm."[13] Solomon desires that his bride "seal" herself with his love.

Seals enclose and protect something, like a letter, a legal record, or the contents of a container. Seals are also used to identify and represent entities, like the official seal of a university, a state, or a government office. Lastly, seals can be decorative, adding artistry and color. Solomon is asking his bride to willingly join him in the river of his eternal love, sealing herself with a love that will protect and enclose her, display her identity as his bride, and add beauty and loveliness to her life.

When we choose to minister to Jesus, we are electing to step into his marvelous love, willingly and permanently sealing ourselves as his cherished bride. We are secure and protected in his love, rejoicing in our

---

13. Song 6a.

identity as his bride and delighting in the joy he adds to our life. Our ministry to Jesus is thus our choice to participate in the overflow of the life-giving, everlasting love of our eternal bridegroom.

THE NATURE OF LOVE: SONG 8:6B-7

In Song 8:6b–7, the bridegroom takes time to describe to the bride the nature of the love she has entered into, identifying four characteristics. Some of the metaphors the bridegroom uses to illustrate his love are surprising, yet they offer incredibly powerful and poignant pictures of the love he has for his beloved partner.

The first trait of the bridegroom's eternal love is that it is unrelenting. In Song 8:6, the bridegroom declares, "Love is strong as death, jealousy is fierce as the grave." The word *jealousy* in this verse can also be translated as *ardor*, which is another word for passion.[14] Why would the bridegroom liken his tender, delightful love to the saddening, unsettling reality of death? Surely there was a more pleasant comparison he could have made!

Truth be told, though, nothing is as unrelenting as death. Who escapes its grip? Have you ever known anyone to cheat death, to come back from the finality of the grave? Wealth, intelligence, power, beauty, youth, strength—none of these has ever saved even one person from eventual demise. Death is the most certain, unyielding reality on earth. Solomon desires that his bride know that his love is as unrelenting and certain as death itself.

Second, the bridegroom announces that his love is as all-consuming as fire—specifically, the fire of God. In verse 6b, he assures the bride that "its flashes are flashes of fire, the very flame of the LORD." The New International Version translates the statement as "it burns like blazing fire, like a mighty flame."

Living in Southern California, I understand the all-consuming nature of fire and how its intense heat can literally incinerate everything it encounters. Several years ago, a terribly destructive fire tore through the mountainous region near the university at which I teach. Driving through the burned-over canyon area soon after, I was stunned to see the complete destruction of literally everything that had been in the path of the fire. The entire area looked like the surface of the moon—the

---

14. ESV text note.

mountainsides completely and utterly bare, with only a handful of blackened tree stumps scattered throughout and a few grotesquely melted road signs. Without a doubt, fire is all-consuming.

But while fire destroys all that it encounters, it also refines and purifies, literally bringing beauty from ashes. When fire burns through metals such as gold or silver, impurities are removed and the metal is refined. Similarly, after the fire in our region, we experienced a spring super bloom—a rare explosion of colorful wildflowers so intense it could be seen from space. Ironically, the destructive wildfires had provided the first condition necessary for the super bloom by awakening seeds and removing the plant life that competed with the flowers for sunlight.

In Song of Songs, Solomon's love for his bride consumes her, drawing all of her into his passionate desire. But it also purifies her, like the fire of a holy God, making her more like her bridegroom and more fully herself. The fire of Solomon's love burns through her heart like "the very flame of the Lord."

Third, the bridegroom's love is indestructible. Notice the hyperbole in his words in verse 7a: "Many waters cannot quench love, neither can floods drown it." Flood waters are an unstoppable force of nature that can destroy property, wash away roads, and drown people and animals who get caught in the current. Flood waters can certainly put out a fire. In fact, water is what firefighters used to eventually extinguish the powerful fire that tore through the region surrounding my university.

However, the bridegroom's passionate fire of love cannot be quenched even by many rivers. What kind of fiery love can survive a flood? The indestructible kind. Solomon's love for his bride is strong enough to withstand anything that comes against it, even its absolute nemesis.

Finally, the love of Solomon is priceless. As he assures his bride in verse 7b, "If a man offered for love all the wealth of his house, he would be utterly despised." Love cannot be bought, as many parents ruefully discover when the costly Christmas presents lie discarded in the corner and the boxes they came in become the favorites playthings. Love can only be given, freely and willingly, without expectation of return. The bridegroom's perfect love is priceless, yet, wonder of wonders, it has been given in all its fullness to the bride. She is the joyful recipient of the most valuable treasure in the universe.

Unrelenting, all-consuming, indestructible, priceless—this is the love of the bridegroom in Song of Songs for his beloved bride. Can we even imagine such a love? Can we truly wrap our minds around a fiery passion that never relents, completely consumes and purifies, can never be destroyed, and is beyond all value?

Of course we can't. Understanding such a love is not humanly possible. Yet this is the love of our bridegroom Jesus, and when we minister in love to him, we step into the flow of this love which pours out of our beloved, into our own heart, and back into his heart. We exist with him in the fire of his unrelenting, all-consuming, indestructible, priceless love.

What does it look and feel like to experience this passionate bridal love of Jesus as we minister to him? You have probably already encountered Jesus' overwhelming love in your own ministry to him, but sometimes we learn even more from examples such as Sarah Jones, an eighteenth-century Virginia Methodist who was consumed with loving Jesus. Her letters and journal reveal her experiences with Jesus' love as she pours out her ministry to him. I believe Jones will serve as an instructive, inspiring illustration of a bride completely devoted to ministering to her bridegroom within the perfect, eternal love that flows from his own heart.

THE PRIVILEGED, COMPLICATED LIFE OF SARAH JONES

Sarah Jones (1753?–94) was destined for an advantaged and securely conventional upper-class life in Mecklenburg County, Virginia. Born into an established family, married to a wealthy planter who owned more than 1,300 acres,[15] mother of both sons and daughters, Jones was perfectly poised to spend her days serenely enjoying the security, status, and privilege that her position as a southern plantation mistress offered. But Jesus had other ideas. A powerful revival among the new and somewhat radical Methodist denomination swept through Jones's region in 1775–76, and Jones was probably converted in its wake.[16] Suddenly, Sarah Jones's comfortable, predictable life among the Virginia aristocracy became complicated.

Jones enthusiastically embraced her new life with Jesus, using her significant resources for the kingdom of God. Becoming a lay leader in the fast-growing Methodist movement in Virginia, she counseled those seeking spiritual advice, supported and hosted traveling Methodist

15. Grasso, *Skepticism*, 68.
16. Grasso, *Skepticism*, 68.

preachers, visited the sick and the poor, exhorted her local congregation, and attended and spoke at regional Methodist Quarterly meetings.[17] Through her commitment to letter-writing, Jones vastly expanded her circle of influence, communicating with Methodist Christians and ministers throughout the area, becoming known for her passion, piety, and leadership. When she died in 1794, the Rev. Francis Asbury, one of the first two bishops of the Methodist denomination in America, preached her funeral sermon, years later identifying Jones as a one of "those female *flames*, and almost martyrs for Jesus."[18]

In addition to her significant public ministry and service, Jones's commitment to ministering to her bridegroom in private devotions was also legendary. For hours each day, she would pray somewhere on her property, and during the night, she would seek Jesus in her prayer room. She often called prayer her "one employment,"[19] despite her many responsibilities at home and among the Methodists. In a letter to her close friend the Rev. Jeremiah Minter (1766–1829), Jones recounts an evening experience of prayer:

> Here I set in an upper chamber with my sparkling Jesus by. All nature is shrouded with the curtain of the night, and all my veins beat with earnest, eager, real life. While others sleep, I feel on real stretch for heaven. Oh, what I feel! I cannot hold my peace.... I looked away toward my Father's house by an eye of renewed faith and saw the blazing doors opened and the Son of God cleaving the starry plains.[20]

Jones enthusiastically adopted Paul's admonition in 1 Thess 5:17 to "pray without ceasing" as a personal goal. In her journal for March 5, 1792, she writes, "Here I renew my vows to consecrate my days and nights and

---

17. Francis Asbury (1745–1816), one of the first two bishops of the American Methodist church, records in his journal Jones's contribution to one of the quarterly meetings in 1786: "We had a gracious time at quarterly meeting, especially at the sacrament: the words of our excellent sister Jones, both in speaking and in prayer, were sweetly and powerfully felt." Asbury, *Journal: 1771 to 1793*, 1008.

18. Asbury, *Journal: 1794 to 1816*, 669. Asbury's journal entry is from 1802, and the italics are his.

19. See, for example, Jones's journal entries for March 13, March 30, April 16, April 27, May 15, May 16, June 7, June 27, July 6, and July 18, 1792 (Jones, Diary). Jones's journal is used with permission from the Special Collections Research Center, William & Mary Libraries, and I have used the transcription of Jones's journal by Chad Sandford, with permission and with limited silent modifications for the reader.

20. Jones, *Devout Letters*, 41–42.

hours to God, begging in sight of angels (I feel it) for strength renewed, for wisdom's eye with prudent hands to steer aright, advance in grace, and learn the heavenly art more full of walking close to God."[21] Jones calls spending time with God her "greatest delight on earth."[22]

Such single-minded passion and devotion to Jesus was bound to bring Jones into conflict with both her family and the aristocratic plantation society of which she was a member. Her husband was the first to challenge Jones, as he did not particularly approve of her religious enthusiasm nor her association with the mostly lower-class Methodists. Reported to be "a man of violent passions and a most ungovernable temper" who "cherished the most bitter and inveterate prejudice against the Methodists," Jones's husband once forbade her from attending the preaching of a traveling Methodist minister and threatened to shoot her when she returned home if she went. But Jones believed God wanted her to attend the meeting and thus went despite the threats. Upon her arrival back home, Jones faced her armed husband calmly and offered a gentle threat of her own with the words, "My dear, if you take my life, you must obtain leave of my heavenly Spouse," quietly removing the weapon from his hand.[23]

According to Jones's journal, few in her immediate family were Christians, and they often criticized both the hours she spent in prayer and her commitment to attend religious meetings. One journal entry records that her "heart felt like splitting" at the opposition she encounters when she desires to attend church.[24] Her husband's rule that their children dress in the elaborate fashion of upper-class society distressed her because she wished they could dress more simply.[25] She often grieved for her adult children who did not follow Jesus. In a journal entry for July 11, 1792, Jones notes that when she visits her married daughter's beautiful estate, she wishes fervently that her daughter, and all her children, would love God.

---

21. Note also this excerpt from Jones's journal for June 27, 1792: "Christ is the altar of my heart, which sanctifies the gift, and I find acceptance in the Beloved. My heart is continually without ceasing upon the patrol, searching every secret corner of the written word, where are hid the riches for more knowledge and wisdom and that fear of the Lord, all the day long, every day, as shall be my employment." Jones, Diary.
22. Jones, Diary, June 28, 1792.
23. Ware, *Sketches*, 167–69.
24. Jones, Diary, June 30, 1792.
25. Jones, *Devout Letters*, 87–88.

The elite society to which Jones belonged also challenged her desire to pursue Jesus singlemindedly. Jones chafed against the custom of social visiting, believing it a waste of time and preferring to spend her hours in prayer and ministry rather than mingling with "the great ones of the earth," as she called them.[26] Even when fulfilling her social obligations, her mind was on her bridegroom: "I dined with that <u>harsh</u>-sounding title of gentlemen and ladies. Had not much place to speak of Jesus, which was grievous."[27]

Jones's passionate public worship was sometimes a bit more expressive than that of her more conventional neighbors: "Got safe to meeting, but, alas, a crowded house appeared hard and insensible. Lord, what is man—a grave, a ditch of sorrow, without you. The preacher preached a good sermon, my heart burned in public prayer while my courage in a congregation felt too great to tell. Great ones by, but Jesus was my <u>mark</u>."[28] At times, even other Methodists criticized her religious zeal. As she writes to her cousin, Methodist minister William Spencer (b. 1764), "Those who cannot endure sound doctrine of self-denial and earnest, constant wrestling [in prayer] cry out, 'This woman is going too far.'"[29]

But what caused Jones the most internal anguish and conflict with both her family and her society was the institution of slavery. Jones's husband had seventy or eighty enslaved persons on his property at one point in his life,[30] but Jones strongly believed the practice to be inhuman and inconsistent with Christianity. She laments in her journal for March 24, 1792, "Although I live with the heavy burden, I do not consent to it. I abhor it; I would flee from it as from the face of deadly serpents."

She believed God's judgment would come on the South because of slavery: "My mind is as solemn almost as death, my soul is clothed with a profound sense of a present, awful, blazing Deity, pointing in glittering streams of keen justice—blood, blood, I will avenge, mine arm shall get victory. Bend, oh nations, bow, oh Virginia, loose the captives, let the mangled objects go, or my sword shall wreak your bowels and be drunk with my fury."[31] Although Jones's husband did eventually become

---

26. See Jones, *Devout Letters*, 23, for Jones's comments on visiting.
27. Jones, Diary, April 2, 1792.
28. Jones, Diary, July 9, 1792.
29. Jones, *Devout Letters*, 59.
30. Grasso, *Skepticism*, 68.
31. Jones, *Devout Letters*, 1.

a Methodist himself, he never consented during Jones's lifetime to release his enslaved workers.[32]

The advantages and resources that Sarah Jones enjoyed in many ways enabled her ministry to both Jesus and others. However, those same privileges also burdened her with familial and societal expectations that caused her much grief and created many obstacles for her pursuit of God. On a daily basis, Jones had to navigate both the privileges and the challenges of her life as a bride of Jesus.

A WRITING LIFE

Modern Christians are blessed that Sarah Jones decided to record and share her life and spiritual experiences through her journals and letters. Although we have only one of her journals extant, which covers the final seventeen months of her life, and one collection of her letters, published ten years after her death in 1804 by her friend Jeremiah Minter, these writings offer us an honest, intimate look into Jones's life with Jesus.

Jones's writing is truly beautiful: she uses descriptive metaphors easily and powerfully, expresses emotion authentically and poignantly, and communicates a passion for God that is inspiring. Perhaps she saw herself as completing the testimony to Jesus' goodness and glory begun by the bride in Song of Songs, for she notes in her journal on November 17, 1792, "I have never written as much as I think of [Jesus'] charity yet, but his smiles are soft, [he] wears the face of a king, and his garments smell of myrrh. There is much to be said of him. The spouse in Song of Songs has not opened all. There is yet something left which only the heart can utter and immortality declare."

Jones's writing is notable for its depth of personal detail and undisguised zeal for her bridegroom that is honestly seldom seen in print. She describes her overwhelming encounters with his love, her unbearable pain at being separated from him, her unquenchable desire to grow in holiness, and her lack of patience with believers who are content with a half-hearted spiritual commitment. Clearly evident in her writings is Jones's keen desire to use every literary device at her disposal to convey to the world her experiences with her beloved. Word pictures, metaphors, detailed descriptions, biblical references and allusions, original poems,

---

32. Initially, the Methodist denomination took a stand against slavery on biblical grounds, but that stance weakened as the institution grew in popularity in America.

excerpts of hymns, exclamation points, and underscores—Jones employs all of these and more to share what Jesus means to her.

And she succeeds in many ways. Her letters were widely read by other Methodists for inspiration and instruction, and her journals were probably also shared. Even today, her words have power. One student in my American literature class decided to use some of Jones's words in her own wedding vows!

But while Jones accomplishes much with her pen as she shares about Jesus, she also admits the limits of human words to express our deepest experiences of ministering to our bridegroom. As she complains to Minter in a letter dated July 21, 1790, "What do words signify or figures mean or nature's voice with all terrestrial things possess to show my pleasures this morning? They faint, grow dumb, and expressive silence points the task beyond their skill. Their language droops; they borrow all that's grand or eloquent below the sun, but all is but a shadow, pale and glimmering."[33] More than any other writer in this book, Jones exhibits the ability to use language to "borrow all that's grand or eloquent below the sun" to write of her beloved, but even she ultimately fails to adequately express more than just a "shadow, pale and glimmering," of what she experiences in her encounters. As she records in her journal entry for May 4, 1792, "My heart felt what my hand could never write until immortal."

SARAH JONES'S MINISTRY OF PLEASURE AND PAIN

Sarah Jones's writings highlight for us one final reality of ministering to Jesus as his bride: such ministry is often accompanied by a bewildering combination of both pleasure and pain. Have you ever noticed that the more you experience of Jesus, the more you want of him? It is a paradoxical truth that the same encounter with our bridegroom that blesses and fulfills us, simultaneously arouses within our hearts even greater desire for him, creating almost as much dissatisfaction as it does satisfaction! Unlike physical demands such as hunger or fatigue, which can be satisfied by food or rest, longing for Jesus seems to increase the more it is fulfilled. Why is this so?

God created the human heart to be in perfect union with Jesus through the power of the Holy Spirit to the Father's glory. This is our eternal purpose, which will be fully accomplished when we wed our

---

33. Jones, *Devout Letters*, 28–29.

bridegroom at the end of time. As the ultimate goal of our lives, Jesus does not simply fulfill a desire or meet a need we have—he completes us, and we find our true life in him. As Luke quotes in Acts 17:28a, "In him we live and move and have our being."

Thus, as we minister in love to Jesus as his bride on this earth, we paradoxically experience both the profound, satisfying pleasure of his presence *and* the desperate, unsatisfied pain of his absence. At the exact moment we are basking in Jesus' perfect love, our hearts are simultaneously being ignited to desire even more of that love, unceasingly and instinctively longing for the day when our mutual love with him is made perfect and complete. As a bride of Jesus, we exist in a crucible of potent, comingling pleasure and pain as we minister to our captivating bridegroom.

Sarah Jones understood and experienced this reality as she ministered in love to Jesus. Her writings are full of what in one place she calls "paradisiacal pleasure and heartbroken pain."[34] In a journal entry for May 5, 1792, Jones writes,

> About 12 [pm], I walked afar to a most lovely retreat all adorned with thick shades while Jesus with his skillful touch drew my impassioned heart to a mighty flame. Oh, my flowing eyes looked around as if my heart would burst in two, crying, oh heaven, heaven, how can I bear it, how can I bear this soul drawn out? What pangs to see Jesus! Oh, I cried, painful pleasure and love, hope, and joy.

In one short journal entry for April 24, 1792, Jones calls herself a "woman that knows sorrow, well acquainted with grief,"[35] yet she ends the entry just sentences later with the pronouncement that she is "amazing[ly] happy." The paradox for Jones occurs, she writes, because "Jesus is always very near me, but he feeds me with strong meat and tears for my drink."[36] In her writings, Jones reveals both the exquisite pleasure and heartbreaking pain experienced by those of us who minister to Jesus as his bride as we await the final consummation of our shared love.

I hope you enjoy reading Sarah Jones. She is one of my personal favorites from the early American period, a woman who was unashamed

---

34. Jones, Diary, April 27, 1792.
35. Jones is referencing Isa 53:3.
36. Jones references Ps 42:3: "My tears have been my meat day and night, while they continually say unto me, Where is thy God?" (KJV).

of her love for her bridegroom and who was relentlessly committed to ministering bridal love to him.

JOURNAL: SARAH JONES'S JOURNAL[37]

Tuesday, March 6, 1792

"Ask and you shall have, seek and you shall find, knock and it shall be opened to you."[38] These words were dropped into my ear as Jesus awoke me. I took hold of them and find enough to confound the world, unbelief, flesh, and devil. If there were ten thousand times ten thousand worlds of beggars, and [they] would only all believe those unchanging words, they might be kings and priests and heirs of heaven. Jesus Christ would not be [challenged] to supply every want and fill us all. Oh, deep words, *fill us all*. Christ is a well of life, but who in heaven or on earth can tell how deep it is.

Oh, what a Fair One, what a Lovely One, what an Only One is my Beloved. If all the worlds of paradises like the garden of Eden were all in one—trees and flowers and smells and colors, all tastes, all joys, all sweetness, all loveliness therein—what would that be when the wonder of heaven and my soul, my matchless Almighty-to-Save Jesus, my lovely Friend, is only spoken of and held up? His beauty and glory have almost killed me this day as well as for several of late.

Oh, could I, oh, could I let my heart be seen. Oh, believe me, my love to Jesus and his burning flaming nearness truly keeps my feeble trembling body on the brink of eternity. I can just bear the insufferable weight of crushing glory. I am chained and fettered with love....

May I not say my every moment is employed to meet God. Never was a soul so hurried for gold as mine for holiness. I believe it is my one employ. I thought once today of resisting the power a little to recover my strength in a

---

37. Selections are from Jones, Diary.

38. Matt 7:7. Jones references Bible passages almost constantly in her writing; I will identify the primary ones.

distant valley as I gazed in heaven, but, oh, I refused, thinking, "Let me die if Jesus will."

Oh, sweet pain, living death. Finding my feeble body unable to walk out, had a horse got and rode out about the fields to meet and converse with God. It appeared as if heaven was as present as earth in the open vision of Jesus, with whom I conversed with flowing tears and assured hope he heard my every breath. I have great trials, but tribulation has worked patience. Great self-denial and resolve in late [spiritual] exercise.

Wednesday, March 7, 1792

"To live is Christ and to die is gain."[39] Very early, faint in the arms of Jesus in the garden where the return of spring and harmony of birds awoke all my quickened powers. I am now after breakfast in a silent chamber, trembling with the infinite weight of falling glory as by ten thousand bullets shot at once, they meet my heart from Jesus' bow. My faith is next to sight; with boldness I ask, assured to receive, and from that rich ocean I hourly live. There are but few that will believe, I fear.

How overwhelmed I am in the sea of Jesus' love. I really don't feel as I can bear much more without bursting my chains and hurling them aside and seeing Jesus as he is. A river of God's untold love from bank to bank has flowed over my soul. How do you think Christ's breathing is just as he pronounces you his fair one[40] and kisses you with the kisses of his mouth?[41] His love, I see, is so kingly, he will not abide a rival, but must have a throne all alone in the soul. . . .

Friday, April 27, 1792

No daring hand nor human pen can paint my joys in God. The fragrant rosy morn perfumes the opening day. I

---

39. Phil 1:21.
40. Song 2:10, 13.
41. Song 1:2.

meet her smiles in haste to cry and watch and pray. Long wrestling opened heaven and spouts of glory poured while swelling fountains full overflowed; the healing virtue rested.

I fasted and spent much of the morning in devotion, but I met with a cruel spear of hard reproach for my retirement [to pray] and dedication. My enemies would daily swallow me up for they be many that fight against my soul. When I am afraid, I cried to the Lord when my heart is overwhelmed; he leads me to a rock that is higher than I.[42] My God performs all things for me; he shall send from heaven and save me from their cruelty for my soul dwells among lions and their tongues are sharp swords.[43]

I keep very patient—at length, walked away to open my burning heart, which almost killed me at the awfulness of realities. I thought much of getting some friend to tell my intricate hidden grief to, but concluded it would be better born in silent death. None, no, not one, knows my acute troubles but God, who counts my groans and puts my tears in his bottle.[44] In God have I put my trust; I will not be afraid what man can do to me.[45]

I know Satan hates my praying breath, but it shall kindle heaps of fire on my adversaries.[46] My work is prayer. I could hardly live near one hour. At 12 [pm], I held down my head on my hands and let the trickling, streaming tears fall on the ground. I said but little; my strength was weakness, but, ah, when I looked so moving at Jesus and asked him how could his beautiful eyes bear my agony, how soft he answered.

I am yet in silent glory and paradisiacal pleasure and heart-broken pain. A riddle, yes—pain and pleasure. Oh, how I want to see Jesus. Oh, Lord Christ, show me, show me more, more, more of your glory. Poor me, when shall I rest? Did not fail to agonize until after ten. I am bound to continue faithful.

---

42. Ps 61:2b.
43. Ps 57:4.
44. Ps 56:8.
45. Ps 56:4.
46. Rom 12:20.

Sunday, May 12, 1792

Early arose and trimmed my lamp, went out, and met the Bridegroom.[47] Infinite pleasures surrounded me, and my heart glowed with the vivifying flame. Boundless glories overwhelm my soul; the new-born light was crowned with blessings bright, while Jesus drew the veil from his dear face and poured celestial beauty down in soft variety and melting charms divine, while I lifted up my voice and sang. Oh, angels, help me sing and sound his praise abroad. Delight crowned my song.

Thursday, July 5, 1792

I arose up this morning to open the door to my Beloved, and my hands dripped with myrrh and my fingers with sweet-smelling myrrh upon the handles of the lock. I opened to my Beloved, and he was not gone, but smiled with beauty.[48] His cheeks were as rows of jewels, his neck with chains of gold appeared,[49] while, solidly charmed, I sprang into his arms and his name poured out as ointment,[50] and his lips dripped as the honeycomb. Honey and milk were under his tongue, and the smell of his garments were as the flowery field.[51] I felt my body made his temple[52] and springing wonders roll anew.

I found the sacred path of holiness still narrow[53] and an absolute necessity for fortitude to run in God's commandments, keep on resignation, and to bear every repeated temptation to discouragement. This is a season of conflict, the hour of temptation, but I find Jesus the new room which at 12 o'clock I entered through faith and agony and dressed all in the needlework of patience.

47. A reference to Matt 25:1–13.
48. Song 5:4–6a.
49. Probably a reference to Song 4:3–4.
50. Song 1:3.
51. Song 4:11.
52. 1 Cor 6:19.
53. Matt 7:14.

Shining with brilliant tears and love, [Jesus] drove my sorrows away and showed me the gates of the city where the King and his people were waiting. I poured out my soul in begging to be ready to go with the Lamb to the marriage.[54] Oh, what sobs and flowing reasons run through my swimming eyes and cut a certain passage above the azure skies. I lodged my spirit, crying close by the ear of God and pointing him to Jesus, who showed his streaming blood. Great things I saw and believed.

Oh, there is a temple in the tabernacle of my testimony where I hope Jesus is seated and keeps the door without a rival. I have got the Morning Star,[55] therefore it is always morning and never night with me. He shines with unspeakable brightness upon me, and I have a peaceable dominion in his favor.

Oh, that all had within mercy's reach. Oh, may a sense of these inestimable blessings produce an increasing conformity to all God's will and a steady attachment to the precepts. My [interaction] with the eternal world and heaven in Jesus' company in a long evening visit defeat altogether a description, and [I was] until after ten o'clock in the bright union of Father, Son, and Spirit, walking in the solitary moonshine in the still, deep-running channel of love, never ceasing. Happy for me that prayer was appointed and pointed to me.

LETTERS: DEVOUT LETTERS; OR, LETTERS SPIRITUAL AND FRIENDLY[56]

To Jeremiah Minter, Minister of the Gospel

My tender brother,[57]

---

54. Rev 19:7–9.
55. Rev 22:16.
56. Selections are from Jones, *Devout Letters*, 39–40, 57–59, 60–62.
57. Jones uses "brother" and "sister" to refer to fellow Christians, not biological siblings.

Just from a throne of grace. In an hour of acute agony, in vehemence of extreme desire for more of God, I plunged in a sea of deep self-abasement and self-abhorrence, and groan the Spirit's speechless prayer for the deepest measure of profound humility in preference to any grace in heaven.

Oh, my brother, I cried repeatedly in a bright cloud of spicy odors, where sleeps my gratitude? In what remote corner of my breast has gratitude reclined her useful head? Why am I not all devotion, every moment a scene of praise to my adorable, matchless, shining, starry Jesus? Awake, awake, gratitude, for God is pleased in bounty to distress you; awake, gratitude, awake, while I call for you!

What course shall I take to extol my lofty and loveliest, my fairest, marvelous, well-beloved Lord Jesus? I am at my wit's end how to have his name made great. Blessed are they who will help me in this arduous, delightful work of praise.

May I challenge time that holds me and my beloved Jesus asunder and cry to him, "Come over the mountains at one stride and fold up the heavens like an old cloak, and shovel time, days, and months out of the way, and make ready in haste the Lamb's wife," for his absence from his church here is as a mountain of iron upon my breast. . . . I long, I thirst to see the long day and high sun of millennial love appear. . . .

Let us learn his name—what is it? The scripture says his name is a well of living water, a well of life, a wedding garment, Shiloh, a heart, a stone cut out of the mountain, the Pascal Lamb, rain and showers, an apple tree, a bundle of myrrh, a cluster of camphire,[58] fuller's soap, a purging fire, a ladder, a rose, a lily, the desire of nations, the door of the sheep, the Ancient of Days, God's Beloved, the bread of life, a branch, the law, the end of the law, a light, a great light, etc., he is the finisher of faith—this makes my heart glad. He is the head of all power, the head of the church, the lion of Judah, and the Amen.

Oh, how am I buried in wonder, swallowed up in ecstatic joy and gladness, to think his name is ointment for every sore, for every complaint, for all my infirmities, for he bears my sickness and weakness[59] and the iniquities of my holiest

---

58. Song 1:14 (KJV).
59. Isa 53:4–5.

things, or I could not see GOD, that composition of bright HOLINESS.

To William Spencer, Minister of the Gospel[60]

January 1, 1790
My very dear brother,

I am just from a throne of grace where I felt such strong and powerful effusion of the Holy Ghost flowing through all my life, and the Angel of the Lord, on whose flaming countenance shone benignity and love, darted such blazes through my soul as sharpened daggers, I felt faint, while rolling tears streamed in sight of heaven. Broad day opened all around while Trees of Life dropped their delicious melons. The fertile soil became a paradise, a garden of sweets, a seat of high felicity, more delightful than rose buds in June.

My dear brother, I love Jesus so much I can [barely] live upon the earth. Oh, he more than draws nigh, and the effulgent beams of his brightness have overcome me. I can't open my eyes [without seeing] the fullness of him who fills all things. I burn, I melt, I blaze, I sicken, all faint with love divine.

Oh, what a heaven, what a heaven I live in; not for one day only, but daily. Celestial fruit on earthly ground and glory more than half-blown I gather.[61] God knows I am happy. Oh, Lord, what shall I render? What shall I bring?[62] I feel I am little, little, less than little, nothing, and Christ is all in all. Oh, had I a hundred hands and tongues, I could never tell what a complete heaven I dwell in.

I pray without ceasing.[63] Walking, standing, sitting, lying down, rising up, eating, drinking, I pray, besides going in private many times a day. And I work on my knees, sometimes,

---

60. William Spencer was Jones's cousin and a Methodist minister. Grasso, *Skepticism*, 79.

61. This may be a reference to a hymn by Isaac Watts, "Come, we that love the Lord," from Book II, Hymn 30, of Watts's *Hymns and Spiritual Songs* (London, 1707).

62. Ps 116:12.

63. 1 Thess 5:17.

till the fire of Jesus' love has taken possession of all my soul and every vein beats with young life and sweet salvation.

I am your solid sister,

S. J.

To William Spencer, Minister of the Gospel

Nov. 18, 1790. Late at night.
My dear brother,

While my heart burned for more of God, I, after much agony and unutterable delight, thought, oh, where are my Father's dear and precious children that I may open the exercises of my fainting soul to? I remembered my dear brother Spencer and heartily believed you dearly love that name which my heart is almost broke to see face to face, without a veil, and hoped it would prove a comfort to me only to talk about him whom my soul loves.

Oh brother, see the blotted tear I have sent you—this is for real possession and all Christ's mind. My fluttering spirit fatigues my breast; see how she struggles to get free. Since I was born, I never had such continual thirst and raging hunger after more righteousness as for some months past. I have had such a pain in my heart to be dissolved and be with Christ, and such a fever for all his mind, I have but few nights for two months past gone to bed at a usual hour, but when all around me are sleeping, my gazing, wrestling, fainting heart is begging, praying, striving, with uplifted hands and swimming eyes, for as much holiness as God Almighty can give me.

Brother, I want more than a little religion. I sicken for enlargement and want my desires and soul in every faculty extended that I may drink seas and rivers and running streams of Jesus' dying love, and what I cannot drink, I want to swim in continually. My Jesus is no broken cistern, but he is a well of life without bottom.

Boundless, matchless, adorable Jesus! Sometimes I feel like my breath would cease in his embraces. And such floods of dying love dashing through my whole frame, I cry, Slay me with flagons [pitchers], comfort me with apples, send them from the

Tree of Life, for I am sick [with] love.[64] *His eyes that are so fitly set have left an arrow in my heart. His cheeks are like a bed of spices, as sweet flowers.*[65] *Oh, when shall I see him in full! He never leaves me, my brother, and I find prayer with much humility will keep him near. I seldom sleep seven hours in twenty-four, and I find diligence is the path to glory....*

Oh, my brother, I want more religion, more than the seeker feels he wants pardon. I believe, because I have tasted his love. I now know he is here, even in my heart. I do not attempt just now to write you how great my exercise at this moment is, as it must be long, but you may guess that Gideon's God is with me.[66] *I want to be holier, I want to be humbler, I want to live in God's will. I must close and am grieved I don't hear from you by letter oftener. Oh, my brother, write to your poor sister,*

Sarah Jones

CHAPTER SUMMARY AND FURTHER READING

Ministering to our bridegroom Jesus is a practice valued and established by God and enabled by the presence of the Holy Spirit in our lives. The personal purity that is required to draw near to Jesus to minister to him matures our love. From the bride in Song of Songs, we learn that ministry to Jesus happens in solitude, requires vulnerability and honesty, and is a valid ministry in and of itself. Like the bride, we are made complete in our bridegroom through our ministry of love.

The bridegroom in Song of Songs reveals that Jesus' perfect love is the source of the love with which we minister to him, and as we step into the overwhelming current of his unrelenting, all-consuming, indestructible, and priceless love, it flows through us, returning to his own heart. Sarah Jones exemplifies for us the dedication required to live a life of ministry to Jesus wherever we are planted, embracing the conjoined pleasure and pain that comes from our ministry of love.

---

64. Song 2:5.

65. Song 5:12–13.

66. The Old Testament story of how Gideon, a judge, military commander, and prophet, delivered Israel from the Midianites is found in Judg 6–8.

To read more about Sarah Jones, see chapter 2 of Christopher Grasso's *Skepticism and American Faith: From the Revolution to the Civil War*, in which Grasso discusses Jones's life and her friendship with Jeremiah Minter. Rhonda D. Hartweg's article "All in Raptures: The Spirituality of Sarah Anderson Jones" and Chad Sandford's master's thesis "Practicing Piety: Sarah Jones and Methodism in 1790s Virginia" also provide background on Jones. For readers interested in how Jones fits into the broader context of eighteenth-century southern American Methodism, some helpful works are Lester Ruth's *Early Methodist Life and Spirituality: A Reader* and Cynthia Lynn Lyerly's "Passion, Desire, and Ecstasy: The Experiential Religion of Southern Methodist Women, 1770–1810" in *The Devil's Lane: Sex and Race in the Early South*.

The published collection of Sarah Jones's letters, *Devout Letters; Or, Letters Spiritual and Friendly*, can be found in the digital collections of most university libraries. The manuscript of Jones's journal is held by the Swem Library of the College of William & Mary and can be viewed on the website of the library's Special Collections Research Center under the title "Sarah Anderson Jones Diary."

8

Bearing His Authority: Julia A. J. Foote
Song of Songs 8:8–14

But now I have grown and become a bride,
and my love for him has made me
a tower of passion and contentment for my beloved.
I am now a firm wall of protection for others,
guarding them from harm.
This is how he sees me—I am the one who brings him bliss,
finding favor in his eyes. . . .
Forever we shall be united as one![1]

THE PASSAGE ABOVE CONTAINS some of the final words of the bride in Song of Songs, and they are powerful words indeed. After beginning her courtship with King Solomon as an immature maiden who cannot find the king on her own and doubts his love for her,[2] she now declares herself to be a "bride" who functions as a "firm wall of protection for others" as well as a "tower of passion and contentment" for her bridegroom. What a transformation! Clearly, her relationship with Solomon has significantly altered who she is and how she functions, and both the community and her bridegroom benefit from the person she has become. She has learned

---

1. Song 8:10, 14b.
2. Song 1:5–7.

to receive the love and blessings of King Solomon and to share them with the king himself and the world.

Of course, we are not completely surprised by this alteration since we have followed the bride through each stage of her growth as Solomon's beloved. We have watched her overcome her initial fear of responding to the king's overtures of love, cheered for her as she chose to pursue her bridegroom and encounter him in all his fullness, and learned from her as she matured in ministering to others and to Solomon. We see that she has become a person of authority, speaking and acting with confidence, conviction, and a sense of her own purpose and influence.

Like the bride in Song of Songs, we, too, have been transformed by our bridegroom Jesus and bear his authority as we minister in his name. We can bless others and our beloved with the strength and assurance that come from our position as his bride. As we end the section of this book devoted to ministering to others with our bridegroom, we will take a closer look at how we can most appropriately and effectively embrace and utilize the authority we bear to minister as a bride of King Jesus.

THE IMPORTANCE OF AUTHORITY

As we learn very early in life, authority is a reality. From the first moments we discover that someone can say no to our desire for a cookie or to cross the street, we begin to recognize that power and influence affect our personal world. As we also learn pretty quickly, authority can be a force for unimaginable good in our lives or, sadly, equally unimaginable pain. Authority exists, and how it is wielded matters.

Authority can be understood as the power to make choices and to facilitate the outworking of those choices by compelling the compliance of others. As Christians, we know that God holds the ultimate authority in the universe and that the authority humans bear, earthly or spiritual, is bestowed by him. Romans 13:1 reminds us of this truth in regard to earthly authority: "Let every person be subject to the governing authorities. For there is no authority except from God, and those that exist have been instituted by God." Earthly leaders receive their authority from God and are accountable to him for how they use it. According to Acts 17:26–27, God establishes all earthly authority and directs the affairs of nations with the ultimate purpose "that [humans] should seek God, and perhaps feel their way toward him and find him."

Spiritual authority, too, comes from God, and those who exert it will be similarly accountable to God for its use or misuse. Spiritual authority is power in the spiritual realm to accomplish the desires of God, resulting in spiritual fruit. God the Father has given Jesus all authority in heaven and on earth, and Jesus has conferred his authority upon us. As Jesus proclaims in Matt 28:18–19, "All authority in heaven and on earth has been given to me. Go therefore and make disciples of all nations, baptizing them in the name of the Father and of the Son and of the Holy Spirit." As believers indwelt by the Holy Spirit, we are endowed with Jesus' authority in the spiritual realm to act on God's behalf with the goal of advancing his kingdom.

As a bride of Jesus, we recognize that our bridegroom's authority is ours by virtue of our marriage bond with him. Our license to act on Jesus' behalf and in his stead is not a result of our gifting, training, skill set, or passion. Instead, it flows from our position as his bride who bears his name and image. Jesus is the guarantor of our spiritual power. Just as gold once backed up the paper currency of this country, so Jesus' perfect authority from the Father backs up the spiritual authority we exercise in his name as his earthly representative.

We have been given Jesus' authority not to accomplish our own agenda, but to fulfill his greatest desire: to bring his kingdom of love to earth, drawing all people to himself. Thus, as we minister with him, we act on his authority and offer the values, power, and blessings of his kingdom to a needy world.

Understanding the spiritual authority we bear as Jesus' bride matures our love for him by reinforcing our identity as his partner and making us confident in our position to minister with our beloved. We know that we are not serving others out of our own power or resources but instead can bless the world because we minister in the authority of our bridegroom. This confidence gives our ministry purpose and efficacy.

Jesus provides a striking example of how recognizing one's spiritual authority produces confidence and effectiveness in ministry. At the Last Supper, shortly before his crucifixion, Jesus washes his disciples' feet, giving them a powerful lesson in humility and assuring them of his love for them. The disciple John describes the event in John 13:1–20:

> Jesus, knowing that the Father had given all things into his hands, and that he had come from God and was going back to God, rose from supper. He laid aside his outer garments, and taking a towel, tied it around his waist. Then he poured water

into a basin and began to wash the disciples' feet and to wipe them with the towel that was wrapped around him.

Just hours before he will undergo the unimaginable humiliation, physical torture, and spiritual agony of his trial and crucifixion, Jesus is still able to notice and meet the needs of those he loves with remarkable selflessness. John gives us a clue to his strength when he notes that Jesus was confident in his authority to minister because "the Father had given all things into his hands" and that he was secure in his identity because he "was going back to God." In the same way, the authority we bear as Jesus' bride can make us secure in him and enable us to reach out to bless others, despite the demands and challenges of our own life.

What does it look like when we minister with the authority we hold as a bride of Jesus? We can learn much on this topic from the bride in Song of Songs. In some of the final verses of the narrative, we encounter three powerful images that help us understand how we can bless and minister to others with the authority of our bridegroom.

A STRONG WALL WITH TOWERS: SONG 8:8-10

Several years ago, my family was blessed to take a trip to Israel. It was the first time I had been to Israel, and personally visiting the sites where so many events in the Bible occurred was moving beyond words. In Jerusalem, we walked atop the sixteenth-century walls that surround the Old City and that replaced numerous former walls that had either been destroyed or fallen into ruin. The current walls travel more than two miles around most of the city and contain both towers and gates.

In the narrative, a wall with towers is the first image offered to reveal the bride's spiritual authority, announced by the bride herself in Song 8:10: "I am a wall, and my breasts are like towers."[3] Walls surrounding ancient and medieval cities were of critical importance. A wall's towers provided vantage points for watchmen so they could protect the city, while its gates offered access points that allowed citizens and visitors to enter and exit.

The key role a city's walls played in both defense and daily life explains why Babylonian King Nebuchadnezzar destroyed the walls surrounding Jerusalem in 586 BC and why Nehemiah worked more than

3. NIV.

one hundred years later to rebuild them.[4] Because of her authority as a bride of King Solomon, the bride in Song of Songs can function as a wall with towers, offering protection to others as well as access to her bridegroom. The bride's ability to shelter and advocate for others pleases the king; as the bride remarks later in the verse, "Thus I have become in his eyes like one bringing contentment."[5]

As Jesus' bride who bears his authority, we, too, can offer protection and assistance. We can function as a tower to keep others safe, encouraging them in faith when they are afraid and protecting them from the stratagems of the devil through prayer and spiritual counsel. In these ways we model Jesus, who came to earth "to destroy the works of the devil," as 1 John 3:8b reminds us.

We also can function as a gate, offering access to our bridegroom through our testimonies of his goodness, power, forgiveness, and love as well as our intercession in prayer. As we protect and help others, Jesus is pleased, and we become "like one bringing contentment" to our bridegroom as we minister in his authority to the ones he loves.

A FRUITFUL VINEYARD: SONG 8:11-12

The second image of the bride's spiritual authority is that of a vineyard. As the bride asserts in Song 8:12, "My vineyard, my very own, is before me; you, O Solomon, may have the thousand [pieces of silver], and the keepers of the fruit two hundred." This statement reveals three important points about the bride's authority.

First, we learn that the bride has resources. A vineyard provides a sustainable, consistent source of income from the fruit it produces. The bride has the produce of her vineyard at her disposal as the bride of King Solomon.

As a bride of Jesus, we enjoy access to the resources of the King of kings! As Paul reminds us in Eph 1:21–23, God has elevated Jesus "far above all rule and authority and power and dominion, and above every name that is named, not only in this age but also in the one to come. And he put all things under his feet and gave him as head over all things to the church, which is his body, the fullness of him who fills all in all."

---

4. See 2 Kgs 25 for the story of Nebuchadnezzar's siege of Jerusalem and the book of Nehemiah for the rebuilding of the walls.

5. Song 8:10b (NIV).

Jesus holds all authority and has been appointed by the Father to lead the church. Our resources for ministry are thus truly limitless, so we need never fear shortage or lack when our bridegroom prompts us to bless and give to others.

Second, the bride has cultivated her vineyard so that it produces fruit. This is a marked change from the beginning of the narrative in which she laments that she has had to work in her brothers' vineyards and so has neglected her own vineyard.[6] Now, through her relationship with her bridegroom, she has learned to nurture her own vineyard and reap its harvest.

We, too, must learn to cultivate our relationship with our bridegroom so that our authority flows from him with integrity and effectiveness. The closer we draw to Jesus and the more our hearts become like his, the more authority he can trust us with and the more organically and powerfully he will work through us. Paul warns believers in Rom 14:12 that "each of us will give an account of himself to God," so we should remember that one day, we will each be held responsible for how we used our bridegroom's authority in this world. Growing ever closer to him will help us immeasurably in deploying his authority with uprightness and honor.

Third, it is notable that the bride in Song of Songs is the owner of the vineyard, not a renter. As she declares, the vineyard is "my very own." In this way, she is unlike Solomon's tenants mentioned in the previous verse who only lease their land: "Solomon had a vineyard in Baal Hamon; he let out his vineyard to tenants. Each was to bring for its fruit a thousand shekels of silver."[7] As the owner of her vineyard, the bride has the authority to decide how to distribute its resources, and she chooses, significantly, to give the first one thousand pieces of silver to her bridegroom. After all, he is her first love and the one who taught her how to tend her vineyard. In this way, she freely offers him the first fruits of her harvest without compulsion. Next, she allots two hundred pieces to those who have tended the land with her, recognizing and appreciating the individuals who have invested in her life and journey to maturity.

In the same way, we are owners of our own vineyard. We are not tenants, working on another's land, compelled to give a determined portion of our harvest to the true owner. No, we *own* the vineyard! Our

---

6. Song 1:6b.
7. NIV.

bridegroom has given it to us. Thus, we can determine the dispersal of our harvest, voluntarily choosing to honor our bridegroom above all others and blessing those who have provided for us as we have grown and matured.

When I began relating to Jesus as a bride, one of the first things that surprised me was how motivated I became to willingly obey and bless him and others. The security of our bridal relationship and the authority it bestowed on me released me from feeling *obligated* to obey him and made me *want* to please him much more strongly and authentically than I had previously experienced. I felt like I couldn't abandon to him my desires, my resources, or my will fast enough.

There is something about the bridal love of Jesus that touches our hearts in such an intense and deep way that we find ourselves absolutely aching to please him out of an overpowering love that springs up within us. This may be part of what Paul had in mind in Eph 3:14–19 when he declares that he prays for believers to be strengthened by "being rooted and grounded in love." Our bridegroom's fervent, fiery love for us as his bride ignites the same reckless love in our own hearts, and we willingly, joyfully, and passionately cast all the fruit of our harvest at his feet that he may enjoy our offering and share it with those he loves.

A POPULATED GARDEN: SONG 8:13

A garden is the third image of the bride's authority, provided by King Solomon when he makes a request of the bride in Song 8:13: "O you who dwell in the gardens, with companions listening for your voice; let me hear it." The garden of love between the bride and her bridegroom has appeared frequently in Song of Songs, notably as the place into which the bride invites Solomon on their wedding day in chapter 4 and in which they consummate their love in chapter 5. Solomon identifies the bride as "you who dwell in the gardens," recognizing the bride's permanent place as his chosen and treasured partner.

But Solomon's words also reveal that the bride is not alone in the garden; she is surrounded by "companions." These individuals are probably the friends who have accompanied the bride throughout the narrative, only casually noticing the budding romance between the bride and Solomon initially but eventually becoming more intrigued, viewing the wedding ceremony with excitement and watching the bride transform from a simple, ill-equipped maiden into a strong, resourceful lover who bears her bridegroom's imperial authority. The fact that her friends are now present with her in the garden suggests that they have become personally interested in the bride's flourishing life with Solomon, perhaps desiring to know him and his bridal love in a deeper way for themselves. Maybe they will be the next ones to begin the journey of embracing Solomon's bridal love!

Finally, we observe that Solomon wishes to hear his bride's voice, reminding us of Song 2:14 in which he makes the same request of her: "O my dove . . . let me see your face, let me hear your voice." In chapter 2, Solomon is attempting to draw out his bride, encouraging her to connect with him by speaking to him and revealing her face. Now, in chapter 8, he asks again to hear her voice, but this time he desires her to speak so others can hear her words. Her speech now has a public component.

What conclusions can we draw about the bride's authority from this image of a garden in which she dwells, surrounded by friends, speaking to them at her bridegroom's request? I would suggest two. First, we see that the bride is using her authority for the purpose for which it was intended—to advance Solomon's kingdom. Her position as his bride allows her to speak to those who are "listening for [her] voice" and share with them what she has learned about her bridegroom—his kindness, his perfect love, his passion for her, his complete trustworthiness. As she shares with her friends her experiences with and knowledge of Solomon, she prompts them to pursue and desire her beloved for themselves.

Like the bride, we bear Jesus' authority for the purpose of advancing his kingdom on the earth. As we mature in our relationship with our beloved, others are naturally drawn into our orbit, attracted by the deepening love we share with Jesus. The presence of people in our life is an opportunity for us to represent Jesus and his desire that all would come to know and love him, joining the family of God.

As Peter reminds us in 2 Pet 3:9, "The Lord is not slow to fulfill his promise as some count slowness, but is patient toward you, not wishing that any should perish, but that all should reach repentance." Jesus desires to be "the firstborn among many brothers,"[8] drawing to himself a people who represent every nation, tribe, and tongue to declare his praises and enjoy his love. At the marriage supper of the Lamb recorded in Rev 19:6–7, the apostle John hears what seems to be "the voice of a

---

8. Rom 8:29.

great multitude, like the roar of many waters and like the sound of mighty peals of thunder" as countless lovers of Jesus all sound forth his eternal praise. It is our honor as Jesus' bride to bear his authority and image and to attract others to him, teaching them to know and love him as their precious bridegroom, creating for Jesus a complete, spotless bride at the end of time.

When we speak of Jesus in community, we speak with authority because we have joined our life to his. We know him, we have spent time with him, we have responded to his voice, and we have pursued him and encountered him. Our intimate position as his bride allows us to testify about him in a deep and compelling way. We are not simply a student speaking of a teacher we have learned from, or a servant sharing about a master we have served. We are an intimate, lifelong, devoted partner sharing about our eternal lover. How can our words *not* carry his authority and move the hearts of our listeners as we share about our bridegroom?

Second, we can conclude that King Solomon's request for his bride to speak authoritatively within community shows his support for her and her ministry. He trusts her to speak on his behalf, to represent him and his interests, and to stir others to seek him.

Remembering that Jesus supports our ministry should encourage us as well. He has given us his authority to build his kingdom, and he trusts us to use it. He delights in watching us follow the guidance of his Holy Spirit as we use our position as his bride to bless the ones he loves, sharing authentically and winsomely about our beautiful bridegroom. We will see others aspire to their own intimate relationships with Jesus as we testify to the bridal love we share with him. Our public testimony will please our beloved and increase his kingdom of love.

Three images of the bride's authority—a wall with towers, a vineyard, and a garden—help us understand our own authority as Jesus' bride. As the narrative of Song of Songs concludes, however, we learn one final point related to authority from the bride's closing words to her bridegroom.

TAKING INITIATIVE: SONG 8:14

The love story of the bride and King Solomon culminates in a final request from the bride: "Come away, my beloved, and be like a gazelle or like a young stag on the spice-laden mountains."[9] The bride's invitation for her lover to come away with her and travel to the mountains of spices is striking in one sense in that Solomon makes the exact same request of the bride at the beginning of their relationship in Song 2:13b: "Arise, come, my darling; my beautiful one, come with me."[10] At that time, the bride refuses his invitation and encourages her bridegroom to journey to the mountains alone, which he does.[11] Now, however, the bride is the one inviting Solomon to join her in traveling to the mountains. How the bride has changed!

The bride's request is notable in another sense in that she feels confident enough in her own bridal authority to take the lead in her relationship with Solomon and to initiate something for them to enjoy together. This is a significant step for the bride as she is no longer only responding to her bridegroom, but is now herself initiating within the relationship. But what should she initiate with her beloved? The bride makes the wise choice to suggest the very thing she knows he has been yearning to share with her—a journey to the mountains. We can imagine Solomon's deep pleasure when his bride excitedly invites him to travel with her to the very place he has longed to take her since the beginning of their relationship.

Have you considered that Jesus might desire that you assume the lead at times in your relationship with him? Taking the initiative in our relationship with our bridegroom makes him feel valued and moves us to deeper intimacy with him. I feel appreciated when my husband takes the initiative to plan something special for the weekend, when he gives me a thoughtful gift for no reason, or when he devotes time and energy to asking about the concerns of my heart. He doesn't have to do these things; he can fulfill his spousal obligations without initiating events or encounters that he knows I will find meaningful. But I feel cherished when he steps up and does something that he knows will bless me.

In the same way, Jesus is pleased when we respond to his initiatives, but he is equally delighted when we take the lead as his loving, mature bride. Our initiative shows him how much we value him and how secure we feel in our authoritative position as his beloved bride.

But, like the bride, what should we initiate? The bride knows her plan to journey to the mountains will please Solomon because he desires

---

9. NIV.
10. NIV.
11. See Song 2:17.

that very thing in his own heart. In the same way, we can allow our bridegroom's wishes and goals to guide us as we take the lead.

Jesus wants to be pursued by the one he loves. Set aside a day to seek your beloved and ask him to draw near to you. Jesus wants to change your heart to be like his. Remind him of his promises to you every morning when you awake. Jesus wants you to be healthy and whole. Invite him to share his thoughts about an area of your heart that needs healing. Jesus wants you to be moved by the things that move him. Ask him for one or two specific desires of his that you can bring before him in daily intercession. Jesus wants you to know him more intimately. Invite him to reveal to you something about himself before you fall asleep each night. Jesus wants to share your daily life. Ask him to take a walk with you, listen to worship music with you, or sit with you as you rest in his presence.

Be proactive in your relationship with your beloved, initiating what you know will please and delight him. He has elevated you to the position of his bride and partner, bestowing upon you his royal authority, so you can feel comfortable taking the lead at times with him.

The bride in Song of Songs has shown us much about the authority we possess as Jesus' beloved partner, so we will turn now to our final early American writer to see how embracing our authority in Jesus can help us minister with persistence and effectiveness. Although this nineteenth-century African American evangelist was born on the late end of our timeline, I simply had to include her as she fits our discussion of bridal authority so brilliantly. Let's take a closer look at a woman who ministered in her authority as a bride of Jesus despite incredible opposition.

JULIA A. J. FOOTE AND THE CHALLENGES OF MINISTRY

Julia A. J. Foote (1823–1901) was born in Schenectady, New York, the daughter of parents who had purchased their freedom from enslavement and had become Christians. At the age of fifteen, while listening to a sermon on Rev 14:3 extolling the new song of the redeemed in heaven, Foote was struck by the reality of her "lost condition," fell to the floor unconscious, and was carried home by friends and placed in bed. Twenty hours of spiritual battle ensued for Foote until she cried to God for mercy and was saved, leaping from her bed singing, "Redeemed! Redeemed! Glory! Glory!" Immediately, Foote "went from house to house" telling her young friends about Jesus.[12] Thus commenced the evangelistic career of Julia A. J. Foote.

The basic details of Foote's adult life can be related quickly and easily. Married in 1841, Foote relocated to Boston, joined a congregation of the African Methodist Episcopal Zion Church (AME Zion), and soon after heard a call from God to become an evangelist.[13] Traveling by boat, stagecoach, train, and horse, Foote preached throughout southern New England, the mid-Atlantic, parts of the Midwest, Oregon, California, and Canada during a career that spanned decades. She spoke in churches, conference meetings, lecture halls, homes, and outdoor venues, publishing an account of her ministry in 1879 as *A Brand Plucked from the Fire: An Autobiographical Sketch*. Foote was ordained as the first female deacon of the AME Zion church in 1884, later becoming the second woman ever to be ordained to the role of elder. She is recognized as one of the most influential preachers in the history of the AME Zion denomination.[14]

Beyond a simple recitation of Foote's accomplishments and experiences lies the reason she is included in this chapter: Foote's unwavering belief in her authority as a bride of Jesus enabled her to overcome opposition to her ministry that would have unquestionably derailed most people. To use a twist on a modern term, Foote's life was one of intersectionality with a vengeance.[15] As an African American female evangelist living during the decades surrounding the American Civil War, Foote encountered racism, sexism, and religious persecution on a scale beyond what we can imagine today.

In her autobiography, Foote records many blatant and brutal experiences of racial prejudice, beginning with her father's capture and enslavement despite being born free and her mother's sufferings at the hands of a harsh enslaver. Even though she was a free woman living in a northern state, Foote herself encountered many insults and injustices during her lifetime: forbidden to receive communion with White parishioners in her own church, barred from education because of an absence of schools for Black students, prohibited from traveling in a stagecoach whenever

---

12. Foote, *Brand*, 9–11, 32–34.

13. The African Methodist Episcopal Zion Church separated from the African Methodist Episcopal Church over issues of race and preaching.

14. Biographical information is taken from Howard, "Foote," 86–93.

15. Intersectionality is a twentieth-century theoretical construct that examines how an individual's social and political identities such as gender, class, race, religion, disability, etc., overlap and combine to create advantages or disadvantages for the individual in society.

a White passenger protested to the presence of a Black passenger, once taken ill after sitting on the deck of a ship all night because Black travelers could not sleep in the cabins, and being asked to preach at a White church that did not allow Black guests to attend the service are just some of the indignities Foote mentions in her autobiography.[16]

Similarly, as a female evangelist, Foote encountered much resistance and ridicule, despite the fact that the Methodist church allowed female preaching at its founding in the eighteenth century. Foote was excommunicated and slandered by her own minister when she first expressed a desire to preach in the community, and her mother informed Foote she "would rather hear you were dead" than hear she was a preacher, although she later supported Foote's ministry.[17] So extensive and troubling were Foote's experiences with sexism during the 1840s and 1850s that in 1879 she encouraged other female evangelists with these words: "Dear sisters who are in the evangelistic work now, you may think you have hard times, but let me tell you, I feel that the lion and lamb are lying down together, as compared with the state of things twenty-five or thirty years ago."[18]

Lastly, Foote was criticized by Christians of both races and sexes for her passion for God. Early in her marriage, Foote's husband expressed his disapprobation of her growing religious commitment: "He said I was getting more crazy every day and getting others in the same way, and that if I did not stop, he would send me back home or to the crazy-house." Foote writes that members of her own church acted in "an unchristian-like spirit" toward her when she pressed forward in her desire for more holiness. Even her friends accused her of being "too forward."[19] It is no wonder one sympathetic contemporary ironically lamented that Foote

---

16. Examples are found in Foote, *Brand*, 9–10, 11–12, 15, 96, 102–3, 108.

17. Foote, *Brand*, 74, 84–85.

18. Foote, *Brand*, 89. Foote references Isa 11:6 and the peace of Jesus' kingdom.

19. Foote, *Brand*, 53, 59, 65. Foote was part of the Holiness movement in Methodism which maintained the traditional Methodist doctrine of Christian perfection, which asserted that a Christian could reach a state of sanctification in which they desired only God's will and did not desire sin. Foote explains her view in her autobiography: "Bless God, we may all have that inward, instantaneous sanctification, whereby the root, the inbeing of sin, is destroyed. Do not misunderstand me. I am not teaching absolute perfection, for that belongs to God alone. Nor do I mean a state of angelic or Adamic perfection, but Christian perfection—an extinction of every temper contrary to love." Foote, *Brand*, 120. This doctrine put her and other Holiness proponents at odds at times with other Methodists. For the origins of Christian perfection in Methodism, see John Wesley, *Plain Account of Christian Perfection* (Bristol, 1766).

was "guilty of three great crimes": "Color," "Womanhood," and being an "Evangelist."[20]

External opposition often produces internal conflict and doubt, and Foote experienced this reality as well. She knew the hostility she would face if she accepted God's call to preach the gospel, and she struggled for months with insecurity and fear, admitting, "When I thought of the difficulties [female preachers] had to encounter, both from [Christians] and [non-Christians], I shrank back and cried, 'Lord, I cannot go!'"[21] Ultimately, Foote pushed past both the external and internal resistance produced by her "crimes" of being a female African American gospel preacher and joined Jesus in ministering his love to the world. How did she do it?

OVERCOMING OPPOSITION WITH AUTHORITY

The secret to Foote's ability to overcome opposition from both without and within can be found in her abiding assurance of her authority as a bride of Jesus. Early in her call to ministry, Foote encountered God's promise in Isa 54:4–5a: "Fear not, for you will not be ashamed; be not confounded, for you will not be disgraced; for you will forget the shame of your youth, and the reproach of your widowhood you will remember no more. For your Maker is your husband, the LORD of hosts is his name." These verses assured Foote that whatever shame, disgrace, or reproach society attempted to heap upon her because of her race, sex, or zeal for God, her favored position as Jesus' bride would enable her to overcome such antagonism for the good of advancing Jesus' kingdom, and she "went forth glorifying God."[22]

In all aspects of her ministry, Foote consistently operated in the authority of her bridegroom Jesus. Describing how the denominational conference ignored her plea for an investigation into her minister's slander when she began preaching, Foote admits, "It is no little thing to feel that every man's hand is against us and ours against every man, as seemed to be the case with me at this time; yet how precious, if Jesus but be with

---

20. Foote, *Brand*, 5–6. This comment is by Thomas K. Doty, editor of the *Mission Harvester*, a monthly periodical which reported evangelical news and happenings. Doty wrote the introduction to Foote's *A Brand Plucked from the Fire*, from which this comment is excerpted. Biographical information is from Wisbey, "Salvation Army," 80.

21. Foote, *Brand*, 67.

22. Foote, *Brand*, 61.

us." Foote trusted her beloved, asserting in her autobiography, "Though opposed, I went forth laboring for God, and he owned and blessed my labors and has done so wherever I have been until this day. And while I walk obediently, I know he will, though hell may rage and vent its spite."[23]

At times, she saw a swift transformation from initial resistance to solid support. In 1855, in Ithaca, New York, one of the church trustees where she intended to minister strongly opposed her, but Foote held firm in faith and experienced God's intervention: "Beloved, the God we serve fights all our battles, and before I left the place, that trustee was one of the most faithful at my meetings and was very kind to assist me on my journey when I left Ithaca."[24]

Foote's unwavering belief in her authority as a bride of Jesus is most clearly revealed in the title of her autobiography, *A Brand Plucked from the Fire*. A brand is a burning stick, and the phrase is a reference to Zech 3, in which the Old Testament prophet Zechariah has a vision of Joshua being commissioned for his role as the high priest of Israel. In Zechariah's vision, Joshua is standing before the angel of the Lord, traditionally identified as preincarnate Jesus, in unclean garments and enduring the accusations of Satan. The angel of the Lord rebukes Satan in Zech 3:2, declaring, "The LORD rebuke you, O Satan! The LORD who has chosen Jerusalem rebuke you! Is not this a brand plucked from the fire?" The angel of the Lord then removes Joshua's filthy clothing, dresses him in clean clothes, and announces, "Behold, I have taken your iniquity away from you, and I will clothe you with pure vestments," assuring Joshua of his God-given authority as Israel's high priest.[25]

Foote's choice of Zech 3:2b as the title of the story of her life and ministry cannot be accidental, for Foote received a vision similar to Zechariah's when God confirmed her gospel preaching. In Foote's vision, Jesus washes her clean in a celestial body of water and dresses her in a white robe, giving her a certificate authenticating her ministry that she is to carry next to her heart. Interestingly, her vision also includes many of the same images we examined in this chapter in relation to the bride in Song 8:8–14. Foote's experience occurs in a garden-like location where she is surrounded by a "whole company" of others. After Jesus cleanses her, everyone is given fruit to eat from a large tree "hung full of fruit," which Foote exclaims tastes "like nothing I had ever tasted before."

23. Foote, *Brand*, 77, 80.
24. Foote, *Brand*, 85.
25. Zech 3:4b.

Foote's vision cements her sense of her bridal authority so deeply that when describing the vision to friends, she instinctively reaches into her bosom for her "letter of authority," as she calls it, realizing then that "it was in my heart."[26]

Foote's assurance of her authority as Jesus' bride enabled her to overcome both outward opposition and inward doubt, never losing her vision for ministry. She opens her autobiography with a bold declaration of her lifelong goal: "My object has been to testify more extensively to the sufficiency of the blood of Jesus Christ to save from all sin."[27] The excerpts below from Foote's autobiography relate the story of her new married life in Boston, her call to minister, her struggle to accept the call, and the vision that enables her to move into her authority as Jesus' sanctified and secure bride. Her experience reveals for us the extraordinary strength and confidence that result from fully receiving the authority our bridegroom Jesus bestows upon us as his partner in ministry.

AUTOBIOGRAPHY: A BRAND PLUCKED FROM THE FIRE: AN AUTOBIOGRAPHICAL SKETCH[28]

A Call to Ministry

[My husband] accepted an offer to go to sea for six months, leaving me to draw half of his wages. To this arrangement I reluctantly consented, fully realizing how lonely I should be among strangers. Had it not been for dear "Mam" Riley, I could hardly have endured it.[29] Her precept and example taught me to lean more heavily on Christ for support. God gave me these precious words: "Be careful for nothing, but in everything, by prayer and supplication, with thanksgiving, let your requests be made known to God."[30] Truly, God

---

26. Foote, *Brand*, 69–71.
27. Foote, *Brand*, 3.
28. Selections are from Foote, *Brand*, 60–61, 65–72, 78, 81–82, 100.
29. "Mam" Riley is a friend of Foote's who appears several times in Foote's autobiography.
30. Phil 4:6.

is the great arbiter of all events and "because he lives, I shall live also."[31]

The day my husband went on shipboard was one of close trial and great inward temptation. It was difficult for me to mark the exact line between disapprobation and Christian forbearance and patient love. How I longed for wisdom to meet everything in a spirit of meekness and fear, that I might not be surprised into evil or hindered from improving all things to the glory of God.

While under this apparent cloud, I took the Bible to my closet, asking divine aid. As I opened the book, my eyes fell on these words: "'For your Maker is your husband."[32] I then read the fifty-fourth chapter of Isaiah over and over again. It seemed to me that I had never seen it before. I went forth glorifying God.

For months, I had been moved upon [by God] to exhort and pray with the people in my visits from house to house, and in meetings my whole soul seemed drawn out for the salvation of souls. The love of Christ in me was not limited. Some of my mistaken friends said I was too forward, but a desire to work for the Master and to promote the glory of his kingdom in the salvation of souls was food to my poor soul.

When called of God on a particular occasion to a definite work, I said, "No, Lord, not me." Day by day, I was more impressed that God would have me work in his vineyard. I thought it could not be that I was called to preach—I, so weak and ignorant. Still, I knew all things were possible with God, even to confounding the wise by the foolish things of this earth.[33] Yet in me there was a shrinking.

I took all my doubts and fears to the Lord in prayer, when what seemed to be an angel made his appearance. In his hand was a scroll on which were these words: "You have I chosen to preach my gospel without delay." The moment my eyes saw it, it appeared to be printed on my heart. The angel was gone in an instant, and I, in agony, cried out, "Lord, I cannot do it!" It was eleven o'clock in the morning,

---

31. John 14:19b.
32. Isa 54:5a.
33. A reference to 1 Cor 1:27.

yet everything grew dark as night. The darkness was so great that I feared to stir.

At last, "Mam" Riley entered. As she did so, the room grew lighter, and I arose from my knees. My heart was so heavy I scarce could speak. Dear "Mam" Riley saw my distress and soon left me.

From that day my appetite failed me and sleep fled from my eyes. I seemed as one tormented. I prayed, but felt no better. I belonged to a band of sisters whom I loved dearly, and to them I partially opened my mind. One of them seemed to understand my case at once and advised me to do as God had bid me or I would never be happy here or hereafter. But it seemed too hard—I could not give up and obey.

One night, as I lay weeping and beseeching the dear Lord to remove this burden from me, there appeared the same angel that came to me before, and on his breast were these words: "You are lost unless you obey God's righteous commands." I saw the writing, and that was enough. I covered my head and awoke my husband, who had returned a few days before. He asked me why I trembled so, but I had not power to answer him. I remained in that condition until morning, when I tried to arise and go about my usual duties, but was too ill. Then my husband called a physician, who prescribed medicine, but it did me no good.

I had always been opposed to the preaching of women and had spoken against it, though, I acknowledge, without foundation. This rose before me like a mountain, and when I thought of the difficulties they had to encounter, both from [Christians] and [non-Christians], I shrank back and cried, "Lord, I cannot go!"

The trouble my heavenly Father has had to keep me out of the fire that is never quenched, he alone knows. My husband and friends said I would die or go crazy if something favorable did not take place soon. I expected to die and be lost, knowing I had been enlightened and had tasted the heavenly gift. I read again and again the sixth chapter of Hebrews.

Authority in Jesus

Nearly two months from the time I first saw the angel, I said that I would do anything or go anywhere for God if it were made plain to me. He took me at my word and sent the angel again with this message: "You have I chosen to go in my name and warn the people of their sins." I bowed my head and said, "I will go, Lord."

That moment, I felt a joy and peace I had not known for months. But strange as it may appear, it is not the less true, that, [before] one hour had passed, I began to reason thus: "I am elected to preach the gospel without the requisite qualifications, and, besides, my parents and friends will forsake me and turn against me, and I regret that I made a promise." At that instant, all the joy and peace I had felt left me, and I thought I was standing on the brink of hell and heard the devil say, "Let her go! Let her go! I will catch her." Reader, can you imagine how I felt? If you were ever snatched from the mouth of hell, you can, in part, realize my feelings.

I continued in this state for some time, when, on a Sabbath evening—ah, that memorable Sabbath evening—while engaged in fervent prayer, the same supernatural presence came to me once more and took me by the hand. At that moment, I became lost to everything of this world. The angel led me to a place where there was a large tree, the branches of which seemed to extend either way beyond sight. Beneath it sat, as I thought, God the Father, the Son, and the Holy Spirit, besides many others, whom I thought were angels.

I was led before them; they looked me over from head to foot, but said nothing. Finally, the Father said to me, "Before these people make your choice, whether you will obey me or go from this place to eternal misery and pain." I answered not a word. He then took me by the hand to lead me, as I thought, to hell, when I cried out, "I will obey you, Lord!" He then pointed my hand in different directions and asked if I would go there. I replied, "Yes, Lord."

He then led me, all the others following, till we came to a place where there was a great quantity of water, which looked like silver, where we made a halt. My hand was given to Christ, who led me into the water and stripped me of my clothing, which at once vanished from sight. Christ then appeared to wash me, the water feeling quite warm.

During this operation, all the others stood on the bank, looking on in profound silence. When the washing was ended, the sweetest music I had ever heard greeted my ears. We walked to the shore, where an angel stood with a clean, white robe, which the Father at once put on me. In an instant, I appeared to be changed into an angel. The whole company looked at me with delight and began to make a noise which I called shouting. We all marched back with music.

When we reached the tree to which the angel first led me, it hung full of fruit, which I had not seen before. The Holy Ghost plucked some and gave me, and the rest helped themselves. We sat down and ate of the fruit, which had a taste like nothing I had ever tasted before. When we had finished, we all arose and gave another shout.

Then God the Father said to me, "You are now prepared, and must go where I have commanded you." I replied, "If I go, they will not believe me." Christ then appeared to write something with a golden pen and golden ink upon golden paper. Then he rolled it up and said to me, "Put this in your bosom, and wherever you go, show it, and they will know that I have sent you to proclaim salvation to all." He then put it into my bosom, and they all went with me to a bright, shining gate, singing and shouting. Here they embraced me, and I found myself once more on earth.

When I came to myself, I found that several friends had been with me all night, and my husband had called a physician, but he had not been able to do anything for me. He ordered those around me to keep very quiet or to go home. He returned in the morning, when I told him, in part, my story. He seemed amazed, but made no answer and left me.

Several friends were in during the day. While talking to them, I would, without thinking, put my hand into my bosom to show them my letter of authority. But I soon found, as my friends told me, it was in my heart and was to be shown in my life instead of in my hand.

Among others, my minister Jehial C. Beman came to see me.[34] He looked very coldly upon me and said, "I guess you will find out your mistake before you are many months older." He was a scholar and a fine speaker, and the sneering, indifferent way in which he addressed me said most plainly, "You don't know anything." I replied, "My gifts are very small, I know, but I can no longer be shaken by what you or anyone else may think or say."

An Unshakable Faith

Though I did not wish to pain anyone, neither could I please anyone only as I was led by the Holy Spirit. I saw, as never before, that the best men were liable to err and that the only safe way was to fall on Christ, even though censure and reproach fell upon me for obeying his voice. Man's opinion weighed nothing with me, for my commission was from heaven and my reward was with the Most High.

The language of 1 Peter 1:7 came forcibly to my mind: "The trial of our faith is much more precious than of gold that perishes, though it be tried by fire." Fiery trials are not strange things to the Lord's anointed. The rejoicing in them is born only of the Holy Spirit. Oh, praise his holy name for a circumcised heart, teaching us that each trial of our faith has its commission from the Father of spirits. Each wave of trial bears the Galilean Pilot on its crest. Listen, his voice is in the storm, and winds and waves obey that voice: "It is I; be not afraid."[35] He has promised us help and safety in the fires and not escape from them.

"And hereby we know that he abides in us, by the Spirit which he has given us." 1 John 3:24. Glory to the Lamb for the witness of the Holy Spirit! He knows that every step I have taken has been for the glory of God and the good of souls. However much I may have erred in judgment, it has

---

34. Jehiel C. Beman (1789–1858) was the pastor of the Boston AME Zion Church which Foote attended. Beman may have objected to Foote's preaching not only because she was female, but also because of Foote's Holiness leanings. For more on Beman, see Housley, "'Yours for the Oppressed,'" 17–29.

35. Foote references John 6:16–21.

been the fault of my head and not of my heart. I sleep, but my heart wakes,[36] bless the Lord.

Since I first entered the vineyard of my divine Master, I have seen many a star fall and many a shining light go out and sink into darkness. Many who have been singularly owned and blessed of God have deserted his standard in the day of trial; yet, through his abounding grace, have I been kept. Glory be to the keeping power of the blood that cleanses me, even me, from all sin!

CHAPTER SUMMARY AND FURTHER READING

Both earthly and spiritual authority are bestowed upon humans by God to accomplish his goals on earth, and bearing authority gives us confidence and effectiveness in ministry. The bride in Song of Songs has matured through her relationship with King Solomon and reveals for us a powerful picture of bridal authority through the images of a wall with towers, a vineyard, and a garden. As Jesus' bride, we bear his authority to minister in his name and with his power, even taking the initiative at times in our relationship with our bridegroom. Evangelist Julia A. J. Foote shows us how the security and strength of our bridal authority enables us to overcome opposition to our ministry and persevere in partnering with Jesus to advance his kingdom.

Foote's autobiography, *A Brand Plucked from the Fire: An Autobiographical Sketch*, can be accessed digitally in the Internet Archive or in William L. Andrews's *Sisters of the Spirit: Three Black Women's Autobiographies of the Nineteenth Century*. Joy A. J. Howard's short article titled "Julia A. J. Foote (1823–1901)" offers background on Foote's life and ministry.

For readers interested in African American preaching in America, see Bettye Collier-Thomas's *Daughters of Thunder: Black Women Preachers and their Sermons, 1850–1979*, as well as *Preaching with Sacred Fire: An Anthology of African American Sermons, 1750 to the Present*, edited by Martha Simmons and Frank A. Thomas, both of which include short sermons by Foote. An extensive collection of writings by nineteenth-century African American women can be found in the thirty-volume *Schomburg Library of Nineteenth-Century Black Women Writers*, edited by Henry Louis Gates Jr.

36. Song 5:2.

Conclusion: John Winthrop

I will sing and greatly rejoice in Yahweh!
My whole being vibrates
with shouts of joy in my God!
For he has dressed me with salvation
and wrapped me in the robe of his righteousness!
I appear like a bridegroom on his wedding day,
decked out with a beautiful sash,
or like a radiant bride adorned with sparkling jewels.[1]

IN SOME BIBLE TRANSLATIONS, chapter 61 of Isaiah is subtitled "The Year of the Lord's Favor,"[2] and with good reason. After prophesying Judah's destruction and exile at the hands of the kingdom of Babylon in chapter 39, the Old Testament prophet Isaiah uses the rest of the book to proclaim the freedom, abundance, beauty, and restoration that will be given by God to his people when he brings them back from their Babylonian captivity. The opening section of chapter 61 ends with God's promise of hope: "All who see them shall acknowledge them, that they are an offspring the Lord has blessed."[3] The final two verses of the chapter, one of which is printed above, is an exuberant song of praise sung by Isaiah on behalf of Jerusalem, rejoicing in what God will do for his people when he restores them.

---

1. Isa 61:10.
2. For example, ESV and NIV.
3. Isa 61:9b.

Isaiah's prediction of Judah's return from exile and full restoration as a nation is also a prophetic picture of the kingdom of God that Jesus inaugurated in part with his atoning sacrifice on the cross and that he will establish in its fullness at the end of time. In fact, Jesus himself reads Isa 61:1–2 in a synagogue in Nazareth, about one year into his public ministry, and applies the passage to himself with the words, "Today this Scripture has been fulfilled in your hearing."[4]

As the bridegroom of the church, Jesus will appear with his bride in their dazzling wedding garments as they are united forever at the marriage supper of the Lamb.[5] The end-time wedding of Jesus and his church will usher in the new heaven and new earth of Rev 21, and God's kingdom will be fully and finally established. The words of the bride in Song 6:3a will be realized in time and space—"I am my beloved's and my beloved is mine"—and we will reign with King Jesus, our perfect bridegroom, through all of eternity.

LESSONS LEARNED

I hope this book has helped you understand and embrace Jesus in his identity as the bridegroom of the church as well as how you can relate to him personally as his bride. His heart is always reaching out to us in perfect love, and his greatest desire is that we would assume our place as his precious, redeemed, eternal partner. Perhaps a short summary of the main points we have learned on our journey together will be useful.

The first section of this book suggests four responses we desire to have to Jesus' overtures of bridal love toward us. First, we awaken our heart to his love, seeking his help and embracing the reality of his passion for us. We rest in the certainty that our beautiful and relentless bridegroom will never cease pursuing us. Second, true love requires the intentional choice of both parties, and so we choose our beloved. As we fall more in love with Jesus, our lovesick heart inspires us to cultivate a habit of saying yes to him. Third, we use the painful longing we have for Jesus as motivation to pursue him, employing our time on earth to prepare for our celestial wedding by deepening our intimacy with him. As an adventurous, entrepreneurial bride, we follow our beloved to new places and purposefully stir up our affections for him. Fourth, we encounter

---

4. Luke 4:16–21.
5. Rev 19:6–10.

Jesus, inviting him into our most private place, giving him our attention, and accepting the productive disruption his love causes as he grows and changes us. These responses to our bridegroom enable us to fully embrace our identity as his beloved bride.

To help our love for Jesus grow into a deep, mature love, we also embrace ministering with him, the focus of the second section of the book. First, we join him in interceding for the ones he loves, embracing the identification and sacrifice that such ministry requires. We release control to him, look to our beloved to strengthen us, and join action to prayer when necessary. Second, we learn to receive encouragement from Jesus to inspire our heart, resisting the urge to minimize or discount his tender affections toward us. Then, we encourage others in unique and authentic ways that will bless them, letting them know they are loved. Third, we minister to Jesus himself by offering him our love, sourced from his own unrelenting, all-consuming, indestructible, and priceless love for us. This valuable ministry, established by God, happens in solitude and requires vulnerability and honesty. Fourth, as Jesus' bride, we bear his royal authority for the purpose of advancing his kingdom on earth. Jesus supports our exercise of his authority and enjoys when we take the initiative in our relationship with him. Through ministering with our bridegroom, our love for him matures, and the blessings of his kingdom are dispersed to the people he created and loves.

Hopefully, as you have read this book, these points and others have dovetailed with your own thoughts and encounters with Jesus. Let's close our study with one final story of an early American Christian. I believe John Winthrop (1588–1649) in his diary sums up for us in a few paragraphs the heart of the experience of Jesus as our bridegroom.

JOHN WINTHROP'S EXPERIENCE OF BRIDAL LOVE

John Winthrop was born in England and trained in the law. As a Puritan, he suffered religious persecution in the 1620s, as the government began to harass dissenting religious groups, losing his government position in 1629 because of his beliefs. In 1630, Winthrop sailed with other Puritans to establish the Massachusetts Bay Colony in America. Winthrop was elected as their first governor and served in that position for more than half of the colony's first twenty years of existence. He is best known today for applying the New Testament phrase "city on a hill" to the Puritan community in colonial America.[6]

Winthrop kept a journal for much of his life, a standard Puritan practice, but he also maintained a separate diary from 1607 to 1637 known as his "Experiencia," which recorded his spiritual experiences. An entry from 1617 finds Winthrop reading through some love letters he shared with his first wife, Mary Forth (married 1605–15), who bore five children and died of complications from childbirth in 1615. Winthrop's reminiscences of his first earthly marriage turn his thoughts to his eternal bridegroom, and his heart is "ravished" with "unspeakable love" as he contemplates Jesus. I think you will be moved by this short excerpt as we conclude our exploration of Jesus' bridal love.

DIARY: "EXPERIENCIA"[7]

Looking over some letters of kindness that had passed between my first wife and me and being thereby affected with the remembrance of that entire and sweet love that had been sometimes between us, God brought me by that occasion into such a heavenly meditation of the love between Christ and me as ravished my heart with unspeakable love. I thought my soul had as familiar and sensible society with him as my wife could have with the kindest husband. I desired no other happiness but to be embraced of him. I held nothing so dear that I was not willing to part with for him. I forgot to look after my supper and some vain things that my heart lingered after before.

Then came such a calm of comfort over my heart as revived my spirits [and] set my mind and conscience at sweet liberty and peace. I thought upon that speech of the church, Song of Songs 5:2: "It is the voice of my well-beloved that knocks," etc. Oh, there's my husband (says the loving wife),

---

6. Matt 5:14 reads, "Ye are the light of the world. A city that is set on an hill cannot be hid" (KJV). Winthrop applies the biblical phrase to the Puritan settlement in America in his "lay sermon" eventually titled *A Model of Christian Charity*. For more on the sermon, see Rodgers, *City on a Hill*. For a biography of Winthrop, see Bremer, *John Winthrop*.

7. Selections are from Winthrop, "John Winthrop's Experiencia," 1:202–4, used with permission of the Massachusetts Historical Society. I am grateful to Michael Ditmore for bringing this excerpt to my attention.

then she runs, then she joys, out of the arms goes the child, away goes every impediment, she has enough that she hears his voice whom her soul loves. Oh, my Lord, how did my soul melt with joy when you spoke to the heart of your poor unworthy handmaid!

Further, when I considered of such letters as my wife had written to me and observed the scribbling hand, the basic harmony, the false slant, and broken sentences, and yet found my heart not only accepting of them, but delighting in them and esteeming them above far more curious [impressive] workmanship in another, and all from [the reason] that I loved her, it made me think thus with myself, "Can I do thus through that drop of affection that is in me, and will not my Lord and husband Christ Jesus (whose love surpasses knowledge and is larger than the ocean) accept in good part the poorest testimonies of my love and duty towards him?" Oh, if I had faith to believe this, how abundant comfort would it afford me in my weakest services since they are sent up to him that looks not at the form or phrase, but finding them to come from one in whom he delights, he accepts with all favor the sincere simplicity of the heart and covers all imperfections with the skirt of his love. Oh, my God, increase my weak faith, I humbly pray.

This affection continued still with me, and the love of Christ was ever in my heart and drew me to be more enamored of him. Then I oft remembered that [promise] in Jeremiah 2:2—"I remembered you with the kindness of your youth and the love of your marriage"—which made me to recall to my view the love of my earthly marriages, which the more I thought upon, the more sensible I grew of the most sweet love of my heavenly husband, Christ Jesus. His spirit persuaded my heart that if I could so entirely effect and delight in such as I had not labored for,[8] only for this consideration—that they were to become a part of myself—[certainly] his love towards me [must] be [of] exceeding measure, [he] that had made me, died for me, sweat water and blood for me, and married me to himself, so as I am become truly one with him. Then I was persuaded that neither my sins nor infirmities could put me

---

8. Josh 24:13a.

out of his favor, he having washed away the one with his own blood and covering the other with his unchangeable love.

This comfort that I had in his sweet love drew me to deal with him as I was accustomed to do with my earthly well-beloved, who being ever in the eye of my affection, I greedily employed every opportunity to be a messenger of the manifestation of my love by letters, etc., so did I now with my dear Lord Christ. I delighted to meditate of him, to pray to him and to the Father in him (for all was one with me), to remember his sweet promises, for I was well-assured that he took all that I did in good part. I considered that he was such a one as should ever be living, so as I might ever love him, and always present, so as there should be no grief at partings.

Oh, my Lord, my love, how wholly delectable are you! "Let him kiss me with the kisses of his mouth, for his love is sweeter than wine."[9] How lovely is your countenance! How pleasant are your embracings! My heart leaps within me for joy when I hear the voice of you, my Lord, my love, when you say to my soul you are her salvation.

Oh, my God, my King, what am I but dust! A worm, a rebel, and your enemy was I, wallowing in the blood and filth of my sins, when you did cast the light of your countenance upon me,[10] when you spread over me the lap of your love and said that I should live. Then did you wash me in the ever-flowing fountain of your blood. You did [dress] me as a bride prepared for her husband; my clothing was your pure righteousness. You spoke kindly to the heart of your most unworthy servant, and my flesh grew like the flesh of a young child.[11]

And now let me ever be with you, oh, my Redeemer, for in your presence is joy, and at your right hand are pleasures forevermore.[12] Shadow me and guide me with your love, as in the days of my marriage, that I may never swerve from you to run after earthly vanities that are lying and will not

9. Song 1:2.
10. Ps 4:6b.
11. Job 33:25a.
12. Ps 16:11.

profit. Wholly yours I am (my sweet Lord Jesus), unworthy (I acknowledge) so much honor as to wipe the dust off the feet of my Lord and his well-beloved spouse in the day of the gladness of their heart,[13] yet will you honor me with the society of your marriage chamber.[14] Behold, all you beloved of the Lord, know and embrace with joy this unspeakable love of his towards you. God is love,[15] assuredly.

CLOSING THOUGHTS

Thank you for joining me on this journey of encountering Jesus the bridegroom and his passionate, eternal, and unconditional love for us, his bride. Learning to relate to Jesus as his bride has been one of the most impactful lessons of my spiritual life, and I am grateful that I could share some of my ideas and experiences with you. I hope this study of Jesus' bridal love has encouraged you to pursue your beloved ever more zealously and to receive and respond to his tender overtures of love toward you. May we all continue to grow in appreciating and enjoying our beautiful bridegroom Jesus.

---

13. Song 3:11b.
14. Perhaps a reference to Song 1:4.
15. 1 John 4:8b.

Bibliography

Aarniokoski, Doug, dir. *Star Trek: Picard*. Season 1, episode 7, "Nepenthe." Aired March 5, 2020, on CBS All Access. https://www.cbs.com/all-access/.

Adams, Jennifer, ed. *In Love with Christ: The Narrative of Sarah Edwards*. Forest, VA: Corner Pillar, 2010.

Addison, Joseph. *The Spectator* 412 (Jun. 23, 1712).

The American Letter-Writer: Containing, A Variety of Letters on the Most Common Occasions in Life. Philadelphia, 1793.

Andrews, William L., ed. *Sisters of the Spirit: Three Black Women's Autobiographies of the Nineteenth Century*. Religion in North America. Bloomington, IN: Indiana University Press, 1986.

Asbury, Francis. *The Journal, 1771 to 1793*, Vol. 1 of *The Journal and Letters of Francis Asbury*, edited by Elmer T. Clark, et al. London: Epworth, and Nashville: Abingdon, 1998.

———. *The Journal, 1794 to 1816*, Vol. 2 of *The Journal and Letters of Francis Asbury*, edited by Elmer T. Clark et al. London: Epworth, and Nashville: Abingdon, 1998.

Augustine, Bishop of Hippo. *Expositions on the Book of Psalms*. Vol. 2. Oxford: John Henry Parker, 1848.

Brekus, Catherine A., ed. *Sarah Osborn's Collected Writings*. New Haven: Yale University Press, 2017.

———. *Sarah Osborn's World: The Rise of Evangelical Christianity in Early America*. New Haven: Yale University Press, 2013.

———. *Strangers and Pilgrims: Female Preaching in America, 1740–1845*. Chapel Hill: University of North Carolina Press, 1998.

Bremer, Francis J. *John Winthrop: America's Forgotten Founding Father*. Oxford: Oxford University Press, 2003.

Brooks, Joanna, ed. *The Collected Writings of Samson Occom, Mohegan: Leadership and Literature in Eighteenth-Century Native America*. Oxford: Oxford University Press, 2006.

Buell, Samuel. *The Excellence and Importance of the Saving Knowledge of the Lord Jesus Christ in the Gospel-Preacher . . . Preached . . . at the Ordination of Mr. Samson Occom*. New York, 1761.

Calcaterra, Angela. "Fire and Chain: Samson Occom's Letters, Anglo-American Missions, and Haudenosaunee Eloquence." In *Literary Indians: Aesthetics and*

Encounters in American Literature to 1920, 47–82. Chapel Hill: University of North Carolina Press, 2018.

Chilcote, Paul Wesley. *Her Own Story: Autobiographical Portraits of Early Methodist Women*. Nashville: Kingswood, 2001.

Collier-Thomas, Bettye. *Daughters of Thunder: Black Women Preachers and their Sermons, 1850–1979*. San Francisco: Jossey-Bass, 1998.

Cotton, John. *A Brief Exposition of the Whole Book of Canticles, or, Song of Solomon*. London, 1642.

The Covenant, and Declaration of Faith, of the Second Church of Christ in Dorchester. Boston, 1828. https://babel.hathitrust.org/cgi/pt?id=hvd.32044086364288.

Davis, Thomas M., and Virginia L. Davis, eds. *Edward Taylor's "Church Records" and Related Sermons*, Vol. 1, *The Unpublished Writings of Edward Taylor*, edited by Joel Myerson. Boston: Twayne, 1981.

Dwight, S[ereno] E. *The Life of President Edwards*. New York, 1830.

———, ed. *The Works of President Edwards*. Vol. 1. New York, 1830.

Edwards, Jonathan. *A Treatise Concerning Religious Affections*. Boston, 1746.

Everson, Elisa Ann. "'A Little Labour of Love': The Extraordinary Career of Dorothy Ripley, Female Evangelist in Early America." PhD diss., Georgia State University, 2007. https://scholarworks.gsu.edu/english_diss/17.

Fletcher, Mary. *Jesus Altogether Lovely: Or a Letter to Some of the Single Women in the Methodist Society*. 2nd ed. Bristol, England, 1766.

Foote, Julia A. J. *A Brand Plucked from the Fire: An Autobiographical Sketch*. Cleveland, 1879. https://archive.org/details/brandpluckedfromoofoot/page/n1/mode/2up.

Foster, Richard J. *Celebration of Discipline: The Path to Spiritual Growth*. Rev. ed. New York: HarperCollins, 1998.

———. *Prayer: Finding the Heart's True Home*. New York: HarperCollins, 1992.

Gates, Henry Louis, Jr., gen. ed. *Schomburg Library of Nineteenth-Century Black Women Writers*. 30 vols. New York: Oxford University Press, 1988.

Grasso, Christopher. *Skepticism and American Faith: From the Revolution to the Civil War*. New York: Oxford University Press, 2018.

Hammond, Jeffrey A. "The Bride in Redemptive Time: John Cotton and the Canticles Controversy." *The New England Quarterly* 56 (Mar. 1983) 78–101. http://www.jstor.com/stable/365312.

———. *Sinful Self, Saintly Self: The Puritan Experience of Poetry*. Athens, GA: The University of Georgia Press, 1993.

Hartweg, Rhonda D. "All in Raptures: The Spirituality of Sarah Anderson Jones." *Methodist History* 45 (Apr. 2007) 166–179. http://hdl.handle.net/10516/412.

Henry, Matthew. *A Commentary on the Whole Bible*. 6 vols. Iowa Falls, IA: World Bible, n.d. First published 1706 in London.

Hogan, Laura Reece. *I Live, No Longer I: Paul's Spirituality of Suffering, Transformation, and Joy*. Eugene, OR: Wipf & Stock, 2017.

Hopkins, Samuel. *The Life and Character of the Late Reverend Mr. Jonathan Edwards*. Boston, 1765.

———. *Memoirs of the Life of Mrs. Sarah Osborn*. 2nd ed. Catskill, NY, 1814.

———. *Memoirs of Miss Susanna Anthony*. 2nd ed. London: Clipstone, 1803.

———. *The Works of Samuel Hopkins*, edited by Edwards A. Park. 3 vols. Boston, 1852.

Housley, Kathleen. "'Yours for the Oppressed': The Life of Jehiel C. Beman." *Journal of Negro History* 77 (Winter 1992) 17–29. https://www.jstor.org/stable/3031524.

Howard, Joy A. J. "Julia A. J. Foote (1823–1901)." *Legacy* 23 (2006) 86–93. https://www.jstor.org/stable/25684497.

John Paul II. *On the Dignity and Vocation of Women on the Occasion of the Marian Year*. Boston: St. Paul, [1988?].

Jones, Sarah. *Devout Letters; Or, Letters Spiritual and Friendly*. Edited by Jeremiah Minter. Alexandria, Virginia, 1804.

———. Sarah Anderson Jones Diary, Special Collections Research Center, William & Mary Libraries.

Lyerly, Cynthia Lynn. "Passion, Desire, and Ecstasy: The Experiential Religion of Southern Methodist Women, 1770–1810." In *The Devil's Lane: Sex and Race in the Early South*, edited by Catherine Clinton and Michele Gillespie, 168–86. New York: Oxford University Press, 1997.

Marsden, George M. *An Infinite Fountain of Light: Jonathan Edwards for the Twenty-First Century*. Downers Grove, IL: IVP Academic, 2023.

———. *Jonathan Edwards: A Life*. New Haven: Yale University Press, 2003.

Mather, Cotton. *Right Thoughts in Sad Hours*. London, 1689.

McCulley, Sue Lane, and Dorothy Z. Baker. *The Silent and Soft Communion: The Spiritual Narratives of Sarah Pierrepont Edwards and Sarah Prince Gill*. Knoxville: University of Tennessee Press, 2005.

Occom, Samson, *A Sermon, Preached at the Execution of Moses Paul, an Indian*. New Haven, CT, 1772.

Osborn, Sarah, and Susanna Anthony. *Familiar Letters, Written by Mrs. Sarah Osborn, and Miss Susanna Anthony, Late of Newport, Rhode Island*. Newport, RI, 1807.

Oxford English Dictionary, s.v. "bridegroom (n.)." https://www.oed.com/search/dictionary/?scope=Entries&q=bridegroom.

Oxford English Dictionary, s.v. "lovesick (adj.)." https://www.oed.com/search/dictionary/?scope=Entries&q=lovesick.

Patterson, Daniel, ed. *Edward Taylor's Gods Determinations and Preparatory Meditations: A Critical Edition*. Kent, OH: Kent State University Press, 2003.

Perkins, Mary E. *Old Houses of the Ancient Town of Norwich, 1660–1800*. Norwich, 1895. https://archive.org/details/oldhousesofantieooperk.

Pitre, Brant. *Jesus the Bridegroom: The Greatest Love Story Ever Told*. New York: Image, 2014.

Poe, Edgar A. "The Philosophy of Composition." *Graham's Magazine* XXVIII (Apr. 1846) 163–67.

Porterfield, Amanda. *Feminine Spirituality in America: From Sarah Edwards to Martha Graham*. Philadelphia: Temple University Press, 1980.

Reed, Michael D. "Edward Taylor's Poetry: Puritan Structure and Form." *American Literature* 46 (1974) 304–12. https://www.jstor.org/stable/2924411.

Ripley, Dorothy. *The Extraordinary Conversion, and Religious Experience of Dorothy Ripley, with Her First Voyage and Travels in America*. New York, 1810.

Roberts, Wendy Raphael. "The Calvinist Couplet: Ralph Erskine's *Gospel Sonnets* and Espousal Poetics in Early Evangelicalism." *Christianity & Literature* 68 (2019) 412–31. https://doi.org/10.1177/0148333119827675.

Robinson, Timothy H., ed. *A Companion to the Song of Songs in the History of Spirituality*. Leiden: Brill, 2021.

Rodgers, Daniel T. *As a City on a Hill: The Story of America's Most Famous Lay Sermon*. Princeton, NJ: Princeton University Press, 2018.

Rubin, Julius H. "Samson Occom and Evangelical Christian Indian Identity." In *Tears of Repentance: Christian Indian Identity and Community in Colonial Southern New England*, 114–59. Lincoln: University of Nebraska Press, 2013.

Ruth, Lester. *Early Methodist Life and Spirituality: A Reader*. Nashville: Kingswood, 2005.

Sandford, Chad. "Practicing Piety: Sarah Jones and Methodism in 1790s Virginia." Master's thesis, College of William & Mary, 2004. https://dx.doi.org/doi:10.21220/s2-xgcp-tx14.

Schellenberg, Annette, ed. *The Song of Songs Through the Ages: Essays on the Song's Reception History in Different Times, Contexts, and Genres*. Berlin: De Gruyter, 2023.

Schwartz, Stephen. *Wicked: A New Musical*. Milwaukee, WI: Hal Leonard, 2004.

Simmons, Brian, and Candice Simmons. *Throne Room Prayer: Praying with Jesus on the Sea of Glass*. Savage, MN: BroadStreet, 2018.

Simmons, Martha, and Frank A. Thomas, eds. *Preaching with Sacred Fire: An Anthology of African American Sermons, 1750 to the Present*. New York: Norton, 2010.

Smith, Alice. *Beyond the Veil: Entering into Intimacy with God through Prayer*. Ventura, CA: Regal, 1997.

Smith, Lisa. *Godly Character(s): Insights for Spiritual Passion from the Lives of 8 Women in the Bible*. Baltimore: Square Halo, 2018.

———. *Hammer & Fire: Lessons on Spiritual Passion from the Writings and Life of George Whitefield*. Baltimore: Square Halo, 2024.

Spurgeon, Charles Haddon. *Spurgeon's Sermons*. 5 vols. Peabody, MA: Hendrickson, 2011. First published as *Sermons of Rev. C. H. Spurgeon of London*. 10 vols. New York: Robert Carter & Brothers, 1883.

Stanford, Donald E., ed. *The Poems of Edward Taylor*. New Haven: Yale University Press, 1960.

Stout, Harry S., ed. *The Jonathan Edwards Encyclopedia*. Grand Rapids: Eerdmans, 2017.

Ware, Thomas. *Sketches of the Life and Travels of Rev. Thomas Ware*. Rev. ed. New York, c1839. https://hdl.handle.net/2027/uc2.ark:/13960/t6736q17f.

Whitefield, George. *The Wise and Foolish Virgins: A Sermon Preached at Philadelphia, 1739*. Philadelphia, 1739.

Wiens, Gary. *Bridal Intercession: Authority in Prayer through Intimacy with Jesus*. Greenwood, MO: Oasis House, 2001.

Winship, Michael P. "Behold the Bridegroom Cometh: Marital Imagery in Massachusetts Preaching, 1630–1730." *Early American Literature* 27 (1992) 170–84. https://www.jstor.org/stable/25056903.

Winthrop, John. "John Winthrop's Experiencia, February to June 1617" [electronic edition]. In *Winthrop Papers Digital Edition*, 1:202–204. Boston: Massachusetts Historical Society, 2024. https://www.masshist.org/publications/winthrop/index.php/view/PWF01d124.

Wisbey, Herbert A., Jr., "A Salvation Army Prelude: The Christian Mission in Cleveland, Ohio." *Ohio History Journal* 64 (Jan. 1955) 77–81.

Won, Jonathan Jong-Chu. "Communion with Christ: An Exposition and Comparison of the Doctrine of Union and Communion with Christ in Calvin and the English Puritans." PhD diss., Westminster Theological Seminary, 1989. ProQuest (8918224).

The Works of Jonathan Edwards. New Haven: Yale University Press, 1957–.

www.ingramcontent.com/pod-product-compliance
Lightning Source LLC
Chambersburg PA
CBHW070251230426
43664CB00014B/2497